# FROM IMMIGRANTS
# TO AMERICANS

# FROM IMMIGRANTS TO AMERICANS
## The Rise and Fall of Fitting In

Jacob L. Vigdor

ROWMAN & LITTLEFIELD PUBLISHERS, INC.
*Lanham • Boulder • New York • Toronto • Plymouth, UK*

Published by Rowman & Littlefield Publishers, Inc.
A wholly owned subsidiary of The Rowman & Littlefield Publishing Group, Inc.
4501 Forbes Boulevard, Suite 200, Lanham, Maryland 20706
www.rowmanlittlefield.com

Estover Road, Plymouth PL6 7PY, United Kingdom

British Library Cataloguing in Publication Information Available

**Library of Congress Cataloging-in-Publication Data**

Vigdor, Jacob L.
  From immigrants to Americans : the rise and fall of fitting in / Jacob L. Vigdor.
    p. cm.
  Includes index.
  ISBN 978-1-4422-0136-1 (cloth : alk. paper) — ISBN 978-1-4422-0138-5 (electronic)
  1. Immigrants—United States. 2. Immigrants—United States—Social conditions.
3. Americanization. 4. Assimilation (Sociology)—United States. 5. United States—
Emigration and immigration. 6. United States—Social conditions. I. Title.
  JV6450.V54 2009
  305.9'069120973—dc22                                                    2009035049

Printed in the United States of America

For Elizabeth

# Contents

# List of Figures and Tables

## Figures

## Tables

# Acknowledgments

THIS BOOK WOULD HAVE BEEN more difficult, if not impossible, to write without the advice, assistance, or influence of many individuals.

First and foremost, I would like to thank the Manhattan Institute, and most importantly Howard Husock, for their initial interest and unbridled enthusiasm for this project. Howard's continuous attention and input played a distinct role in the shaping of this book. Thanks also go to Lawrence Mone and other members of the Institute's leadership for their support, and to Mark Riebling for taking great care to read through and comment on the manuscript's first draft. I owe a significant debt to all the staff members who worked tirelessly on behalf of the project: Erin Crotty, Ed Craig, Bridget Sweeney, Ben Gerson, Michael Barreiro, Donna Thompson, Lindsay Young-Craig, Jana Hardy, and Dan Hay.

Several other organizations have either directly supported this book or my earlier research projects on immigration. The Smith Richardson Foundation, and especially Mark Steinmeyer, bear the most direct responsibility for making this book possible. I am also grateful to the William T. Grant Foundation, and particularly Bob Granger and Ed Seidman, for supporting my effort and providing me a forum to discuss the project. The Annie E. Casey Foundation has also sponsored this work, and the Russell Sage Foundation funded the research project that opened the path to this one.

Ideas developed in isolation have much difficulty taking root, and I am grateful to many fellow scholars for informing and improving this research. The Manhattan Institute assembled a distinguished board of advisors to the project, including Tamar Jacoby, Phil Kasinitz, Lawrence Mead, Dowell

Myers, Pia Orrenius, Jeff Passel, Peter Skerry, and Stephan Thernstrom. The expertise and insight of this group was of phenomenal importance.

At my home institution of Duke University, another set of colleagues provided helpful comments on this work. I am grateful to Noah Pickus, Paula McClain, Jose Saldivar, Emilio Parrado, and community members who attended the Kenan Institute symposium on immigration policy in April 2008. I'd also like to thank my colleagues Charles Clotfelter, Phil Cook, and Helen Ladd, who have contributed immeasurably to my progress on this project and others.

A portion of my work on this book occurred while I was a visitor at the Australian National University in Canberra. I am grateful to Andrew Leigh for hosting my visit and providing key insights, and to Bob Gregory, Deborah Cobb-Clark, Tim Hatton, and Yuji Tamura for extensive discussions of the economics of immigration and immigration policy. While in Canberra, I presented many of the findings in this book at the Department of Immigration and Citizenship, and I am grateful to chief economist Mark Cully and other attendees who provided helpful comments.

The actual research for this book would not have been possible without the research assistance of Parul Sharma, and the extensive historical data resources provided by Steve Ruggles and the Integrated Public Use Microdata Series (IPUMS) project at the Minnesota Population Center at the University of Minnesota.

This book also owes its existence to the early and continued influence of David Cutler and Edward Glaeser, my former advisors and current colleagues at Harvard. My initial forays into the study of immigration were also informed by interactions with George Borjas and Glenn Loury.

And finally, a special category of thanks goes to my wife, Elizabeth. As a professionally trained economist, she was uniquely positioned to provide expert commentary on the material in this book, and to make the process of writing it much easier.

# Introduction

SHORTLY AFTER COMPLETING the rough draft of this book, I visited a public elementary school in my hometown of Durham, North Carolina. Like many parts of the United States, Durham's ethnic profile has changed dramatically over the past decade or two. Twenty years ago, the city was roughly half white and half black, with virtually no foreign-born residents save those working or going to school at the local universities.[1] A walk through this school demonstrated just how much change has occurred since then.

Situated at one vertex of the so-called Research Triangle, Durham has drawn highly skilled workers from around the globe, to work in the burgeoning software and pharmaceutical industries centered in office parks just outside the city limits. The region's rapid growth has fueled heavy demand for workers in the construction and service industries—and many of these jobs have been filled by an unprecedented wave of migrants from Mexico and Central America.[2] A city once known for barbeque and cigarettes is now nationally renowned for its taquerias.[3] My son, a second-grader, has already shared a classroom with children born on five continents.

On the wall outside my son's classroom, the students in the room next door had posted short essays in response to a question asked by their teacher: "Is the United States a 'melting pot' or a 'salad bowl'?" There were answers on both sides of the issue, many of them capturing impressive nuances—how today's immigrants are blending in certain respects, but remaining distinct in others. As one might expect from a group of eight-year-olds, the responses focused largely on clothing and food, with a few references to speaking English mixed in. None of them mentioned citizenship, or intermarriage, or living in an ethnic enclave neighborhood.

My preschool-age daughter, tagging along for the visit, asked me why I had stopped to read the responses so carefully. "Because," I responded, "this is what my book is about." That statement stretched the truth a bit—I'll have little to say about clothing and food here—but the basic idea is quite similar. And like the nuanced answers students gave to their teacher's question, the basic message is mixed. On average, today's immigrants are fitting in quite well compared to their predecessors. Averages, however, do not tell the whole story. The experiences and trajectories of some modern immigrants are largely without precedent in American history.

The changes evident in the population of Durham since 1990 mirror broader, and somewhat longer-term, shifts in the nation as a whole. In 1970, only about one in every twenty U.S. residents had been born abroad. The roughly ten million immigrants included a million Italian-Americans, and more than a half-million each of Canadian, British, German, and Polish natives. For every American resident born in either Latin America or Asia, at least two were born in Europe.

Since then, the number of foreign-born residents of the United States has just about quadrupled. At the same time, the balance between Europeans, Latin Americans, and Asians has more than reversed. Cities like Durham, with little legacy of immigration in previous eras, found themselves at the center of the transformation.

These trends, charted in figure I.1, raise many questions. Why did this change happen, and why did it happen when it did? How fundamental a change in American culture and society will occur as a consequence of this demographic shift? Are these immigrants bifurcating society, or blending into it? To extend the second-grader's analogy just a bit, are modern immigrants destined to join the "melting pot" or "salad bowl," or will they be left out?

The number of books on the subject of immigration in the United States has grown almost as rapidly as the immigrant population itself. The difference between this book and the many other worthy efforts to describe immigrant assimilation can be summed up in a three-word declaration: it is comprehensive. To answer these basic questions, it compares the experiences of immigrants over a period of more than 150 years—from 1850 to 2007. There are many older books about pre-1920 immigrants, and quite a few about post-1960 immigrants, but precious few that try to measure the two groups using the same yardstick.

This book analyzes a wide range of indicators, considering how immigrants through the ages have fared in the labor market, acquired English skills, be-

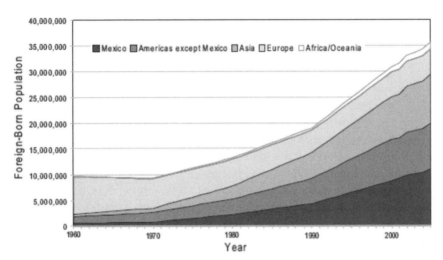

**FIGURE I.1.**
**The Foreign-Born Population of the United States, by Region of Birth, 1960–2005**

come citizens, moved out of enclave neighborhoods, and married outside their own ethnic group. There has been quite a bit of work on most of these subjects individually, but relatively little has attempted to integrate findings across these dimensions, and none over so extensive a time period.

The only potential drawback to being a comprehensive study is the possibility of presenting the reader with too much information—with so many trees to look at, we might be at a loss to see the forest. To avoid this pitfall, the book provides a framework, drawn from basic economics, that helps to explain both why immigration has surged and how immigrants behave once they arrive. The framework isn't restricted to "old-fashioned" supply-and-demand economics, either. It integrates important lessons from psychology and sociology into a unified model. Drawing on this evidence, and using this framework, this book finds that:

1. The post-1970 wave of immigration reflects the confluence of several independent events. After nearly a half-century of severe restrictions on immigration, U.S. policy was relaxed significantly in 1965. Civil war and other calamities pushed emigrants from many nations. Once the initial round of migrants had arrived, a "snowballing" effect, driven partly but not entirely by official policy, brought more and larger numbers from a wide array of countries. The United States has clearly witnessed waves of immigration before, but never from so many nations in such a narrow timeframe. When rapid immigration occurs, the degree of cultural

distinction between the average foreign- and native-born resident of the United States increases.

2. Newly arrived immigrants in the early twenty-first century are on average more integrated than their predecessors. They are more likely to speak English and more likely to live in an integrated neighborhood. Over time, they make economic progress comparable to their predecessors, and in at least some cases intermarry and become naturalized citizens at high rates. Paradoxically, the greater integration of newly arrived immigrants contributes to the common perception that immigrants are not "fitting in."

3. The average does not tell the whole story. Immigrants from Mexico comprise roughly one-third of the foreign-born population, and as a group they lag significantly behind in economic terms, and in rates of language acquisition and naturalization. The lack of legal status for many Mexican immigrants explains part of the disparity, but other forces are at play as well.

4. Across the centuries, immigrants to the United States can be sorted into two basic categories. Economic or *job-seeking* migrants are drawn primarily by the promise of higher wages in the United States—even a minimum wage job in the United States pays more than the per capita income in 141 other nations.[4] Economic considerations are a factor for *home-seeking* migrants as well, but their primary motivation is to escape war, persecution, or the consequences of poor policy in their origin country.[5]

5. The incentives for home-seeking migrants to assimilate are stronger, primarily because they have little prospect of returning to their home country. Home-seeking migrants also tend to arouse fewer nativist passions; the great episodes of anti-immigrant sentiment in the United States have generally been focused on job-seeking immigrants. Home-seekers are also offered certain advantages under current immigration policy. For all these reasons, home-seekers tend to have rapid rates of assimilation.

6. Immigration policy influences immigrant assimilation both directly and indirectly. Policy determines which immigrants can enter legally, and which can become citizens. Those given favorable preference through policy also have stronger incentives to integrate themselves culturally and economically.

7. Immigration policy has on net raised the costs of assimilation between 1900 and the present day. The persistence of assimilation in spite of these higher costs implies that immigrants, on average, attach greater value to membership in American society than their predecessors.

8. Of the many recently proposed alterations to immigration policy, most will have at best little impact on immigrant assimilation. Some proposals actually threaten to widen the economic, civic, and cultural gaps between the native- and foreign-born. An assimilation-friendly immigration policy would integrate a system of rewards for taking steps toward integration.

The book begins by putting some basic groundwork in place. Chapter 1 lays out the conceptual framework, and discusses the sources of historical and contemporary information. Chapters 2 provides a baseline for analysis of current trends, by collating factual information about traditional-wave immigrants a century or more ago, and describes in detail the factors that contributed to the "snowballing" phenomenon.

From there, the book proceeds to evaluate the progress of modern immigrants in historical context, along economic, cultural, and civic dimensions. Chapter 3 focuses on the labor market, where immigrants have traditionally held an advantage relative to the native-born. This advantage extends to some, but not all, contemporary immigrant groups. Chapter 4 considers language. The English skills of newly arrived immigrants are better now than they were a century ago, but the rate of learning for nonspeakers appears low by historical standards. Chapter 5 analyzes citizenship. Average naturalization rates have changed little over time, but a combination of factors has led to particularly low rates for certain groups. Chapter 6 examines residential integration. Modern immigrants are on average more likely to live in an integrated neighborhood, but those who enter an ethnic enclave are less likely to leave it. Finally, chapter 7 shows that intermarriage between immigrants and natives of a different ethnic group have always been rare, except for those groups with few cultural distinctions from the majority.

Having considered the evidence, chapter 8 talks policy. Immigration is a heated issue, and will continue as such so long as the American economy maintains its advantage over so much of the world. Immigration policy, traditionally seen as a method of regulating the flow of people across the nation's borders, can also be used as a tool to promote assimilation. This concluding chapter considers the implications of various extant policy proposals for the assimilation of immigrants in the United States, and proposes an alternative designed with the explicit goal of encouraging assimilation. The alternative policy is not a pie-in-the-sky dream, but rather a realistic proposal that draws on regulations currently in place in other nations.

# 1

# An Immigrant's Decision

Land being thus plenty in *America*, and so cheap as that a labouring Man, that understands Husbandry, can in a short Time save Money enough to purchase a Piece of new Land sufficient for a Plantation, whereon he may subsist a Family; such are not afraid to marry; for if they even look far enough forward to consider how their Children when grown up are to be provided for, they see that more Land is to be had at Rates equally easy, all Circumstances considered.

> Benjamin Franklin (1751), *Observations Concerning the Increase of Mankind* (italics in original)

THE ORIGINS OF modern economics are generally traced to Adam Smith's publication of *The Wealth of Nations* in 1776. Franklin's passage quoted above, however, illustrates a clear application of economic thought to the question of immigration. As long as there have been migrants, there have been efforts to understand the motives and forces underlying their actions and behavior.[1] And the framework most often applied to this behavior is fundamentally an economic one. Migrants move when they perceive that the opportunities available to them in some other land are superior to the ones they face at home. Likewise, the choices they make once they have elected to move can be understood as efforts to generate the greatest opportunity for themselves and their offspring.

Franklin's central argument in his three-thousand-word treatise *Observations Concerning the Increase of Mankind* was that Great Britain would do well to continue populating the colonies; he draws a clear contrast between the economic opportunities available in the colonies and in the mother country. "Labour is no cheaper now, in Pennsylvania, than it was 30 years ago, tho' so many Thousand labouring people have been imported," he wrote. The increase in population did not lead to any real scarcity in opportunities because the road to economic self-sufficiency, which in the eighteenth century meant owning one's own farm, was so easily trod, and the prospects for yeoman farming so plentiful. Franklin argued that the earnings of British laborers, by contrast, were incredibly meager, to the point where a manufacturer's costs to hire a British worker were lower than the costs of employing a slave in America.

Two hundred and fifty years later, the incredible contrasts in economic opportunity between the United States and other nations can still be made. In 2008, the U.S. gross domestic product (GDP), equal to the value of all goods and services produced within the nation's physical borders in a year, amounted to $48,000 per resident, according to the Central Intelligence Agency's *World Factbook*.[2] Though eclipsed by a few smaller nations, each either oil-rich or a center of finance, the output of the average worker in America is more than four times the CIA's estimated world average. In sixteen nations, primarily located in sub-Saharan Africa, GDP per capita is less than $1,000 per year.

Now, to be fair, the value of everything produced in the United States in a given year is not distributed equally to all residents of the country. As in all economies, there is a concentration of wealth and income among a fortunate minority. But even for the world's least skilled, poorest workers, the American labor market offers opportunities that simply cannot be matched in many other nations. A worker earning the 2008 federal minimum wage of $6.55 per hour, working forty hours per week for fifty weeks in a year, will earn $13,100 before taxes. The minimal reward for full-time work in the United States beats the average income in 141 nations, and is more than double the average in the world's most populous nation, China. Even if these earnings were to be used to support a family of four, the resulting $3,275 per capita beats the average in sixty-four nations, including the world's second most populous nation, India. Any legal job in the United States is thus superior to the typical alternative for billions of potential immigrants throughout the world. Not surprisingly, then, millions of foreign-born aliens would jump at the chance for legal access to the American labor market. Millions more have made the jump even in the absence of legal access. Although many aspects of life in the United States have changed over the past quarter millennium, the basic arguments regarding the rationale for migration, and the behavior of migrants once they have arrived, have not.

To argue that an economic model explains both migration and the behavior of migrants is not to deny that nonremunerative considerations play a role in these human decisions. Not every immigrant comes to the United States with the sole purpose of making money. There are other things available in this country that are tragically scarce in other regions of the world. The United States has a stable, democratically elected government that (with a few noteworthy and lamentable exceptions) has a strong track record of promoting equal rights and freedom from political, ethnic, or religious persecution. The nation's institutions of higher education offer opportunities to learn and train that cannot be matched even in many of the world's most developed countries. The economic perspective is flexible enough, though, to incorporate factors such as religious or political persecution. Migrants pursue not only economic opportunities, but the opportunity to live or worship in peace.

This chapter will review the basic economic framework for thinking about an individual's decision to move to a new country, and an immigrant's decision to blend in to their adoptive home. The term most often applied to this framework, particularly by noneconomists, is *rational choice*. Rational choice models presume that individuals make decisions by weighing the costs and benefits of various actions, and choosing the alternative that provides the most favorable combination of substantial benefits and limited costs. Although informal rational choice arguments can be seen in many historical writings, the formal use of this framework to describe human behavior dates to the groundbreaking work of economist Alfred Marshall in the late nineteenth century.[3]

Relative to economists, sociologists have undoubtedly devoted more attention to human migration and the experiences of immigrants. The discipline of sociology has developed its own models to explain the behavior and experiences of migrants. While sociological models have a rich scientific tradition and decades if not centuries of empirical observation to substantiate them, there is an important distinction between the way economists and other social scientists produce theoretical models. The rational choice model is a general-purpose framework, capable of application to nearly every human decision, from the choice to abandon one's homeland in search of a better standard of living to the choice of what to have for dinner on any given night. The model does have its drawbacks: there are certain types of behavior that are famously difficult to explain in the context of a rational choice model, and the framework presumes that people possess a high degree of cognitive sophistication to predict and evaluate the long-range consequences of their actions.

Sociological models, by contrast, are relatively ad hoc in nature.[4] A sociological model of migration or assimilation is not easily applied to unrelated decisions. Specialization is not necessarily a negative feature, however; it is possible that the use of a more specific theory generates insights that other approaches might miss. In this chapter we'll give a full hearing to the essential sociological theories of migration and assimilation, and ultimately show that they can be incorporated into a more traditional economic rational choice model. The rational choice model is vastly enriched by incorporation of sociological perspectives.

This chapter will apply the rational choice perspective to two choices: the decision to migrate and the decision to assimilate. The first discussion will illuminate the basic distinction between two types of migrants: those who effectively choose to abandon their homeland, and those who migrate purely for economic reasons. The differences between the two types will carry important implications for the second discussion. Put simply, "home-seeking" immigrants face strong incentives to assimilate relative to job-seekers. These distinctions will in turn carry implications for public policy.

The chapter closes with a discussion of data and methods that sets the stage for the next five chapters of the book, which examine a series of assimilating behaviors for immigrants to the United States between the mid-nineteenth and the early twenty-first centuries.

## Theories of Migration

A scientific model of human migration, or of the behavior of immigrants in their adoptive homeland, must explain why some choose to migrate and others don't, where immigrants choose to settle, and why some adapt quickly to the circumstances of the host society and others do not. Using these criteria, scientific efforts to model migration date back to the nineteenth century.

In 1885, German-born geographer Ernest Ravenstein delivered an address to the Statistical Society of London titled "The Laws of Migration."[5] Ravenstein's lecture followed a written treatise he had published nearly a decade before, and was itself followed by a second lecture in 1889.[6] While much of the text of these articles and lectures focuses on a relatively dry set of statistics concerning internal migration in Great Britain in the late nineteenth century, Ravenstein did use the data to induce a series of patterns which he hypothesized governed migration more generally.

To a modern eye, Ravenstein's generalizations appear quite basic. The majority of the laws enumerated by later scholars boil down to one: in late nineteenth-century Britain, the locus of economic opportunity was in rapidly industrializing cities, and these opportunities drew in migrants, most of them from nearby areas.[7] To be sure, there were some lesser observations: that females migrate more often than males, and that for every flow of migrants from points A to B there is usually a flow from B to A as well.

It is not clear, however, that these various laws have applied universally to human migration in other times and other places. But the main point is already familiar to us, that differences in economic opportunities across space create powerful incentives for movement. As Benjamin Franklin's writings suggest, the same point would have found general agreement a century before Ravenstein wrote it.

Nearly a century after Ravenstein first formulated the laws of migration, a young economist completing dissertation work at the University of Chicago formally introduced the rational choice model of human migration. Larry Sjaastad, the grandson of Norwegian immigrants who participated in the significant wave of Scandinavian migration in the 1880s, would eventually publish this work in one of the top journals in the field.[8] Sjaastad's work builds on Ravenstein's in many respects, but offers insights that can explain some seeming anomalies from the German-British geographer's time and his own.

Sjaastad conceptualized migration as "an *investment increasing the productivity of human resources*, an investment which has costs and which also renders returns"[9] (emphasis in original). The costs, generally borne at the time of migration, include both the tangible costs of moving, the loss of income associated with discontinuing work in one's place of origin, a prime example of what economists refer to as an *opportunity cost*, and a set of intangible or "psychic" costs associated with abandoning "familiar surroundings, family, and friends."[10] Presuming that these costs rise as the contemplated migration increases in distance allows one to explain one of Ravenstein's laws, the modern "gravity model" of migration.[11] The returns, which accrue over time spent in a new location, relate primarily to the tangible standard of living available in that location, which is affected primarily by income, but also by price levels and the intangible qualities of a place that economists refer to as amenities.[12] As we will soon see, the distinction between tangible and intangible costs and benefits to migration is important for classifying immigrants and explaining differences in their behavior.

Realistically, we can't presume that migrants make choices knowing perfectly what will happen to them in the event they move. There is uncertainty and risk associated with any choice, and migration often entails leaving a certain position in the home society for a more uncertain, but possibly greater, position in the destination. A rational choice framework operates under the presumption that individuals can properly assess these risks when making their decisions. As we'll see below, one of the primary arguments against this model is that people might not possess such powers of assessment.

The basic rational choice framework offers explanations for a number of migration-related phenomena. Migration is most likely to occur when individuals are young, because a young worker can expect to reap the returns of his or her move for a longer period of time. The "bidirectional" migrant flows noted by Ravenstein occur when the set of opportunities for one do not match those of another.[13] For example, in certain depressed areas there are very few opportunities for unskilled laborers. At the same time, a skilled professional such as a physician or lawyer might find no shortage of work in the same area.[14] For unskilled workers, there are enormous differences in earning potential between most Latin American countries and the United States. A highly skilled worker, on the other hand, may be able to find unparalleled opportunity in Latin America.[15] Bidirectional migration could also reflect differences in the value that certain groups place on amenities. At a subnational level, couples often move from city to suburbs when their children reach school age, and then move back to the city when they become "empty-nesters."[16]

A further implication of the rational choice model of migration is that a potential migrant's decision depends on the decisions of others. Migrants who move to a new country alone face different costs and benefits than those who move to a nation where a community of fellow migrants already exists. A preexisting community of migrants can ease some of the psychic costs of moving, but can influence real costs as well. Migrant networks make it easier to collect information about potential destinations, and to find work or housing upon arrival.[17] There is considerable evidence supporting the "network theory" of migration.[18] The importance of networks can explain the typical progress of immigration waves, both the current wave depicted in the introduction and the historical waves we'll learn about in the next chapter. Immigration waves start with a few pioneers; once this small initial group has established a network, a much larger group of migrants can take advantage of it.[19]

Sjaastad's work has been highly influential, serving as the basis for considerable subsequent work on migration. But there are certain aspects of migration not incorporated into the model. In some cases, migration is not the outcome of an individual's own decision. Human history offers countless examples of forced migration, many if not all of them regrettable. The Atlantic slave trade, the partition of India in 1947, and the displacements associated with totalitarian regimes in the mid-twentieth century all caused migration to occur without invoking the individual decision process Sjaastad envisioned.

Migration in response to war or partisan strife represents a more ambiguous case. On the one hand, refugees often make a conscious choice to relocate, invoking the sort of cost-benefit analysis Sjaastad ascribes to migrants in general. On the other hand, refugees may be incorporating factors into their analysis that effectively make the decision for them. The line between rational choice and forced migration is fuzzy. From a purely detached analytical perspective, it is clear that the rational choice model of costs and benefits can be applied to the typical refugee. If the alternative to becoming a refugee is certain death, the economic model would simply note that the benefits of migration are infinite, or in any case equal to the refugee's valuation of his or her own life. A gruesome calculation to be sure, but one with many precedents in economic thinking.[20]

The rational choice theory of human migration, expanded to consider the case of individuals who either *de jure* or *de facto* have no choice but to migrate, offers no bright line distinction between home-seeking or job-seeking immigrants. All immigrants arrive because the expected returns to migration exceed the costs. For some, the excess of returns over costs is quite large; for others the difference is more slight. But the amount of excess varies continuously, at least in theory.

A useful way of thinking about the distinction takes advantage of Sjaastad's enumeration of both tangible and intangible benefits and costs.[21] For a purely economic migrant, the monetary return to migration is sufficiently large to offset the costs, but the nonmonetary return may not be. For example, some migrants may choose to move in spite of the fact that they place high sentimental value on their home, or exhibit a great distaste for the place they are moving to. In either case, economic considerations are sufficient to outweigh any distaste they have for moving, at least in the short run. At some point down the road, perhaps when they exit the labor force, or when they have amassed enough savings to improve their living standard wherever they choose to live, their intent is to return home. Of course, this is presuming that the migrant's preferences don't vary over time, and they might. One might learn to love one's adopted homeland.

For the more traditional migrant, the intangible considerations do not offset the monetary rewards; rather, they amplify them. For these migrants, the allure of the new territory is strong, and their allegiance to their initial location is weak. Refugees, whose political allegiance to their initial home has been severed by war or radical shift in government, fall into this category. A new territory can be quite alluring for groups that consider themselves outcasts in their home country; such an appeal is largely responsible for the initial colonization of the United States.[22]

Figure 1.1 summarizes this typology of immigrants. For some potential migrants, both tangible and intangible considerations favor the home country. The potential migrant faces a better standard of living in their home country, and places a higher value on the intangible aspects of residence in that territory as well. This type of potential migrant will presumably refrain from moving, unless some form of domestic catastrophe alters the balance. When tangible considerations favor moving, but intangible considerations do not, the migrant can be classified as a "job-seeker." An alteration in economic

| Tangible costs and benefits: | Intangible costs and benefits: | |
|---|---|---|
| | Favor home country | Favor destination country |
| Favor home country | Will not migrate. | Migrate if intangibles are sufficient to offset tangibles; "home-seeker" |
| Favor destination country | Migrate if tangibles are sufficient to offset intangibles; "job-seeker" | Definitely migrate; "home-seeker" |

**FIGURE 1.1**
**A Typology of Immigrants**

circumstances, either in the destination or origin, might lead this migrant to reverse his earlier decision.[23]

When both intangible and tangible factors favor moving, the migrant can be classified as a "home-seeker." In some cases, the intangible factors can change over time in either the origin or destination, which might in turn lead the migrant to move back to their origin. But a change in tangible circumstances does not carry the same implications for this type of migrant.

Finally, in some cases migrants may face a decline in monetary living standards upon moving, but also a large improvement in the intangible aspects of life. A migrant willing to accept a lower standard of living purely to enjoy the intangible aspects of living in a certain place is here classified as a "home-seeker" as well, even though the use of a common term does not fully acknowledge the differences between the two types. Throughout history, there are relatively few examples of mass migrations that involved individuals accepting inferior economic opportunity in exchange for some intangible amenities. Retirees often choose to relocate to places with poor labor market prospects, but so long as their pension benefits do not vary by location they actually face no economic loss. In fact, the lower cost of living in economically less-vibrant areas might make them better off.

This typology makes clear how changes in immigration policy can influence not only the volume of migrants to a host nation, but also the motives of those who choose to enter. A policy that offered purely financial inducements to migrate, such as an offer to refund tax money paid into state-funded retirement programs, would presumably attract job-seekers ahead of home-seekers. Policies promoting religious tolerance and other intangible aspects of society, conversely, would differentially attract home-seekers.

## Theories of Assimilation

Historically, the scholars most responsible for tracking the integration of immigrants into society have been sociologists. If we maintain the convention that theories explain differences across persons, time, or places, then much of the early work on assimilation must be described as atheoretical. Sociologist Robert Park, a prominent early scholar of assimilation, wrote in 1926 that the process was "progressive and irreversible."[24] If the process is considered inevitable, then there is really no variation to explain. The so-called Chicago school scholars of the early twentieth century thus devoted their efforts not to explaining why assimilation might occur in some instances and not others, but rather to a basic description of the process.[25] Their output was not so much a theory of why something occurs but a model of the way it occurs.

In 1964, sociologist Milton Gordon's *Assimilation in American Life* introduced the most completely enunciated and complex descriptive model of the assimilation process.[26] Gordon identified distinct dimensions of assimilation and argued that different aspects of the process occurred in a specific order. Gordon also introduced the possibility that the ultimate outcome of the assimilation process was not inevitable: that groups might persist in a less-than-perfectly assimilated state over generations. While this represented a clear innovation in the modeling of assimilation, it stops short of a true theory explaining why assimilation might occur in some cases but not others.

Gordon's work was accompanied by other studies of immigrants and their descendants in the 1960s, which concluded that even after decades or generations of residence, group members maintained a distinct cultural identity.[27] The idea that America was a "melting pot," where individuals of varying origins were transformed into a single homogenized prototype, seemed to be refuted by these findings. These positive findings—that full assimilation doesn't really happen—promoted a more normative conclusion, that full assimilation isn't really something to be longed for anyway. From these origins, the celebration of diversity in social science and the academy more generally burgeoned.

Diversity and assimilation are not, in fact, mutually exclusive. The view that assimilation necessarily means the elimination of all dimensions of variability between two groups, and the establishment of one group as the ideal, is overly simplistic. To begin with, no single ethnic group is perfectly homogeneous: members of any given group exhibit variation in aptitude, taste, and habit. Referring to a group as "assimilated" cannot therefore imply that all variation between it and some reference category has been eliminated, as the reference category itself is heterogeneous. Rather, it must imply that the heterogeneity exhibited by one group matches well with the heterogeneity exhibited by a second group.

Taking the argument even further, among the many dimensions along which persons might vary, only a relative few matter from society's perspective. To preview an example from chapter 4, economist Edward Lazear argues that linguistic barriers impede trade.[28] This theoretical work has been supplemented with a great deal of empirical evidence documenting difficulties in societies marked by linguistic fractionalization.[29] Thus, there is a compelling argument to be made that linguistic assimilation is beneficial to society. There is no corresponding argument, however, that society's interests are best served when members are forced to eat the same food, or worship on the same day of the week, or use the same language in the privacy of their own home. Indeed, assimilation can be both beneficial along some dimensions and detrimental in others. The elimination of culinary diversity, for example, would be viewed negatively by most.

Finally, it should be noted that the study of assimilation need not elevate one particular ethnic group as a standard which must be emulated. Assimilation is fundamentally the erosion of critical differences between groups, and changes in the status of any group can be conducive to the goal—this is one of the central points that the work of Richard Alba and Victor Nee has brought to the table. Commonality of language, for example, is a justifiable societal goal, but there is not necessarily a rule for which language should be set forward as the standard. As another example, we will learn in chapter 3 that there are several immigrant groups that outperform the average native-born worker in the labor market. Surely our societal goal would not be to reduce the performance of these groups, but rather to bring the native-born population up to the same standard.

Even though assimilation acquired something of a bad reputation after the 1960s, several true theories of the phenomenon—explanations of why the process occurs in some cases but not others—have emerged in the social science literature in the post-Gordon era. These theories are often not mutually exclusive, and focus on a wide range of factors, from personal to societal. Rational choice theory, applied to this case, would argue that immigrants weigh the costs and benefits of specific actions on the path to assimilation, and take those actions when the anticipated benefits exceed the costs. The rational choice framework has indeed been applied to the question of assimilation, and it is generally considered one of a number of competing theories.[30] As we will see, however, the alternative theories can actually be incorporated into the rational choice framework, making it a form of "unified theory" of assimilative behavior. Alba and Nee, in their book *Remaking the American Mainstream,* refer to the "unified" version of rational choice theory as a "thick" version.[31]

To begin, consider what Alba and Nee would consider the "thin" version of rational choice theory. An individual immigrant choosing, for example, whether to become a naturalized citizen faces certain costs associated with the decision. As we'll discuss more thoroughly in chapter 5, the naturalization process requires some familiarity with American government and history, as well as monetary fees. The benefits of naturalization include effective immunity from future changes in immigration policy, the right to place certain family members in the queue for legal permanent residence, and the right to vote, run for elected office, and participate in other elements of civic life.[32] To a large extent, these costs and benefits can be translated into actual monetary values. Fees are expressed in dollars, and the cost of a civics course can be measured in tuition and the value of foregone work. The right to legally bring family members into the country introduces the possibility of improved family income. Immunity from future changes in immigration policy reduces the likelihood of forced return to one's home country, and the benefit of that could be computed as the difference in living standards between the United States and the other nation. The decision reflects the ratio of costs to returns: if the latter exceed the former, then the immigrant naturalizes.

A similar weighing of costs and benefits attends, in theory, each assimilative decision immigrants make: the decision to learn English, the decision to move away from an ethnic enclave neighborhood, the decision to sign up for training on the job or at school, or even the decision to marry. A critical element of each decision, which we'll expand on in a moment, is that the costs are largely borne immediately, while the benefits accrue over time. The immigrant choosing to naturalize can't be sure that his or her relatives will want to migrate to the United States, and he or she can't be sure of what will happen if they do. They can't be sure that U.S. policy will continue to maintain preferences for relatives in the future. In the event that a migrant later chooses to exit the country, the benefits may be negated entirely. Just as the decision to migrate must incorporate uncertainty regarding future benefits, so must decisions to assimilate.

Because the benefits of assimilation are negated upon exit from the destination country, immigrants who expect to remain in a country for a brief period face very weak incentives to assimilate. The attractiveness of any immigrant's return option will presumably be related to the differential in living standards between origin and destination. For migrants who escaped dire poverty to come to the United States, the prospect of return will be relatively unattractive, and the incentive to assimilate correspondingly high. The return option will be more attractive, in general, when the cost of transport between the origin and destination is small.

Political scientists, psychologists, and other social scientists have formulated numerous critiques of the rational choice model.[33] One of the broadest critiques addresses the presumption that people universally possess the ability to estimate the value of uncertain benefits accruing in the future, and properly incorporate them into a present decision. Suppose I offer you the following proposition: in one year, I'll flip a coin. If it comes up heads, I'll give you $100. If it comes up tails, you get nothing. How much would you be willing to pay today for the right to participate in the gamble? To calculate this rationally, you first determine the expected value of the gamble ($50). You then have to make a decision about how much risk you're willing to accept. If you are risk neutral, that means you consider $50 and a 50 percent chance of getting $100 rather than nothing to be exactly the same thing. If you are risk averse, then even $48 or $49 for sure might be preferable to the 50 percent chance of $100. Once you have an idea of the fixed amount that you consider equivalent to the 50 percent chance of $100, you have to discount that back to the present: think about how much money you'd have to put in an interest-bearing bank account now in order to have that fixed amount in one year, after deducting all relevant taxes on interest payments. Rational choice theory does not assume that individuals explicitly write down these calculations when making this type of decision; it just assumes that they act as though they do.

One straightforward and general criticism of rational choice theory, then, is that people can't always be expected to think quite so clearly about things. Recent literature in behavioral economics has pointed out many different situations where people's behavior appears to violate the maxims of rational choice theory. Dropping out of high school, for example, appears to be an irrational decision, given the substantial differences in the earning power of dropouts and high school graduates.[34] Smokers often state intentions to quit but then fail to follow through.[35] Workers put their money in a particular mutual fund if it is the default option in their 401(k) plan, but not if it isn't.[36] In this particular case, immigrants may rationally calculate that assimilation is in their best interests but then fail to follow through.

The general response to these basic challenges of the tenets of rational choice has not been to abandon the framework, but to extend it in simple ways to enhance its realism. The concept of "bounded" rationality implies that the basic method of weighing costs and benefits is a valid representation of decision-making processes, but that individuals will only go so far to measure costs and benefits.[37] Workers don't opt out of their default 401(k) option because the potential gain from picking a better option is not worth the substantial time it takes to figure out what that better option might be.

When undertaking decisions with long-run consequences, individuals don't bother tallying up the precise expected value of those consequences because it requires too much effort to enumerate them and estimate the probability that each actually comes to pass.

The boundedly rational immigrant, then, might be expected to underassimilate, because the costs of assimilation are generally borne in the present while the benefits accrue over a long period of time. Some individuals may assimilate less than others because they are less willing to sit down and seriously evaluate the long-run consequences. An easy way of summarizing this effect, then, is that the costs associated with the decision to assimilate incorporate the costs of actually evaluating the decision.

Beyond the bounded rationality critique, which applies to most any decision, there are two sociological critiques of rational choice specific to immigrant assimilation. The first is that cultural factors matter—that characteristics of specific immigrant groups may make the path to assimilation easier or more difficult. The second is that institutional factors matter; official policy can have as much bearing on the process as any individual decisions. Just as the rational choice model can be enriched to consider the fallibility of human decision making, so can it also be extended to incorporate these cultural and institutional considerations.

Immigrants belong to national origin or cultural groups with varying degrees of distinctiveness from the native-born majority. Allegiance to these groups may sometimes stand at cross-purposes with assimilation. Steps toward assimilation can be perceived as movements away from an immigrant's own cultural heritage.[38] This conflict is most obvious in cultural decisions. To state an obvious example, parental pressure to marry within one's own religious or ethnic group can pose a significant barrier to intermarriage, typically seen as one of the ultimate signals of integration into broader American society. Only one in five hundred Mexican-born adults currently residing in the United States, for example, is married to a person of non-Mexican heritage.[39] Patterns of dress, worship, and language use at home might also invoke conflicts between origin and host society.

From a rational choice perspective, these cultural ties serve as additional costs associated with certain forms of assimilation. By adopting the native language, or choosing to marry a native-born spouse, the immigrant risks a degree of estrangement from a cultural community. So long as this cultural bond carries value to the individual immigrant, the loosening of that bond is costly. Unlike most costs of assimilation, which are borne up front, the costs of cultural estrangement accrue over the long term.

Some decisions carry little of this cultural baggage. The decision to naturalize, for example, need not ostracize an immigrant from his or her national origin group, especially as the United States generally takes a permissive attitude toward dual citizenship.[40] The decision to learn English for use outside the home also signals little disengagement from the group. In some cases, groups place a positive value on assimilation.[41] And, of course, not all immigrants place a high value on cultural bonds. For this type, the decision to take steps toward cultural assimilation will be easier.

Not all the barriers to assimilation for specific immigrant groups are imposed by the group itself. Historically, many immigrant groups have experienced discrimination of one form or another. The right to become a naturalized citizen, for example, was restricted on the basis of race until the mid-twentieth century. Immigrants can also face discrimination in the labor market, which would impede their economic adjustment into the mainstream. Historically, the existence of prejudice and discrimination against immigrants has been strong enough that Milton Gordon considered the erosion of each to be specific steps on the path to assimilation. From a rational choice perspective, prejudice and discrimination introduce additional costs of taking steps toward assimilation. In some cases, these extra costs are effectively infinite, as was the case when naturalization was prohibited to certain classes of immigrants.

The reference to official immigration policy as a determinant of the costs and benefits of assimilating introduces the institutional critique of rational choice theory. Government policies, which are beyond the control of any one individual, have an undeniable effect on assimilation decisions. Practices not officially codified into policy can also have an impact. From the rational choice perspective, policies determine the menu of costs and benefits associated with specific decisions. Government policy can more or less directly determine many costs and benefits of naturalization. Government can also provide inducements to learn English or take additional steps toward cultural assimilation.[42] Workforce policies can also influence economic assimilation. One can even argue that government influences the costs and benefits of intermarriage, by establishing higher naturalization priorities for the spouses of citizens, or by issuing certain rulings regarding the rights of married couples.

Immigrants from specific countries of origin face common sets of returns to assimilation. Culture determines some of these returns; pressure to marry within one's ethnic group, for example, varies across cultures. Policy determines others; immigration law in the United States often treats aliens differently depending on their country of origin.[43] Expectations regarding duration of stay, which directly impact the expected benefits of assimilation, are to a large extent governed by country-specific factors. For traditional home-seeking migrants, the prospects of a speedy return are slim, and the incentives to assimilate are therefore great. For job-seeking migrants, the expected duration of stay is lower and the incentives to assimilate correspondingly lower.

Figure 1.2 summarizes the "thick," or "enhanced," rational choice model of an immigrant's assimilation decision. The basic decision rule is derived directly from rational choice theory: take a step toward assimilation so long as the benefits of that step exceed the costs. The enhancement of the basic model comes from the realization that the set of benefits and costs may include factors not ordinarily associated with the typical economic decision. The "traditional" set of costs and benefits includes those things that could most readily be evaluated in a quantitative framework. Many of these traditional costs and benefits accrue in the long run, and thus expectations

|  | Potential Costs | Potential Benefits |
|---|---|---|
| Traditional short-term | --Tuition for courses in naturalization or English --Government-imposed fees | Personal satisfaction. |
| Traditional long-term: valuation depends on expected duration of stay in the host country | --Loss of citizenship or other privileges in the origin country. --Increased difficulty of re-integration in the origin country. | --Better employment prospects --Option to bring relatives into the country legally --Option for civic participation in many forms |
| Bounded rationality | Evaluating the payoffs accruing at future dates, estimating the probability they will occur, discounting that expected value back to the present. | Few if any. |
| Cultural | --Potential for ostracism from native cultural group --Obstacles associated with prejudice and discrimination by natives. | Cultural groups can place a positive value on assimilation. |
| Institutional | Institutions govern many traditional costs | Institutions also determine many traditional benefits. Non-governmental institutions can ease the path to assimilation or provide benefits to those who choose to assimilate. |

**FIGURE 1.2**
**The Costs and Benefits of Assimilation**

regarding an immigrant's duration of stay in the host country factor directly into their evaluation.

Beyond the traditional costs and benefits are three additional categories. Costs associated with bounded rationality include the cost of actually engaging in the evaluation in the first place. These costs are high for those immigrants with neither the time nor inclination to think carefully about them. In some cases, however, the perceived benefits are substantial enough that no careful calculation is necessary.

Cultural costs are rooted in the potential ostracism associated with actions that appear to increase the social distance between an individual and his or her cultural group. There may also be cultural benefits, however, for individuals belonging to groups that place a high value on assimilation. Finally, institutions enter into the equation not so much by introducing new costs or benefits but by determining the value in other categories.

The rational choice model, suitably enhanced, offers a range of predictions for which types of immigrants, under which circumstances, will be most likely to take steps toward assimilation—for example, learning to speak English, becoming a naturalized citizen, moving out of an ethnic enclave neighborhood, or intermarrying. The next five chapters of the book will document the consistency (or lack thereof) between these predictions and actual patterns of assimilation. The evidence, drawn from more than a century's worth of statistical information on immigrants in the United States, along with this conceptual framework, will help us to think about the trade-offs incorporated in immigration policy, and how policy changes might alter both the flow of migrants to the United States and the experiences of those migrants once they arrive. Before proceeding to that discussion, however, it is worth spending some time talking about where the data for this analysis come from.

### Tracking Immigrant Decisions through History

This book certainly does not represent the first effort to track the assimilation of immigrants in the United States. As the preceding discussion of the theory of assimilation indicates, many prominent sociologists have studied the progress of specific groups in specific communities or at particular points in time. The roster contains many illustrious names: Park and Burgess of the Chicago school, the mid-century work of Glazer, Moynihan, and Lieberson, not to mention the more recent landmark studies of Alba and Nee, as well as sociologist and historian Joel Perlmann.[44]

This book expands on these earlier works by considering a wider array of assimilation indicators and a broader time span, and by judging assimilation by following cohorts of immigrants over time, rather than assessing their status at a single point in time. The entire exercise is made possible by the availability of data, dating back to the mid-nineteenth century, from the U.S. Census Bureau.

Article 1, section 2, of the U.S. Constitution mandates that the government conduct a decennial enumeration of the population of each state, for purposes of apportioning representatives in Congress. Since the originally ratified Constitution mandated that apportionment be based on the sum of free persons and three-fifths the total number of slaves, the census had to do more than just count the number of bodies in each state. It had to sort them by category.

From this basic beginning, the scope of the census expanded over time. The first published census report in 1790 reported population totals for states, counties, and in some cases towns, then proceeded to name every single head of household in the entire nation and describe the composition of their household. Sixty years later, the exhaustive names were no longer published, but the Census Bureau had begun collecting additional information for everyone enumerated: their birthplace, whether they attended school, whether they could read or write, what occupation and industry they worked in if they worked for pay, the value of real estate they owned, and what specific city they lived in if they lived in a city. Another sixty years after that, the Census Bureau had added questions about the year of immigration for the foreign-born, citizenship status, not just the city of residence but the ward within that city, and the ability to speak English. Another sixty years after that, and in every enumeration between 1970 and 2000, the Census Bureau collected additional information on educational attainment, income, the number of hours worked per week and weeks worked per year, and a host of information on the housing unit a family lived in: the value if owned, the monthly rent if rented, utility costs, kitchen facilities, the presence of nine different household appliances or conveniences, and so on.

The gradual broadening of the census from its original mandate to all-purpose social survey certainly had its drawbacks, but from the perspective of a researcher interested in gaining a snapshot into the life and standing of individuals and families at various points in history, it provides a treasure trove. After 2000, the Census Bureau decided to retrench and reduce the scope of questions asked in the decennial census. At the same time, though, the Bureau began administering the annual American Community Survey (ACS), which collects a rich array of data from a representative sample of American households. From a statistical perspective, having detailed information on just 1 percent of the U.S. population is just about as good as having the same information from 100 percent of the population.

The responses individuals give to the census or ACS, stripped of personally identifying information such as name or address, are in many cases available to the public. All the ACS responses are available for public use, and a representative sample of census responses for the years 1850–2000, with only a couple of exceptions, are available as well. The work of releasing this information to the public, in a format that makes it relatively easy to use, has been undertaken by the Minnesota Population Center, at the University of Minnesota. The Integrated Public Use Microdata System (IPUMS) project has enabled not only the study of immigrant experiences across centuries, a task to which we will soon turn, but a host of other important historical and contemporary research projects.[45]

Figure 1.3 provides a list of important pieces of information about immigrants or the native-born collected by the Census Bureau through history and made available through the IPUMS project. The presence of this information makes the entire exercise, a tracking of the progress and experiences of immigrants over time, feasible. There are certain important gaps in the dataset, however, which introduce limitations. The absence of information on year of immigration in census enumerations before 1900 makes it impossible to track the progress of migrants as they spend more time in the United States. Citizenship and English-speaking ability, two critical measures of assimilation, are not reliably available until the twentieth century as well. As will be discussed in chapter 5, the measurement of language ability also changes in important ways over time.

| Variable | Years available |
|---|---|
| Birthplace | 1850-2007 |
| Year of immigration | 1900-1930; 1970-2007 |
| Citizenship status | 1870; 1900-1950; 1970-2007 |
| Ability to Speak English | 1900-1930; 1970-2007 |
| Labor force participation | 1850-2007 |
| Occupation | 1850-2007 |
| Income | 1940-2007 |
| Marital status & spouse characteristics | 1850-2007 |

**FIGURE 1.3**
**Data Items Available Through the IPUMS Project**

The IPUMS data consist of the actual survey responses that individuals give when they fill out census or ACS forms. The Census Bureau also reports summary statistics for all the individuals residing in specific geographic areas. In 1910 and 1920, census data provide a count of the foreign-born population, by country of birth, at the ward level in major cities. Between 1960 and 1990, a count of foreign-born population by country of birth is available at an even finer level of geography, known as a census tract.[46] Census tracts usually contain around four thousand people, and thus come relatively close to capturing actual neighborhoods. Information on where immigrants of specific nationalities reside within cities allows us to study the tendency for the foreign-born to live in ethnic enclaves, in chapter 7.

The census and ACS are far from perfect; the census does not collect information on whether immigrants reside in the United States legally, nor does it ask respondents about specific civic behaviors such as voting. More detailed surveys of immigrant behavior, such as the polls conducted and released by the Pew Hispanic Center, are available for the present, but there is no historical analogue from the nineteenth or early twentieth centuries for purposes of comparison.[47]

While it is the Census Bureau's mission to report data that are representative of the entire population of U.S. residents, it is well known that certain people either fail to return their census forms or actively avoid being enumerated. Immigrants in general, and illegal immigrants specifically, are likely to fall in this category of "undercounted" residents. Illegal immigrants may refuse to cooperate because they fear that the information they share might be reported to immigration authorities. In reality, the Census Bureau is statutorily prohibited from sharing information with other government agencies. It might be difficult to convince a skeptical respondent of this, however.

The Census Bureau employs statistical methods to try to counteract undercounting.[48] And according to independent assessments, the problem of undercounting has receded in recent years, even as the population of immigrants has risen.[49] Nonetheless, undercounting poses a threat to the accuracy of conclusions drawn from census data. The threat is likely to be modest, however, as even for relatively hard-to-survey groups the undercount rate amounts to a few percentage points.[50]

A final caveat worth bearing in mind is that information reported in the census, whether derived from interviews with census-takers or mail questionnaires, is self-reported. The Census Bureau is not responsible for independently verifying the accuracy of claims. There are clear cases where data accuracy is a problem; for example, it has been shown that individuals have a tendency to overstate their educational attainment.[51] Specific concerns about the accuracy of the data will be addressed as they arise.

# 2

# A Historical Overview of Immigration to the United States

The bosom of America is open to receive not only the Opulent and respected Stranger, but the oppressed and persecuted of all Nations and
Religions; whom we shall welcome to a participation of all our rights and
privileges, if by decency and propriety of conduct they appear to merit
the enjoyment.

> —George Washington (1783), letter to the Volunteer Association
> of the Kingdom of Ireland Lately Arrived in the City of New York

SINCE THE COLONIAL ERA, America has offered a persistent plethora of
economic opportunities to would-be immigrants. The nation's attitudes
toward immigrants, however, at least as evinced by its statesmen, have vac-
illated over time. For over two centuries, natives of the United States have
looked suspiciously on certain types of migrants, even while welcoming
others. George Washington's letter of thanks to an organization of Irish immigrants at the close of war with Britain foreshadows many of the themes
we'll encounter in this chapter's survey of migration and the native response.
Washington does not offer an unconditional welcome to potential immigrants, but rather imposes expectations of behavior. These expectations
would be codified in the nation's first naturalization law enacted seven years
later, and have remained ever since.

Tellingly, and befitting a nation originally populated by religious dissidents,
Washington's welcome is not offered to tired, poor, huddled masses, but rather
to "the oppressed and persecuted."[1] The "Opulent and respected Stranger" is
welcome as well. Throughout American history, there is a recurring theme of

openness to politically motivated "home-seeking" immigrants, impelled to migrate because they are not accepted in their homeland, accompanied by resistance to migrants who appear to be arriving for no reason except to improve their economic lot in life. This hesitation to accept economically motivated migrants tends to be accentuated when the group in question bears some ethnic distinction from the native population.

For an early statement of opposition to immigration of the "wrong" kind, we need look no further than Benjamin Franklin's 1751 treatise quoted at the beginning of chapter 1. Franklin's final sentences express concern that the great opportunities available in the colonies would attract not British subjects, but rather immigrants of much less desirable origins. German immigrants, or more specifically "Palatine Boors," in Franklin's vitriol, were singled out as the greatest threat.[2]

Franklin lumped most Germans ("the Saxons only excepted") together with natives of Spain, Italy, France, Russia, Sweden, Africa, and Asia, calling the lot inferior to "White People."[3] But Palatine immigrants of the eighteenth century were distinct not only because of their complexion, but also their rationale for migration to the United States. Whereas the canonical American colonizers were religious dissidents seeking freedom of worship, the Palatines fled what is now southwestern Germany in the early eighteenth century for more purely economic reasons: their population was too great to be supported by local agriculture, and the governing regime imposed consfiscatory taxes.[4] This was not a group facing some specific persecution or calamity. Rather, the Palatines seemed more like simple arbitrageurs, purely exploiting differences in living standards across nations. The Palatines were thus one of the earliest waves of "job-seeking" migrants to arrive in America, and the opposition they inspired would resemble negative reactions to later immigrant groups from other parts of the world.

From the nation's colonial origins to the present day, the United States has offered opportunities and a standard of living difficult to match in most other parts of the world. In the colonial era, abundant natural resources and the absence of barriers to land ownership offered migrants the promise of agricultural self-sufficiency. The nineteenth century witnessed the undertaking of vast infrastructure projects, from regional canals to transcontinental railroads, and the beginnings of industrialization, both of which created opportunities for unskilled workers willing to engage in hard manual labor. And for most of this time period, there were absolutely no restrictions on immigration to the United States. Only in 1882, with the passage of the Chinese Exclusion Act, was the concept of an "illegal immigrant" invented.

Even as manufacturing jobs began to dwindle in the United States in the late twentieth century, unskilled or semiskilled workers could still find opportunities in services, construction, and other industries. At the same time, highly skilled workers often could find the best market for their talents in the United States. Through the ages, government in America avoided policy failures, rooted in calamitous errors of central planning or sheer kleptocracy, that erased opportunities in less fortunate nations. Government policy did, however, impose broadening restrictions on access to the American labor market, with the national origin quotas of the 1920s, and the restrictions on the number of visas available after the quotas were dropped in 1965. As restrictions on immigration and the existence of superior economic opportunities persist, while the costs of transportation and communication drop, illegal immigration has become a more salient policy issue.

Just as the force of gravity pulls water toward the sea, economic opportunity has drawn a flow of migrants to the United States over more than four centuries of history. And just as humans have seen fit through the ages to alter or restrict the flow of streams, so have political factions in this country sought to manage the flow of immigrants. The benefits of immigration to the migrant, discussed by Franklin and elucidated more completely in chapter 1, are quite clear. The benefits to the remainder of society, however, are more uncertain. As we'll discuss more thoroughly in chapter 3, the entry of new immigrants poses a threat to some natives, who effectively profit from the scarcity of workers and landowners in this country. The easing of this scarcity creates benefits, however, for other members of society. Therein lies the root of political conflict over immigration policy.

As we review the history of immigration to the United States in this chapter, we will see repeated cycles leading up to the present day. A new immigrant group arrives in substantial numbers, provoking concern and in some cases legislation. Over time, immigration by that group slows to a trickle, the group quietly joins the mainstream, and the great consternation that accompanied the group's initial arrival begins to look quaint in hindsight. The greatest opposition, as suggested by our attentive study of Washington and Franklin, has been associated with those immigrants drawn by economic opportunity alone, and not because they seek to escape persecution, repression, or natural calamity in their home country.

If extrapolated to the current day, the lesson of history would appear to be that worries over the immigration of any particular group are misplaced. We don't worry about the Germanization of the American population now; hence we might rationally anticipate that "Mexicanization" will be comparably laughed off in one hundred years' time.

Our review of history will also point out, however, some important points of departure. The waves of immigration that occurred before 1920 were remarkably uncoordinated across nations of origin. Both information and people traveled slowly in that era; ocean passage was costlier and likely more hazardous.[5] Immigration from specific countries was often precipitated by famine, war, or other specific events. By contrast, the immigration wave that has occurred since 1970, with a few exceptions, appears more coordinated—more clearly a function of changes in American immigration policy than of conditions in any specific foreign country. In many cases, there has been no catastrophic precipitating event. In the modern era, travel is quicker and cheaper, and information spreads more rapidly.

The rise of rapid, inexpensive travel, and instantaneous communication regarding the availability of opportunities in specific occupations in particular places, has expanded the ranks of economically motivated "job-seeking" immigrants, the modern descendents of the Palatines. Among them are unskilled laborers born in Mexico or nearby Latin American countries, as well as skilled workers for whom citizenship and national allegiance have become anachronistic concepts in an era of globalization. A Canadian citizen, with an advanced degree from an American university, might work for an investment bank, shuttling back and forth between New York, London, or other financial centers. At the same time, a Mexican national might travel from region to region, following agricultural harvests, construction work, or other opportunities. Both reside in the United States alongside home-seeking immigrants, who like their historic predecessors come to the United States to flee persecution, bloodshed, or abject poverty in their home countries with the intention of raising their descendants as Americans.

In the remainder of this chapter, we'll extend our analysis of the motives of major immigrant groups, and popular reaction to those groups, from the early eighteenth century to the early twenty-first century. Of course, this description of the history of immigration to the United States will pale in comparison to the volumes that have been written previously.[6] Our goal here is not so much to be comprehensive as to point out important patterns in the experiences of specific immigrant groups and in popular reaction to those groups.

### The Irish, the Germans, and the Know-Nothings

While migration of non-British subjects to the American colonies was clearly an issue as early as the mid-eighteenth century, serious study of the foreign-born in the United States is difficult to conduct in the period prior to 1850. In that year, the Census Bureau, charged with interviewing every resident of the United States decennially, started asking every individual where they were born. Published census statistics thus start tracking the foreign-born in earnest at that time. In 1850, there were over two million immigrants in a nation that counted only twenty-three million inhabitants. Over 85 percent of these immigrants, however, came from just three nations: Great Britain, Ireland, and Germany. While it is not possible to track the precise date of arrival for immigrants enumerated in the 1850 census, other historical statistics indicate that some four hundred thousand English immigrants arrived between 1825 and 1850, along with close to one million Irish and a considerable number of Germans.[7] As figure 2.1 indicates, immigration from each of these countries was building to a crest that would occur at least two decades hence. Thus the story of immigration in the United States is probably not grievously damaged by the absence of systematic data in the early days of the republic.

The decades immediately before and after 1850 witnessed rapid immigration from Germany and Ireland. The event traditionally associated with the onset of Irish immigration to the United States was an agricultural disaster in the mid-1840s, in which a fungal infection destroyed a large portion of the potato crop. Many of the nearly one million Irish immigrants in the United States as of 1850 had likely arrived in the few years since this calamity.[8] Rapid immigration from Ireland persisted through 1870. The case of Ireland represents a phenomenon we associate with some of the nation's earliest settlers and repeated over time: an initial event precipitates migration, but the wave of migration crests some years after this event. As we discussed in chapter 1,

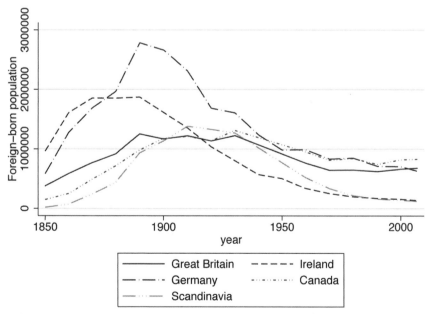

**FIGURE 2.1**
**Major Groups of the Late Nineteenth Century**

the transit of an initial group of "pioneering" migrants opens up a network of information for others, effectively reducing the cost and uncertainty of their own migration.[9]

We know from our study of Franklin's comments that substantial migration from the states that would evolve into modern Germany took place as early as the eighteenth century. A very clear wave of immigration crests after 1850, however, as the total population of German-born residents of the United States more than tripled between 1850 and 1890. The origins of this wave lie in civic and political unrest in the states that would become Germany, culminating in broad revolts in 1848.[10] This wave of German immigration slows in the decades of the 1860s and 1870s, only to spike again after 1880. This last surge of immigration from Germany is at least in part attributable to a wave of Jewish immigration, sparked by incidents in Russia in the early 1880s, which spread throughout Eastern Europe and lasted through the early twentieth century. We will soon see that large-scale migration from Russia, Poland, and Hungary began around this time. The Census Bureau did not record information about religious affiliation or ethnic heritage in this era, so immigrants can only be identified by their country of origin.

Virtually all the mid-nineteenth century immigrants from Ireland, and a sizable proportion of the pre-1880 German immigrants, were Catholic. The principal anti-immigration movement of the time, the Know-Nothing party, objected primarily to this religious affiliation. The Know-Nothings achieved some electoral success in the mid-1850s, particularly in Massachusetts, where the party won a number of statewide races in the election of 1854.[11] The rising tide of Know-Nothingism alarmed, among others, Abraham Lincoln, who wrote in a letter in 1855: "How can anyone who abhors the oppression of negroes, be in favor of degrading a class of white people? . . . When the Know-Nothings get control, [the Declaration of Independence] will read 'all men are created equal, except negroes, and foreigners, and Catholics.'"[12] The expression of certainty here ("when" rather than "if") may be a rhetorical flourish, but reveals a fear, if not necessarily an expectation, that the party's populist message would quickly spread throughout the nation. In fact, the movement would soon founder, as other emergent political movements of the era, including the Republican Party, splintered the coalition over slavery and other issues. The anti-immigrant movement may also have dissipated because the German and Irish immigrants of the mid-nineteenth century fit the basic mold of the "oppressed and persecuted." The Irish Catholics were fleeing not only famine but British rule, and the Germans could point to civil conflict as the root of their movement. They showed quick loyalty to the United States, in part by serving in large numbers in the Civil War. Economic historians Dora Costa and Matthew Kahn, in their study of the behavior and experiences of Civil War soldiers both during and after the conflict, note that German-origin Union soldiers had particularly low rates of desertion.[13] As such, they could arouse a certain sympathy that later waves of migrants would not be able to tap.

After the Know-Nothing episode, the public expression of anti-immigrant sentiment entered a period of dormancy until the late 1870s, when it would be reignited by a numerically much smaller wave of immigration from China and Japan. A "knee-jerk" assessment of this opposition might point to the racial distinctions between these immigrants and the white majority. While racism clearly played some role in the treatment of Chinese and Japanese immigrants, it is also true that the root causes of immigration from these nations were economic rather than political.[14]

### The Slowly Growing Groups: Canadians, British, and Scandinavians

While the population of Irish and German immigrants grew rapidly in the 1850s, waves of immigration from Canada, Great Britain, and Scandinavia were also underway. Whereas the Irish wave clearly crested in 1870, and the non-Jewish German wave by 1880, these other movements proceeded more slowly, reaching plateaus between 1890 and 1910. In some cases, these immigration waves can be traced to specific precipitating disasters, but in most the root cause of migration is primarily economic. The absence of organized opposition to these migration waves could reflect two aspects. First, immigrants from northern Europe may have enjoyed greater acceptance on the basis of their ethnicity. Second, the slow nature of their group's growth may have permitted immigrants to stay "below the radar," in modern parlance, arousing little attention from the native majority.

In Sweden, the most important single origin country within Scandinavia, official restrictions on emigration were lifted in 1860.[15] Swedish restrictions would have also applied in Norway during the period of union between the two nations, which began in 1814. Immigration from Denmark was sparked by the visit of Mormon missionaries to that nation around 1850, and by the transfer of Schleswig and Holstein to Prussian rule in the 1860s.[16] Accounts of the causes of Scandinavian migration refer to these precipitating events, but also cite standard concerns of rural dislocation and industrialization as impetuses.[17]

The comparatively slow crest of the Scandinavian immigration wave, and the lack of organized opposition to these economically motivated migrants, may owe something to the rural distribution of the immigrant population in the United States. Whereas Irish and German immigrants were found in large numbers in the growing cities of the late nineteenth century, Scandinavians were more likely to take root in rural areas, in many cases taking advantage of the Homestead Act of 1862.[18] Danish migrants were drawn disproportionately to Utah.[19] Urbanicity may be conducive to rapid migration, as information about specific opportunities can be more readily broadcast to a wider group of potential migrants. An urban immigrant could encourage his entire village to come work at a specific factory in the United States; a rural farmer could offer only more generic information about the types of opportunities available to potential migrants.

Nineteenth-century immigration from Canada to the United States represents a clear example of economic migration. There is no obvious policy change or catastrophe that precipitated an immigration wave. Rather, most migration between the countries reflected short-distance moves, most often from Quebec and the Maritime provinces to New England, Michigan, and other locations close to the border. The process of industrialization, affecting both nations in this time period, shifted the locus of opportunity from rural to urban areas. While many rural Canadians moved to cities such as Halifax and Montreal, quite a few more took advantage of new opportunities south of the border. In some cases, labor agents from New England actively recruited Canadians to work in unskilled mill positions.[20] Anti-Canadian sentiment was recorded in some instances, especially as Canadian immigrants were sometimes brought in to break trade unions operating in New England mill towns.[21] The limited geographic scope of migration, along with the high degree of cultural similarity between Canadians and Americans, most likely limited any potential backlash.

British emigration to the United States also occurred at a relatively steady pace, with three small but distinct waves between 1840 and 1893.[22] The repeal of the Corn Laws, a set of agricultural tariffs propping up landowning interests, in 1846 is often invoked as the original impetus for British migration at mid-century.[23] While agricultural workers were heavily represented among emigrants of this era, industrial workers and miners also arrived in significant numbers.[24] The rate of migration slowed from 1850 until 1880, at which point a brief resurgence brought the number of British natives in America to a plateau that would last until World War II. This resurgence coincided with the beginning of a wave of British emigration to other commonwealth nations, including Canada, Australia, and New Zealand.

This larger wave of departure from Great Britain is typically attributed to rapid natural increase of the population: as in other industrializing nations at other points in time, mortality rates decreased while birth rates remained relatively constant for a time.[25] Although economically motivated, British immigrants inspired little in the way of organized opposition. Their capacity to blend in to the host society led historian Charlotte Erickson to label the British as "invisible immigrants."[26]

As noted above, it would not be accurate to state that the late nineteenth century was completely devoid of organized opposition to immigration. The Chinese Exclusion Act of 1882, initially intended to be a temporary ban on Chinese immigration, was strengthened and renewed repeatedly over time until its ultimate repeal in 1943. Immigration from China attracted much stronger legislative opposition than European immigration, in spite of the fact that there were sixty European-born foreigners in the United States for every one born in China as of 1880. In light of this evidence, it is difficult to deny that race played some role in inspiring the Chinese Exclusion Act. The Chinese shared economic motivation and a modest rate of immigration with these slowly growing groups, and were regionally concentrated much as the Canadians were. Yet they inspired a much more virulent congressional response.

### The Penultimate Wave: Southern and Eastern Europeans

Emigration from Germany, Ireland, and the remainder of northern and western Europe drove a trebling of the foreign-born population of the United States between 1850 and 1880; the growth rate during this period was nearly identical to that observed more recently between 1970 and 2000. Aside from the flash-in-the-pan Know-Nothing movement and opposition to the numerically insignificant wave of immigration from China, this immigration caused little in the way of civic debate. In the thirty years after 1880, growth in the foreign-born population would actually slow, doubling rather than tripling. This slower growth started from a much larger base population, though. The net arrival of some seven million immigrants by 1910 would occasion a popular uprising that culminated in the imposition of severe official restrictions on immigration beginning in 1920. These restrictions would in turn bring all waves of immigration to a crashing halt, to revive only in the period since 1965.

The distinction, of course, is that the composition of the immigrant population changed substantially after 1880. Although the population of Scandinavian and British Americans increased during the 1880s, the growth of these groups fell dramatically after 1890. At the same time, as shown in figure 2.2, the 1880s mark the emergence of new waves that would build dramatically through 1910. These new waves of immigrants from Eastern and Southern Europe inspired a virulent reaction from the native-born community. As we

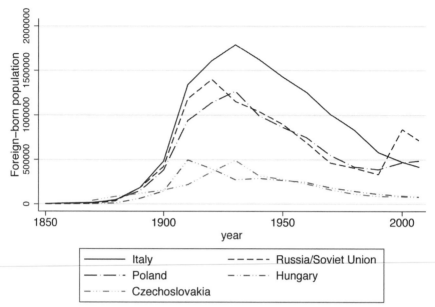

**FIGURE 2.2**
**Major Groups of the Early Twentieth Century**

might expect by this point, the participants in this immigration wave were distinctive not only for their ethnicity but also for their main motivations for migrating. In particular, the largest single country-of-origin group of the early twentieth century, Italians, constituted the largest cohort of "job-seeking" migrants in American history up until the contemporary wave of migrants from Mexico.

Not all post-1880 immigrants fall into the "job-seeking" mold. We have already referred to one precipitating incident provoking immigration in the years just after 1880. The 1881 assassination of Alexander II in Russia led to social unrest that culminated in ethnic violence, with Jews in the Ukraine, Poland, and other regions at the periphery of Russian influence the primary targets.[27] This wave of pogroms in turn provoked Jewish emigration from the region. By the time that restrictions on immigration were imposed in the 1920s, about three of every ten Eastern European Jews had relocated to the United States.[28] As noted above, the U.S. Census Bureau does not permit the tracking of immigrants by ethnic group, only by birthplace. Figure 2.2 shows that the number of immigrants from Russia and Poland was negligible in 1880, but began a steady rise after that date.

Jewish immigrants in the United States faced discrimination and prejudice, but rarely if ever did this escalate to full-blown violence. As in Europe, the group was associated with a full set of stereotyped characteristics, and their reluctance to intermarry and adopt certain other typically "American" habits was noted by contemporary observers.[29] Nonetheless, the rise of Jewish immigration inspired relatively little official concern. When the Immigration Act of 1917 imposed a requirement that aliens over sixteen years of age be able to read in some language prior to admission, Hebrew and Yiddish were the only foreign languages specifically enumerated.

Jewish emigrants from Eastern Europe were joined by members of other ethnic groups. Polish Catholics, who saw their homeland divided by Prussia, Russia, and Austria from the late eighteenth century until the end of World War I, were driven to depart by a number of factors at the end of the nineteenth century. Those living under German rule were relegated to second-class citizen status by the Constitution of 1871. Bismarck's "Kulturkampf" policies promoted the use of the German language and placed restrictions on Polish clergy. The great wave of Polish immigration was thus initiated primarily by politically motivated Poles living in the region of German occupation.[30]

The peak of emigration from the Russian- and Austrian-controlled portions of Poland occurred at a later point in time.[31] Political repression played at least some role in emigration from the Russian-controlled territory. The czar's government imposed religious and cultural restrictions comparable to those imposed by Bismarck; these restrictions helped lead to a series of general strikes collectively referred to as the Revolution of 1905–1907. The strikes also had economic antecedents, however, related to the traditional problems of rural dislocation and industrialization.[32] Thus, even though the ultimate response to this unrest was military occupation, it is not clear that emigration from Russian-controlled Poland should be considered purely political in motivation. Austrian-occupied Galicia was another major source of immigrants late in the wave of Polish migration; economic considerations were the major impetus in this more politically hospitable region.[33]

The mixed rationales for Polish migration also led some observers to lump them in with other groups whose presence in the United States more clearly reflected economic circumstances, particularly Italians. Sociologist Edward Alsworth Ross, the originator of the distinction between "home-seeking" and "job-seeking" immigrants, would be pilloried for his stereotyping and sweeping generalizations in the modern era. Ross, writing in 1914, noted a tendency for Poles to be "clannish" and to "cling to their old speech and traditions" and attributed it to the cultural suppression they had escaped in Germany and Russia.[34]

In the history of immigration to the United States, there is no parallel to the growth of Italy as an origin country. Between 1870 and 1910, the number of Italian-born residents in the United States grew by a factor of seventy-eight.

To exhibit an analogous trend, the number of Mexican-born residents in the United States would have to increase to nearly sixty million in 2010 from its base of seven hundred sixty thousand in 1970. The actual total will likely be less than one-fourth that number. The rapid rate of Italian immigration was startling to observers at the time. Edward Alsworth Ross stated that the population of Italian immigrants had "shot up like a Jonah's gourd."[35] Ross further opined that "one sees no reason why the Italian dusk should not in time quench what of the Celto-Teutonic flush lingers in the cheek of the native American."[36] An impressive statement, which not-so-subtly conveys the notion that natives of Italy are to be considered racially distinct and inferior, while simultaneously granting a measure of acceptance to the millions of Irish and Germans still residing in the United States at the time.[37]

Both contemporary and modern accounts of emigration from Italy cite persistent, long-run economic factors as the principal causes.[38] At a time when other nations were industrializing rapidly, Italy continued to be a more agrarian nation, and a relatively unsuccessful one at that.[39] Italians left in large number not only for the United States, but also to other parts of Europe and South America. As late as the 1890s, the number of Italians migrating to Brazil and Argentina exceeded the number moving to the United States.[40] Italian migrants to the United States were disproportionately natives of the less-developed southern portion of the country, while migrants to the rest of Europe and South America were more likely to hail from the north.[41]

The foreboding imagery associated with Italian immigration by observers like Ross may in part reflect the failure of this group to conform to the traditional American narrative of immigration, traceable to the arrival of the Pilgrims in 1620. This was not a group facing some specific persecution or calamity, who found themselves with little choice but to seek out a new homeland. Rather, like many smaller groups before them, the Italians seemed more like simple arbitrageurs, purely exploiting differences in living standards across nations. Consistent with this impression, Italians had a higher rate of return or onward migration relative to other groups of the same era.[42] This created a new set of concerns for contemporary observers. A flow of political migrants might be expected to cease once political conditions had changed, but economic migrants would presumably continue to flow until living standards in origin and destination were equalized. As Ross himself wrote, "An outflow of political exiles comes to an end when there is a turn of the political wheel; but a stream squeezed out by population pressure may flow on forever."[43]

Some lesser national origin groups of the period share the economic motivation of Italians and many Poles, including the wave of Hungarian immigrants which peaked in 1910. Concern regarding the characteristics and volume of immigration began to stir restrictionist passions around the turn of the century. Congress passed four different bills imposing literacy tests on immigrants between 1896 and 1917; each one was vetoed. On the fourth attempt, Congress finally overrode President Wilson's veto. The first system of national origin quotas followed four years later, and the second three years after that. Reflecting the perceived undesirable nature of immigration flows in the years after 1890, the quotas enacted by the Johnson-Reed Act in 1924 were tied to the size of a group's population in the 1890 census. Colorado congressman William Vaile, speaking in favor of the adjustment to the quota system, specifically referred to Italy and Poland as two countries of origin from which immigration deserved to be further restricted.[44]

A simple glance at figure 2.2 might lead one to believe that the quotas had little immediate impact, as the population of individuals born in Italy, Poland, and Czechoslovakia was in fact higher in 1930 than it had been in 1920. Net immigration to the United States likely would have been much higher in these years, however, given the dislocations associated with the collapse of the Austro-Hungarian and Ottoman Empires at the end of World War I, and the Russian Revolution of 1917. After 1930, immigration from all the source countries studied to this point began a long-term decline, which in some cases has persisted to the present day.

## Summarizing the Lessons of History

History provides us with several lessons. As argued in chapter 1, there are two prototypes for waves of immigration to the United States. Traditional waves of "home-seekers" tend to be spawned by certain political events or natural catastrophes. For the greater part of American history, the great expense and hazard associated with an ocean voyage implied that only those aliens facing the direst of circumstances in their own nation would attempt the journey in large numbers. While these migrants have often encountered discrimination or outright opposition to their presence in the native population, the dominant themes in their experience relate to acceptance and eventual assimilation.

The "job-seeking" or economic migrants differ along a number of dimensions. No single precipitating factor explains the rise of these waves; their motivation instead lies in the existence of persistent differences in living standards between origin and destination. Economic migrants are more likely to return to their origin or move onward to a third destination. Finally, popular opposition to immigration—from Franklin's rant about the "Palatine boors" to Ross's fear of an "Italian dusk"—centers more squarely on economic migrants.

The distinction between traditional and economic migrants is more than a purely academic observation. As we discussed in the preceding chapter, differences in initial motivation translate into differences in the incentives for immigrants to assimilate into American society. Immigration policy can be used as a tool either to encourage or discourage assimilation; the choice of incentives carries important implications for the type of emigrant who will choose to settle in the United States, and ultimately for the degree of cohesion in American society.

### Were the Quotas Good or Bad?

One can point to the relative lack of concern about Italian Americans, Hungarian Americans, or other specific groups in the early twenty-first century and claim either that the immigration quotas of 1921–1965 were unnecessary, or that they were crucial to the successful assimilation of an unprecedented wave of migrants. History does not afford us the luxury of observing what would have happened in the absence of restrictions. Answers to the counterfactual question will always be rhetorical, based on opinion more than evidence.

We can, however, make some more definitive statements about the impact of the quotas on the nation as a whole. The economic opportunities that attracted immigrants, rooted in the industrializing cities of the Northeast and Midwest, did not dry up after the quotas were passed. Rather, the heavy demand for unskilled and semiskilled labor persisted and began to draw on a new source of workers, residents of rural areas, particularly from the American South.[45]

The immigration quotas undoubtedly carried a humanitarian toll. During World War II, potential refugees, including the infamous Jewish passengers on the S.S. *St. Louis*, were precluded from entering the United States.[46] It is unclear that the United States would have maintained an open door policy in the absence of quotas; public opinion at the time of the *St. Louis* incident expressed sympathy for the refugees but generally opposed the option of allowing them to disembark.[47]

If it is correct to think of American policy as favorably disposed toward traditional "home-seeking" immigrants, but not job-seekers, the basic issue with a policy such as quotas is that it is not really capable of making a distinction between the two. Precipitating events are difficult if not impossible to forecast. Using national origin as the basis for distinction, as the quotas did, might get things approximately right at a given point in time, but unforeseen events will always threaten to disrupt the balance. Of course, the inference that only "job-seeking" immigrants inspire opposition, though consistent with historical evidence, may not be entirely accurate. Other factors specific to the 1850s and the first two decades of the twentieth century may have made those periods particularly susceptible to anti-immigrant sentiment.

## Extrapolating to the Present Day

The system of national origin quotas first enacted in 1921 effectively placed a barrier in the path to residence for many immigrants for more than forty years.[48] In 1965, Congress passed and President Johnson signed the Hart-Celler Act, which while retaining restrictions on the overall number of immigrants admitted to permanent residency, eliminated the system of national origin quotas. The Hart-Celler Act also clarified and extended a set of preferences for the children, spouses, and parents of a native-born or naturalized U.S. citizen, which added an official dimension to the more fundamental network mechanism that has created distinct migration waves for the duration of human history.

Notably, immigration since 1965 has featured prominent examples of more traditional "home-seeking" groups as well as groups whose motivation is more purely economic. The great wave of Cuban emigration followed Fidel Castro's ascent to power in 1959; immigration from the Philippines spiked in the 1970s as Ferdinand Marcos subjected the nation to a near-decade of martial law. The fall of South Vietnam in 1975 initiated a period of rapid immigration. Armed conflict in Colombia has resulted in that nation being one of the primary sources of immigrants from South America.

In many other cases, the choice to immigrate to the United States appears to be driven primarily by economic circumstances. Migration from Mexico, the majority of Central America, India, China, Korea, the Dominican Republic, and Jamaica has transpired in the absence of clear natural or political precipitating events. Since 1965, these nations have witnessed orderly transfers of power. To the extent that specific events have been associated with the impetus to migrate, they have been economic in nature. Mexico's repeated devaluation of the peso, for example, has been cited as a cause of immigration from that country.[49] Evidence on the number of border apprehensions of illegal immigrants shows clear spikes in the aftermath of devaluations in 1982 and 1994.[50]

While the historic rationale for economic migration, to take advantage of the higher wages available for unskilled or modestly skilled workers in the American labor market, still holds for many groups, two new rationales have emerged. First, the United States has attracted a class of highly skilled "superstar" immigrants whose earnings are tied directly to the size of the market in which they work.[51] As the United States has the world's largest consumer marketplace, this nation is a natural destination for these workers, representing fields as diverse as finance, technology, and professional sports. Second, the expansion of higher education in the United States has attracted many migrants interested in pursuing opportunities for advanced training that are not available in their own countries. Figure 2.3 shows that a third or more of adult immigrants recently arriving from several nations, including China, Taiwan, Japan, and Korea, reported being enrolled in school. The pursuit of higher education is quite clearly not a major factor for many other groups, including immigrants from Mexico and Central America.

The distinction between traditional and economic migrants is not always clear cut. Many immigrants are likely motivated by a combination of factors. Specific examples of recent migration waves, which in some cases have generated public debate, highlight this blurred distinction. The onset of civil war in El Salvador in the early 1980s led to a clear break in the trend of emigration from that nation. Migration from the whole of Latin America has risen dramatically since 1980, however, and it is unclear exactly how many fewer migrants would have arrived in the absence of war. Similarly, political motivations for emigration from Haiti can be cited from the rise of Francois Duvalier in the late 1950s to the overthrow of Jean-Bertrand Aristide in 1991.

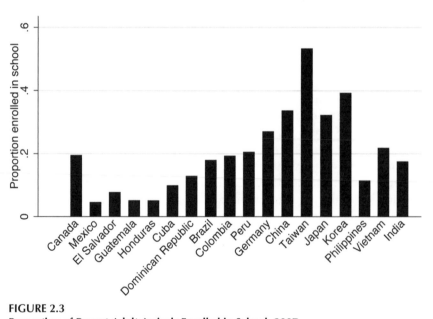

**FIGURE 2.3**
**Proportion of Recent Adult Arrivals Enrolled in School, 2007**

Haiti is also a desperately poor country, however, and significant migration from the Dominican Republic and Jamaica has occurred in recent years without any significant political turmoil.

In all, the parallels between past and present waves of immigration are clearly visible. At the same time, there are important differences that might make the experience of earlier immigrants to the United States dissimilar from those of contemporary migrants. The goal of the next five chapters is to explicitly measure modern and historical immigrant cohorts against one another, to uncover and explain any significant differences in the process of assimilation between past and present.

# 3

# Fitting In Economically

TWO OF THE MOST SPIRITED DEBATES regarding the impact of immigration in contemporary society are tied to the labor market. The first regards the impact of immigration on the earnings of natives. It is often argued that immigration leads to a net decrease in employment opportunities for native-born workers. Immigration can also increase employment opportunities under some circumstances, however. The second debate concerns the fiscal impact of immigration: whether immigrants pay their fair share in taxes, in relation to the value of services they receive from the government.

Information on the economic assimilation of immigrants can contribute to both debates. From a theoretical perspective, the labor market impact of immigration depends on the degree of complementarity between immigrants and natives in the labor market. If the workers we "import" completely replicate the skills already available in the native-born population, then the vision of immigrants and natives competing for the same jobs is close to reality. If, however, immigrants bring skill sets that are in relatively short supply in the United States, there may be benefits to native-born workers. Immigration policy in the United States, which will be discussed more thoroughly in chapter 5, offers encouragement to highly skilled foreign-born workers, for whom there is a relatively short and straightforward path to legal permanent residence.

Tax revenues in the United States are derived largely from levies on income and wealth. The progressivity of the income tax implies that individuals who earn more in the labor market will be more likely, in general, to pay an amount that equals or exceeds the value of services provided by government.

Although immigrants have not been eligible for most forms of welfare assistance since 1996, the targeting of various government programs to lower-income residents provides another link between the income and net fiscal impact of immigrants. Tracking the economic progress of immigrants thus allows us to infer whether they are on a trajectory to become net contributors to the public budget, relieving native-born taxpayers of the burden of supporting government.

### The Labor Market Impact Debate

Basic economic theory tells us that the disparity in living standards across countries reflects the fact that the value of work done by the typical employee in this country exceeds that in other nations. The value of work done by American workers reflects a balance between opportunities for employment and the availability of employees qualified to take advantage of those opportunities. When the number of opportunities exceeds the number of people qualified to take advantage of them, the reward associated with these opportunities naturally rises. If more students want to learn to play the piano, and the number of piano instructors does not rise, existing instructors could raise their hourly rates and still expect to keep their schedules full.

When the number of qualified workers increases, but opportunities do not, the opposite pattern should apply. For example were a boatload of piano teachers to arrive at port in a small city, it would instantly become more difficult for individuals in that profession—whether newly arrived or not—to find work. The market for piano instruction would become a buyer's market, with any potential customer with even the slightest interest in learning to play able to access competent instruction at a very modest price.

The arrival of new piano teachers would thus be harmful to existing piano teachers, yet beneficial to potential customers. Other parties stand to benefit as well. If the availability of cut-rate piano lessons encourages more people to learn to play, the manufacturers of pianos might well see an increase in demand for their product. The manufacturers, in turn, can use their windfall to expand their operations, or to pay handsome dividends to their owners—or, if they are a publicly held company, shareholders. Piano tuners might also expect to see an improvement in their business.

This simple example encapsulates economists' views regarding the impacts of immigration, and begins to illustrate the complexity impeding a complete accounting of whether immigration is beneficial. Immigrants' arrival can trigger wage cuts in some industries, wage increases in others, and will tend to improve the return to capital—the shareholder dividends in the above example. The benefits and costs are not spread evenly throughout the population. Native-born workers facing new competition (in this case, the piano teachers) will suffer, while those who do not (piano makers and tuners) stand to benefit. Capitalists (the piano factory owners and shareholders), as well as consumers with no direct employment connection to the industry in question, benefit as well.

Were we to sit down and add up all these various benefits and costs, we would undoubtedly find that from a purely economic perspective, immigration benefits the winners more than it costs the losers. Economist George Borjas, generally an outspoken critic of relaxed immigration laws, came to this conclusion in a 1995 summary of the economic arguments surrounding immigration policy.[1] Updating Borjas's back-of-the-envelope calculation with more recent data suggests that immigrant participation in the labor market generates net benefits on the order of $57 billion per year.[2]

The benefits of immigration are diffuse, largely spread to consumers and shareholders throughout the economy. The costs, however, may be concentrated to the extent that immigrants compete with specific types of native-born workers. Figure 3.1, which we'll discuss in more detail below, shows evidence that immigrants are disproportionately represented in lower-skilled occupations. Economic theory thus predicts that the main negative

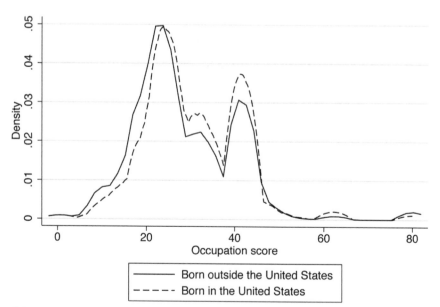

**FIGURE 3.1**
**Labor Market Skills in 2007**

impact of immigration would be to reduce the wages earned by less-skilled native-born workers. It is often asserted that immigrants work in jobs that native-born workers will not accept.[3] The basic economic counterargument, however, is that in the absence of immigration wages and salaries for these occupations would rise to the point where native-born workers would be willing to accept them.[4]

Perhaps surprisingly, there is an active debate among labor economists regarding the magnitude of the impact of immigration on wages. The basic counterargument to the economic logic presented above is that the alternative to having immigrants work in a specific job at a low wage is not to pay a native worker more to do the same work, but to have the job done in a foreign country where wages are lower. This is clearly a realistic scenario in the manufacturing industry, which has been exporting jobs for decades. In service industries, however, the case is more difficult to make. Companies can outsource appliance and automobile manufacturing, but they can't so easily outsource appliance and automobile repair.

The economic debate over the wage impact of immigration can be summarized as an intellectual sparring match between George Borjas and fellow labor economist David Card. Both specialize in empirical analysis, the use of data to address economic issues. Both marshal data in support of their viewpoints, neither questions the veracity of the other's data, yet their views are irreconcilable. How is this possible?

The challenge facing anyone who hopes to infer the impact of immigration on the labor market is that we don't know what the modern labor market would look like without immigrants. The best we can do is make a educated guess. One method of guessing assumes that in the absence of immigration the modern United States would look similar to the way it did at some point in the past, when there were fewer immigrants in the labor market. As immigrants have grown more numerous, what has happened to native-born workers?

This is the Borjas strategy. As it turns out, as immigration has expanded since the 1960s, inequality among native-born workers has grown. That is to say, the entry of immigrants into the low-skilled labor force has been accompanied by a general degradation of the economic standing of low-skilled American-born workers.[5] The Cardian rebuttal to this evidence is not to question the basic facts, but to argue that other trends in the American economy since the 1960s, including the outsourcing of jobs to other countries, the increasing mechanization of the workplace, and the increasing premium placed on highly skilled workers, matter more than the rise of immigration.[6]

Card's evidence is based on a different strategy.[7] Rather than compare America with immigrants today to America without immigrants a half-century ago, the basic idea is to compare, using contemporary data, cities with immigrants to cities without immigrants. In this type of comparison, Card finds that natives do just about equally well in their local labor markets regardless of how many immigrants have entered.[8] The typical rebuttal to this evidence once again does not question its veracity but rather proposes an alternative explanation. The typical argument is that immigrants choose to locate in the areas with the strongest local labor markets. The native workers in those markets look like they are doing fine, but in reality they might be doing even better in the absence of immigration.

The challenge of finding a consensus answer to this most basic of economic questions illustrates a broader point: with so many moving parts in the national economy, it's hard to know what the effect of any single component might be. Despite the inconclusiveness of the evidence, however, few would argue that immigration is a win-win scenario from the labor market perspective. That importing more workers reduces the wages of at least some existing workers is basically a consensus view. The debates center on how large that reduction might be.

### The Fiscal Impact Debate

Does the value of taxes paid by immigrants exceed the value of services they receive from the government? Of course, a simple answer to this question would obscure much detail. There are undoubtedly many immigrants who contribute more than their fair share, and others who do not. The same could be said for the native-born population. But the net impact of immigration on the public budget is still an issue of great concern.

Prior to the passage of welfare reform legislation in 1996, some evidence pointed to elevated rates of welfare receipt among immigrants.[9] Welfare reform reduced immigrants' eligibility for benefits. The net impact of welfare reform on benefit receipt by immigrants has not been reliably estimated, though one study shows that immigrants responded to reduced eligibility by increasing their labor supply.[10] Even if they do not take up welfare benefits, uninsured immigrants often rely on charitable provision of health care.[11] State and local governments often face cost burdens associated with providing services, most notably public education, to both legal and illegal immigrants.[12]

Immigrants contribute to the revenue side of the government budget in various ways. Most aliens who reside in the country temporarily pay taxes into the Social Security and Medicare trust funds without collecting benefits upon retirement.[13] Demographer Dowell Myers has argued that continued immigration could ameliorate impending fiscal problems associated with the aging and retirement of the baby boom generation.[14] Highly skilled immigrants are more likely to make net fiscal contributions at the national and local levels. Finally, immigration has helped fuel the resurgence of several formerly declining cities, leading to higher property values and property tax revenue.[15] Overall estimates of immigrants' net fiscal contribution vary widely, with some studies concluding that immigrants are a net drain on public budgets, and others finding that they are net contributors.[16]

## The Relative Status of Immigrants in 2007

Figure 3.1 provides some basic background on the distribution of occupational skills among native- and foreign-born male workers in the labor market as of 2007. The measure of skills, explained in greater detail below, is a numeric index based on occupations, the occupation score. The distribution of skills in the foreign-born workforce is represented by the solid line, and the native-born distribution by the dashed line. The plot's first impression is of similarity: the two distributions are nearly identical to one another. Upon closer inspection, there are some important differences. Relative to native-born workers, those born outside the United States are overrepresented on the left-hand side of the graph, clustered in low-skill occupations including farm laborers and restaurant waitstaff. They are also overrepresented on the far right-hand side, largely because there are a large number of foreign-born physicians in the United States. The foreign-born are underrepresented at occupation score levels between 25 and 45, which correspond generally to jobs requiring some combination of skill and experience, including accountants, engineers, and managers.

On the basis of this evidence, one could conclude that immigration poses little threat to moderately-to-highly skilled workers and a great threat to the unskilled. Indeed, this exact conclusion has been reached by authors of several prior studies.[17] But figure 3.1 is but a snapshot. It tells us little about whether the skills of newly arrived immigrants have been improving or declining, or what if any progress immigrants make in acquiring new skills after arriving in the United States. It also does little to place the fortunes of immigrants in historical context. Evidence presented later in this chapter will provide greater detail along these lines.

Comparisons of the labor market performance of succeeding waves of immigrants have been published before, as have analyses of the progress that foreign-born workers make as they spend more time in the American labor market.[18] The findings here will largely corroborate this existing work, which has established that the average occupational skill level of immigrants declined from the 1970s to the 1980s, then rebounded in the 1990s.

Comparatively less work has compared the experiences of modern immigrants with those of the early twentieth or mid-nineteenth centuries, largely because of a lack of data. This chapter will offer such a comparative analysis, taking advantage of recently released data on the occupations of immigrants in the United States between 1850 and 1930. The long-term trends turn out to be more fascinating than the short-term fluctuations in immigrant skills. In 1910, the average immigrant worked in a higher-paid occupation than the average native. Even the lowest-skilled immigrants arriving from Southern and Eastern Europe enjoyed an occupational advantage over the average native.[19] Italians and other immigrants benefited from their disproportionate location in cities, which offered economic opportunities that would gradually shift the American population away from rural areas over the course of the twentieth century. Indeed, immigrants on the whole fared worse than native-born urban dwellers in 1910, but much better than rural natives.

The average immigrant of 2007 was slightly ahead of his 1910 predecessors, but behind the average native. The overall skill level of the workforce grew over the intervening century, much more rapidly within the native-born population. There is considerable dispersion across immigrant groups in the early twenty-first century; several groups have average skill levels in excess of the native-born.

Finally, we will find some evidence of economic assimilation transpiring as immigrants spend more time in the United States. First-generation immigrants both now and in the past have experienced modest improvements in their economic fortunes over the first decade or two in residence.[20] The common pattern is not so much a rags-to-riches story as one of modest moves up the occupational ladder, such as a promotion from an unskilled laborer's position to that of a machine operator or foreman. In some cases, these improvements are magnified by the fact that less successful immigrants are more likely to exit the country. There is some limited evidence that the most recent cohorts of immigrants, those arriving after 1995, are experiencing slower rates of economic assimilation, but it is too early to definitively state that the process has fundamentally changed. Thus, while the economic starting positions of the immigrant population have both declined on average and grown more dispersed over time, evidence indicates that the process of economic assimilation has changed very little.

## What Is the Decision?

Motivational speakers may disagree, but economists don't really think that someone "decides to succeed," at least not directly. The true economic choices are not between success and failure, but between the present and the future, or between alternatives with varying levels of risk and return. Advancement at the workplace often requires a significant time investment, in the form of working longer hours, earning higher education degrees, or investigating alternative options at competing firms. There are many situations where the road to economic success involves taking chances: moving to a new city where opportunities are available but not guaranteed, moving from a secure but relatively low-paying position to one that offers both a higher salary and a greater risk of termination. Even simple investment decisions, such as earning a postsecondary degree in one's spare time, are imbued with risk. Degrees and other labor market credentials offer the promise of advancement, but not a guarantee.

Labor market success is thus not the direct observation of the outcome of a decision, but rather a reflection of a number of decisions made at multiple points in time, beginning with the decision to enter the host country in the first place. Since most of these decisions involve risk, there will always be some individuals who experience setbacks. When analyzing the immigrant population as a whole, we can determine whether those setbacks are sufficiently uncommon that the overall trajectory is toward improved outcomes.

In addition to these personal setbacks—being unable to find work in one's chosen specialty area, or being passed over for a promotion because there was a more meritorious candidate—some immigrants may face obstacles to labor market advancement because of their race or national origin. The existence of labor market discrimination in earlier eras, though a topic of controversy in some cases, is impossible to categorically deny.[21] We will learn in chapter 5 that racial restrictions on immigration itself persisted into the middle of the twentieth century. In modern times, there are concerns regarding discrimination against Hispanic immigrants.

Labor market discrimination is an easy thing to suspect but a difficult thing to prove. Data may demonstrate, for example, that immigrants earn less than their native-born counterparts, even taking into account the differences in average education and experience levels. But the remaining difference could be due either to actual discrimination or to difficult-to-observe characteristics that distinguish immigrants from natives. For example, the datasets used to investigate the existence of labor market discrimination often have very limited information on English-speaking ability.

Social scientists often attempt to investigate discrimination by conducting "audit" studies, responding to real job advertisements with resumes for fictitious job candidates with randomly assigned names of varying ethnic origin. Some studies go so far as to send in trained pseudoapplicants with varying appearance but nearly identical fabricated credentials. Discrimination is inferred in these studies when resumes or candidates associated with one ethnic or racial group are offered a job, or invited for an interview, less frequently than others. Several prominent studies have found such evidence.[22] It is unclear, however, whether the lessons of these studies can be generalized across labor markets or ethnic groups.

The analysis here will offer no definitive evidence on whether or to what extent labor market discrimination restricts the economic progress of immigrants. Changes in discriminatory patterns over time—rather than any difference in the actual behavior of immigrants themselves—represent one possible explanation for why some cohorts may experience more success than others.

## Measuring Economic Status through the Ages

As noted above, the economic status and progress of immigrants in the United States have been studied extensively for cohorts arriving in the 1960s or later. Comparatively little work has attempted to compare the experiences of these cohorts to earlier waves of immigrants, largely because the rich economic data available in the past few decades did not exist a century ago. Administrative records from the Social Security Administration (SSA), used in several recent studies of immigrant labor market progress, obviously did not exist prior to the establishment of that agency.[23] The decennial census began asking respondents about their earnings and other economic indicators in 1940. Prior to 1940, there are very few opportunities to observe systematic information about the economic fortunes of American residents, whether native- or foreign-born.

Social scientists have derived a number of substitute measures of economic status based on occupation. The Census Bureau has recorded the occupations of at least some respondents in every enumeration since 1850. Current occupations are recorded for all employed persons; for those currently unemployed or out of the labor force, the census records the last occupation. Before 1940, occupations were not recorded for individuals who had retired. In more recent years, occupations are not recorded for those who had not worked for a period of five years or more.

One of the more straightforward methods of translating qualitative information on occupation into a quantitative measure of economic position is to assign each individual the income typical of those in their occupation. Researchers affiliated with the Integrated Public Use Microdata Sample (IPUMS) project at the University of Minnesota have done exactly this. For every individual reporting an occupation in any census since 1850, or in the American Community Survey after 2000, the IPUMS project assigns a

**TABLE 3.1**
**Occupation Scores of Common Occupations**

| | |
|---|---|
| Farm laborer | 9 |
| Waiters and waitresses | 11 |
| Cooks (except private household) | 15.5 |
| Gardeners | 17 |
| Janitors | 19 |
| Laborers, not elsewhere classified | 20 |
| Musician/music teacher | 20 |
| Professional nurses | 21 |
| Operative, n.e.c. | 23 |
| Farm foreman | 23 |
| Salesman, n.e.c. | 24 |
| Truck driver | 25 |
| Clerical and kindred workers, n.e.c. | 25 |
| Teachers, n.e.c. | 27 |
| Policeman | 32 |
| Fireman | 33 |
| Accountant | 38 |
| Managers, n.e.c. | 42 |
| Personnel/labor relations | 43 |
| Industrial engineers | 45 |
| Lawyers and judges | 62 |
| Physicians | 80 |

number equal to the median income of individuals in that occupation in the 1950 census, measured in hundreds of 1950 dollars. The resulting *occupation score* ranges from zero for unemployed persons to 9 for farm laborers, to 80 for physicians. Table 3.1 provides a sampling of occupation scores for a selection of common occupations.[24]

The occupation score provides a basic sense of where an individual would stand in the income distribution if he or she were in the same occupation in 1950. There are a couple of caveats associated with this measure. First, some occupations available in 1950 (e.g., electrical engineer) did not exist in the mid-nineteenth century. Similarly, some important occupations of the present day (e.g., software developer) did not exist in 1950. The IPUMS project made their best effort to translate occupations backward and forward in time, but this is inherently a difficult process. It is much more straightforward for timeless occupations, including physicians, lawyers, waitresses, and so forth.

A second caveat is that the relative standing even of long-term occupations changes over time. In 1950, the American income distribution was at a historic point, the tail end of what economic historians Claudia Goldin and Robert Margo refer to as the "Great Compression."[25] The difference in income between unskilled and highly skilled occupations was remarkably small, a function of strong demand for unskilled labor coupled with increases in the supply of skilled workers during the 1940s. Economic inequality after 1950 would increase fairly steadily for the next half-century or more, with only periodic breaks.

The occupation score will thus tend to understate the differences in economic standing of skilled and unskilled workers, and to give a misleading picture of the economic progress of disadvantaged groups during times of increasing inequality. An immigrant group with average occupation scores consistently around 20, for example, would most likely be experiencing relative decline since 1980, a period of rising inequality. Measures of income inequality are much harder to compute in the nineteenth or early twentieth centuries, but available evidence suggests that the period between 1913 and 1920 was marked by decreasing inequality, while inequality rose during the 1920s.[26]

In some sense, the failure of the occupation score to trace broad movements in the income distribution is actually advantageous. It allows a direct observation of the extent to which immigrants are moving into more skilled work as they spend additional time in the United States. Their true economic fortune depends on both this transition and the broad trends in economic inequality over which they individually have little control. These trends may influence the size of the gap between skilled and unskilled workers, but they generally do not alter the ranking of occupations.

A final caveat regarding the occupation score is that it makes no distinction between individuals who are gainfully employed, those unemployed, and those who have actually left the labor force for a period of time. Gauging economic progress by occupation, then, threatens to overlook problems of unemployment or underemployment. To some extent, this problem can be addressed by restricting attention to those individuals who report participating in the labor force at a given point in time, and supplementing the analysis of occupational standing with information on labor force participation.

Over the course of American history, the occupational standing of immigrants has improved in an absolute sense but declined in a relative sense. Table 3.2, which reports the mean occupation scores for male workers belonging to prominent immigrant groups at specific points in time, shows that the typical immigrant in the mid-nineteenth century held a low-to-moderately skilled position, with average occupation scores in the range of common laborers or operatives.[27] There is remarkably little dispersion across the major immigrant groups of the day, with average occupation scores in a narrow range between 20.5 and 22.5.

Immigrants of the early twentieth century were slightly better off, with the least skilled groups obtaining positions comparable to the most skilled immigrants of a half-century earlier. Remarkably, the immigrants of this era

**TABLE 3.2**
**Average Occupation Scores of Prominent Immigrant Groups**

| Country of Origin | Year | Mean Occupation Score |
|---|---|---|
| Ireland | 1860 | 21 |
| Germany | 1860 | 22.1 |
| United Kingdom | 1860 | 22.4 |
| Canada | 1870 | 20.8 |
| Ireland | 1910 | 25 |
| Germany | 1910 | 24 |
| Austria | 1910 | 23 |
| Russia | 1910 | 25.2 |
| Italy | 1910 | 22.7 |
| *United States* | *1910* | *22.1* |
| Mexico | 2007 | 23.4 |
| Philippines | 2007 | 28.6 |
| India | 2007 | 36.9 |
| China | 2007 | 32 |
| Korea | 2007 | 33.6 |
| Cuba | 2007 | 30.1 |
| El Salvador | 2007 | 24.9 |
| *United States* | *2007* | *30.4* |

held better-paying jobs, on average, than their native-born counterparts. This pattern reflects a combination of immigrants' disproportionate location in industrializing cities and the existence of better job opportunities in those cities relative to rural areas. Roughly 70 percent of the native-born workforce resided in rural areas or small towns in 1910, whereas only 45 percent of the immigrant population lived in such areas. Urban-dwelling immigrants actually compare negatively to native-born workers in urban areas. The greater economic opportunities available in industrializing cities would cause a massive migration from rural areas to cities over the next four decades.

In the early twenty-first century, immigrants find themselves simultaneously better off than their foreign-born predecessors of prior generations, yet further behind their native-born counterparts. Between 1910 and 2007, the average occupation score for the native-born rose eight points, from 22 to 30. For the average immigrant, the increase was only five points over this period. In stark contrast to earlier periods, considerable dispersion of the fortunes of immigrants has also emerged. Immigrants from Mexico and Central America find themselves in economic positions quite comparable to immigrants of the preceding century, which places them well behind the native-born average. Certain groups, including immigrants from Cuba and the Philippines, have remained fairly close to the native-born average. Immigrants from China,

Korea, and India find themselves in occupations that on average outstrip the native-born norm.

This basic information confirms the existence of a widening gap between the average occupational skills of the native- and foreign-born populations in the United States, and a second gap between the labor market outcomes of high- and low-skilled immigrants. This background information is both striking and important, as it documents the emergence, for the first time in history, of a group of immigrants at a substantial economic disadvantage relative to the native-born. It does not, however, address the question of assimilation—whether immigrants show evidence of improving their status over time.

## The Great Obstacle to Studying Assimilation

Assimilation is a process whereby an individual belonging to a particular social group becomes more similar to members of other groups over time. Logically, the ideal way to measure it would be to track the experiences of individuals over time. In other words, the ideal study of assimilation would use *longitudinal* data. In fact, the ideal study would examine information on an immigrant's entire life trajectory—what situation did the individual face in his or her country of birth, what happened after emigration, and what more happened in the event he or she decided to move to a third country or back home. To ensure that the experiences of immigrants in the dataset are representative of the entire population, the study would examine information of this sort for a large number of immigrants—and for good measure, a large number of native-born residents as well.

Unfortunately, this ideal longitudinal dataset does not exist. To study assimilation thoroughly, social scientists must ultimately make one or more compromises that threaten the validity of their conclusions. This study is no exception. Before reviewing any evidence, it is important to consider the problems associated with using suboptimal data to study the phenomenon of immigrant assimilation.

Like many prior studies, this one makes use primarily of what is known as *repeated cross-section* data.[28] Unlike longitudinal datasets, which follow the exact same individuals over time, repeated cross-sections take snapshots of different individuals at each point in time. The basic challenge of using repeated cross-section data to study immigrants is that the underlying population is quite likely to shift over time: among those immigrants in the country today, some portion will be elsewhere in a few years, and the set that chooses to leave may not look identical to the set that chooses to stay.

Suppose all we wanted to track over time was immigrants' age. In repeated cross-section data, we can't track the age of an individual person over time, so our best alternative is to follow a well-defined group. For example, we could track the age of immigrants who arrived in the United States in 1979. One might expect this to be a simple exercise: if the average age of immigrants who arrived in 1979 were twenty-two, we would expect these individuals to show up with an average age of twenty-three in the 1980 census, thirty-three in the 1990 census, and so forth.

In fact, we might not find this pattern, for two reasons. It is true that by asking a different group of 1979 arrivals for their age in each census, we would naturally expect to observe some variation each time. Statistically speaking, this is sampling error. Every survey has an associated margin of error, and the IPUMS microdata are no exception. With large enough samples, though, the margin of error should be small. There were over six thousand immigrants with an arrival date of 1979 as late as the 2006 American Community Survey. With a sample that large, we wouldn't expect the actual average age to be more than a half-year off of what an earlier survey would lead us to expect.

The second and more fundamental problem with repeated cross-section analysis is not statistical in nature, rather it has to do with human behavior. Only a fraction of the 1979 arrivals present in the 1980 census will stick around long enough to be counted in the 1990 census. An extreme example will make the issue clear. Suppose that there were one million arrivals in 1979, half of them eighteen years old and the other half thirty-eight. Overall, the average age for this group would be twenty-eight. Suppose further that all the young immigrants return home during the 1980s, so that only the older ones are left. The average age of the 1979 arrivals measured in 1990 would then be forty-eight. To the naive observer, it would appear that this group of immigrants managed to age twenty years in just one decade.

This example is, of course, preposterous. But the concern, when applied to other indicators of assimilation, is very real. For example, several researchers have addressed the question of immigrant economic advancement by measuring how the difference in earned income or wages between immigrants and the native-born changes as immigrants spend more time in the United States.[29] In general, these studies find evidence that the gap between natives and the foreign-born shrinks over time. Two phenomena could produce this pattern. The first is assimilation—over time, immigrants learn how to be more productive workers in the United States and get better, higher-paying jobs. The second would be selective emigration: a tendency for a certain type of immigrant to exit the country at a more rapid rate. In the contrived example above, selective emigration occurred—the young exited, the old did not. The concern in the case of economic assimilation is that immigrants who do poorly in the American labor market, and hence earn low wages, will be more likely to exit than those who do well.

There have been several recent efforts to gauge the severity of this problem, by tracking the number and type of immigrants in a given cohort who exit the United States, or by using some form of longitudinal data to track the labor market outcomes of immigrants who actually remain in the United States over long periods of time. Both methods indicate that a substantial number of immigrants in recent cohorts have moved on, and the latter method suggests that these exits cause repeated cross-section analyses to overstate the amount of labor market success that immigrants experience as they spend more time in the United States.

The United States does not directly collect information on the number of immigrants exiting the country each year. There have been multiple recent attempts to infer the number of exits on the basis of existing data. Economists George Borjas and Bernt Bratsberg compared 1980 census data on year of entry with INS data on the number of immigrants admitted each year, and conclude that about 20 percent of immigrants arriving in the 1970s were out of the country in 1980.[30] Sociologist Guillermina Jasso and economist Mark Rosenzweig used demographic methods to infer the number of exiting immigrants between 1960 and 1980; their methods indicate that for every ten new arrivals in either the 1960s or 1970s, roughly four immigrants chose to exit.[31]

Beyond documenting the existence of outmigration, some studies have documented the tendency for certain groups, or certain individuals, to be more likely to exit. Borjas and Bratsberg found that immigrants from more proximate nations and wealthier nations were more likely to return, while those from Communist countries were less likely to return.[32] This pattern fits squarely into the cost-benefit model of immigration described in chapter 1: immigrants place a higher value on residence in the United States when their fallback option—their country of origin—is less desirable. In chapter 5 we will observe one implication of this, that naturalization rates tend to be highest among immigrants from the poorest nations.

Suppose that less-successful migrants are more likely to exit the United States. Then, repeated cross-section analyses will tend to show that the earnings of migrants are improving relative to natives, even if no individual immigrant experiences any progress. Longitudinal studies can, at least in theory, check this hypothesis, by seeing whether the degree of improvement in a fixed cohort over time matches the amount of apparent progress in a repeated cross-section. Several studies have employed some form of longitudinal analysis to investigate this question.

Economist Barry Chiswick made the first foray, by tracking the progress of a group of immigrants born between 1907 and 1921, who lived consistently in the United States for a period beginning in 1965.[33] Chiswick found no evidence that the progress for this cohort was different from the impression one would glean from following cross-sections in the census. Chiswick's chosen cohort was unusual though, consisting of middle-aged men who either came to the United States as young children or as adults during a period when immigration was severely restricted. We might not expect members of this group to leave the United States in significant numbers.

Four more recent studies have used longitudinal data to document tendencies for lower-earning immigrants to outmigrate, and thus for cross-sectional evidence to overstate the degree of progress experienced by long-term members of a cohort. George Borjas studied a longitudinal sample of natural and social scientists and engineers, finding that even within this highly skilled group there was a tendency for immigrants "who did not perform well" to exit the country.[34] Wei-Yin Hu linked a representative survey of American residents born between 1931 and 1941 to administrative earnings from the Social Security Administration spanning the period 1951 to 1991.[35] Two subsequent studies, one by Darren Lubotsky and the other by Harriet Duleep and Daniel Dowhan, followed a similar strategy, linking comparable administrative data to multiple datasets.[36] All three studies found a rate of earnings growth for immigrants tracked longitudinally that was substantially below estimates derived from repeated cross-section analysis.

Each of these studies can be subjected to some criticism. The Social Security Administration's records, for example, might not capture the full extent of immigrant income. Above a certain income level, earnings are not subject to taxation to fund the Social Security program, which implies that the actual income of high-earning individuals is not precisely recorded. Additionally, when immigrants work "under the table," in jobs that do not result in the reporting of income to the Social Security Administration, their true earnings may be understated, if they are even stated at all.[37] In spite of these critiques, the overall body of evidence on the nature of immigrant selection out of the labor market is compelling, and completely consistent with a rational view of immigrant behavior—and worker behavior more generally.

The longitudinal analysis of immigrants to this point has been confined to the study of recent decades, largely because of the difficulties associated with securing longitudinal data in early years. Recent efforts to digitize information available in nineteenth-century census enumerations have introduced a new opportunity. In 2009, the Minnesota Population Center took advantage of recent efforts to digitize the entire 1880 census to make available a dataset linking individuals residing in the United States in 1880 and at least one other decade between 1850 and 1930. This introduces perhaps the only opportunity to determine whether the differences between longitudinal and cross-

**TABLE 3.3**
**Immigrant Occupational Progress in the Late Nineteenth Century**

| Nation | Repeated Cross-Section | | | Longitudinal | | |
|---|---|---|---|---|---|---|
| | *1870* | *1880* | *Change* | *1870* | *1880* | *Change* |
| Canada | 20.9 | 22.5 | +1.6 | 20.2 | 21.2 | +1.0 |
| United Kingdom | 22.9 | 23.5 | +0.6 | 21.7 | 23.3 | +1.6 |
| Ireland | 21.8 | 22.5 | +0.7 | 21.3 | 21.6 | +0.3 |
| Germany | 22.6 | 23.1 | +0.5 | 22.9 | 23.6 | +0.7 |

sectional analyses of immigrant progress evident in the late twentieth century are also present in the early nineteenth.

Table 3.3 presents information on males born between 1815 and 1852 in one of four foreign nations, the United Kingdom, Ireland, Canada, and Germany, who resided in the United States in either 1870 or 1880.[38] The first three columns focus on average occupation scores computed from repeated cross-section samples, which utilize information on separate sets of immigrants in each year. The final columns rely on a longitudinal sample: individuals for whom the MPC matched records in 1870 and 1880. If less-successful immigrants were more likely to depart in this era, we would expect the repeated cross-sections to overstate gains over time; we would also expect the set of individuals observed longitudinally to have higher occupation scores than the full set of immigrants observed in any one cross-section.

Perhaps surprisingly, these patterns are not uniformly found in the nineteenth century data. Occupation scores are in most cases slightly lower in the longitudinal data. The longitudinal data exhibit greater occupational improvement for two groups, and smaller increases for the other two. Neither the repeated cross-sections nor the longitudinal samples show much occupational upgrading over time, with six of the eight estimated gains at one point or less.[39] The overall impression in these historical data, then, is of uneven or irrelevant selective emigration and only modest improvements in the labor market outcomes of immigrants over time.

Why does nineteenth-century data fail to resemble more recent analyses? There are a couple of potential explanations. First, the costs of return migration were higher in an era of more expensive transportation. Thus the impulse of the unsuccessful immigrant to exit the country may have been countered by a simple economic inability to afford a return or onward journey. As noted in the preceding chapter, a considerable proportion of nineteenth-century migrants were politically motivated, indicating that their return option was not viable. Finally, note that the nineteenth-century data do not include information on year of immigration—the Census Bureau did not collect that information for immigrants until 1900. Thus another form of contamination may impact cross-sectional estimates: the entry of new immigrants. In practice, the amount of new immigration to the United States was limited in the 1870s; the population of European-born immigrants increased by 1.8 million in the 1850s and 1.1 million in the 1860s, but only eight hundred thousand in the 1870s. Nonetheless, the new arrivals of the 1870s may have been disproportionately skilled relative to those arriving in earlier decades. This evidence that the process of selective emigration may have changed over time will be important to remember as we review evidence on the progress of immigrant cohorts at varying points in the twentieth and early twenty-first centuries.

From a societal perspective, does it matter whether immigrant cohorts make real progress, or only appear to make progress because unsuccessful members of the cohort leave? While it is difficult to argue that this distinction is completely irrelevant, either mechanism can be viewed positively from the perspective of the host society. When unsuccessful immigrants exit a country, society is potentially relieved of a net fiscal burden, given the progressive nature of taxation and transfer programs in the United States and most developed countries. When immigrant cohorts fail to post economic progress over time, there are likely to be negative ramifications for society whether the root cause is a failure of individual migrants to improve their lot or a failure of unsuccessful immigrants to move on.

Overall, then, while selective emigration serves as a great challenge to the academic study of immigrant assimilation, it poses less of a concern to a society whose primary objective is to ensure that those immigrants who choose to remain have enjoyed at least some measure of success. In any event, it is important to remember when reviewing the evidence in this and later chapters that in almost all cases measures of immigrant assimilation will confound two sources of apparent progress: real progress and selective emigration.

## Reviewing the Evidence on Economic Assimilation

So far, we have established that immigrants of the early twenty-first century, while better off than their predecessors in an absolute sense, have as a group fallen behind the native-born in terms of occupational standing. Splitting the group by country of origin, the story is more mixed, with immigrants from East and South Asia in particular outpacing the native-born while immigrants from Mexico and Central America lag the furthest behind. We have also seen evidence that selective emigration was less of a factor a century or more ago, during a period where return or onward journeys from the United States were much costlier than they are now. The remaining piece of the puzzle concerns the relative rates of progress at different points in time. We have already seen that the rate of occupation score improvement for nineteenth-century immigrants was at most one or two points per decade. How do later waves of immigrants compare?

Figure 3.2 presents two graphs derived from repeated cross-section analysis of six cohorts of immigrants drawn from varying points over more than a century. The first cohort consists of immigrants arriving in the United States between 1896 and 1900. The second cohort arrived between 1906 and 1910. The remaining cohorts belong to the contemporary wave of immigration that followed the passage of the Hart-Celler Act in 1965: arrivals from the late 1970s, late 1980s, late 1990s, and between 2001 and 2005. These cohorts are tracked across decennial census samples from 1900 to 2000, and then in American Community Surveys after 2000. In each case, the analysis focuses on male immigrants who arrived in the United States at age eighteen or above, and who were between twenty-one and sixty-five years of age in the indicated year.

Consistent with the evidence in table 3.2, the evidence indicates that the arrivals of the late twentieth century held better-paying occupations, on average, than those in the previous immigration wave. Upon entry, the mostly

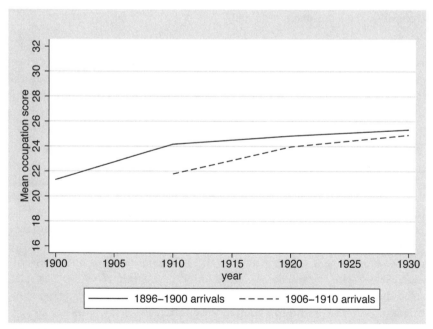

**FIGURE 3.2A**
**Occupation Score by Cohort, 1900–1930**

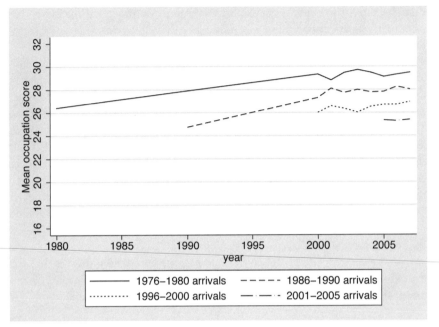

**FIGURE 3.2B**
**Occupation Score by Cohort, 1980–2007**

European immigrants of the early twentieth century had average occupation scores around 22; the largely Latin American and Asian immigrants of the later period posted average scores at entry around 26. Consistent with prior literature, there is evidence of a dip in occupational skills for immigrants arriving in the 1980s relative to the immediately preceding and following cohorts.[40]

For those cohorts observed for at least a decade, progress in average occupation scores over time follows a relatively uniform pattern. After twenty years, cohorts post averages that are three to four points higher than the initial levels. This occupational upgrading is roughly equivalent to a promotion from an unskilled laborer's position to that of an operative, or from an accountant's position to that of a mid-level manager. For most cohorts, progress is concentrated in the first decade after arrival. These gains are thus not necessarily inconsistent with the smaller increases found in the nineteenth-century data, since the nineteenth-century cohort by necessity combines newly arrived immigrants with those who had been in the country for many years.

The two most recent cohorts of immigrants, arriving in 1995 or later, do not demonstrate occupational improvement on the same trajectory as earlier cohorts. This might signal a fundamental change in the economic experience of immigrants or a change in selective return migration. These two explanations are impossible to distinguish without longitudinal data, but either trend—slower progress among immigrants, or a reduced tendency for less-successful immigrants to depart—could be viewed negatively.

Further evidence of a slowdown in the rate of immigrant economic progress can be seen in figure 3.3, which tracks the labor force participation of these same six immigrant cohorts over time. In the early twentieth century, foreign-born males almost always participated in the labor force, though there is some evidence that the onset of the Great Depression took a toll on participation in 1930. With the exception of that year, labor force participation rates are in excess of 95 percent for both the 1896–1900 and 1906–1910 cohorts.

In more recent cohorts, labor force participation is never observed to reach the 95 percent level. Upon arrival, 14 to 21 percent of adult males report no attachment to the labor force. Given the high prevalence of higher education students in the population of recently arrived adult immigrants, this is perhaps not surprising. Rates of labor force participation do rise rapidly for these

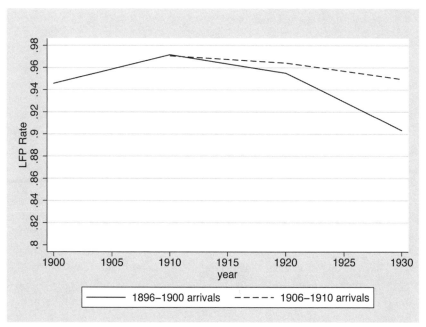

**FIGURE 3.3A**
**Labor Force Participation Rate by Cohort, 1900–1930**

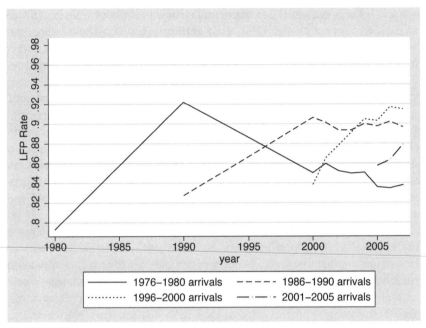

**FIGURE 3.3B**
Labor Force Participation Rate by Cohort, 1980–2007

cohorts over their first full decade in residence, but appear to stall in the 90 to 92 percent range, even showing significant decline in the cohort arriving in the late 1970s.

The low rate of labor force participation among immigrants in the late-1970s arrival cohort is actually not all that remarkable in comparison with the rate among native-born workers. As of 2007, the cohort of immigrants who arrived as adults in the 1975–1980 period is at least forty-five years old. Among forty-five- to sixty-year-old American-born males, the labor force participation rate is even lower than the 83 percent figure posted by immigrants in this cohort—76 percent. Thus, while the decline in labor force participation among older immigrants is noteworthy, it does not necessarily differentiate them from the native-born.[41]

We have already observed significant heterogeneity in the economic standing of immigrants from different origin countries in recent data. Is there a comparable degree of heterogeneity in the rate of economic assimilation? The remaining evidence in this chapter considers four specific case studies, chosen to represent variation along a number of dimensions. The contrast between immigrants from Mexico and India reflects stark differences in economic standing. Immigrants from Vietnam add variation in the initial motivation for emigration. Finally, the experience of early twentieth-century Italian immigrants adds historical detail.

## Mexico

As immigrants from Mexico constitute the largest single country-of-origin group, it is not surprising that their economic progress mirrors that of the foreign-born population as a whole. Recent cohorts have entered with average occupation scores comparable to those of unskilled laborers and have posted gains of three to four points within the first decade or two (figure 3.4).[42] Mexican immigrants generally have labor force participation rates higher than the immigrant population as a whole, particularly in their first years in residence (figure 3.5). This pattern is entirely consistent with the finding in chapter 2 that few of these immigrants enroll in institutions of higher education. The cohort of Mexican immigrants arriving in the late 1970s has exhibited a recent decline in labor force participation that mirrors the immigrant population as a whole.

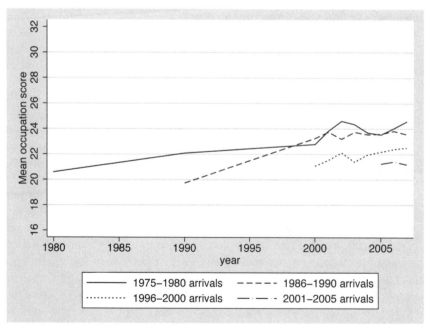

**FIGURE 3.4**
**Occupation Score of Mexican Arrivals over Time**

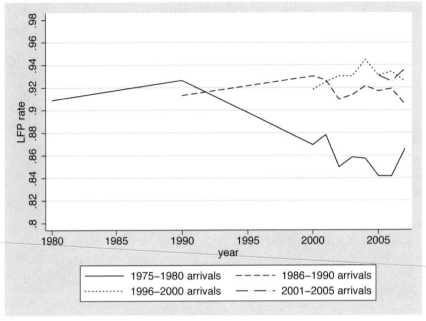

**FIGURE 3.5**
**Labor Force Participation of Mexican Arrivals over Time**

## India

Consecutive cohorts of immigrants from India have exhibited very different patterns in the labor market. Those arriving in the late 1970s started their working careers in relatively high-skilled positions, with a mean occupation score equivalent to that of an accountant, but posted little if any increase in occupation score for more than two decades (figure 3.6). The increases posted by this group since 2000 likely reflect the ascension of some members into senior management positions. More recent cohorts have shown both lower starting positions and more immediate improvements, with the late 1980s cohort in particular gaining nearly six points on the occupation score scale over their first full decade. This may reflect the moderately high rates of school enrollment among newly arrived adults. College and graduate school students most likely engage in relatively menial employment until they complete their degrees. Labor force participation rates for all four cohorts are at or above the average for all immigrants, with the oldest cohort displaying a now-familiar peak in 1990 followed by a decline (figure 3.7).

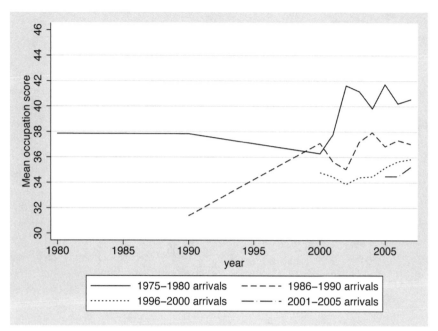

**FIGURE 3.6**
Occupation Score of Indian Arrivals over Time

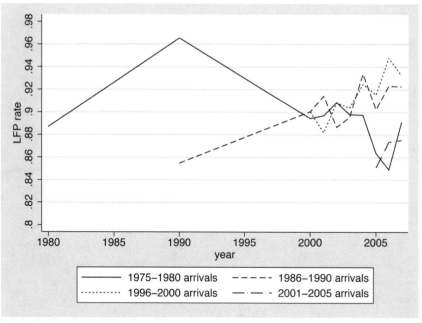

**FIGURE 3.7**
Labor Force Participation of Indian Arrivals over Time

## Vietnam

Immigrants from Vietnam occupy an intermediate rung on the economic ladder. Their patterns of progress in occupation score improvements is roughly similar to that of Mexican immigrants, with cohorts posting gains of four to five points over a decade or two (figure 3.8). The main difference between the groups is in starting point: upon entry into the American labor market Vietnamese immigrants have tended to occupy positions that Mexican immigrants will only attain after one or more decades in the United States. Labor force participation rates are generally low for adult males in this group (figure 3.9). The low initial levels may be a function of enrollment in institutions of higher education. Rates for older cohorts in recent years are relatively similar to those of native-born males in similar age groups. We will learn in chapter 5 that the rate of naturalization is very high among immigrants from Vietnam; the similarity of labor force participation between native-born and Vietnamese males may reflect a set of factors

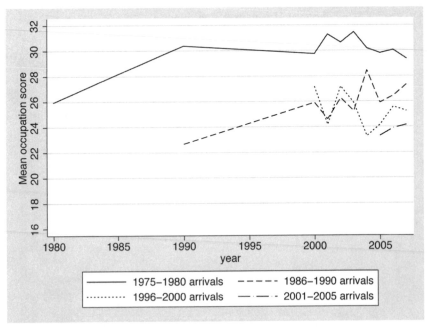

**FIGURE 3.8**
**Occupation Score of Vietnamese Arrivals over Time**

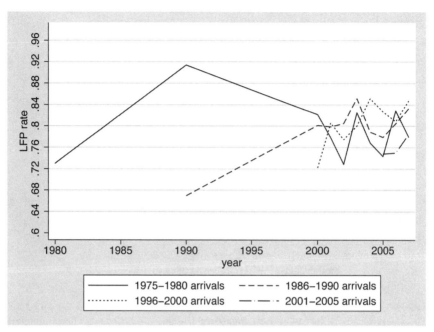

**FIGURE 3.9**
**Labor Force Participation of Vietnamese Arrivals over Time**

common to citizens and permanent residents—particularly eligibility for disability insurance—that other groups lack.

### Italy

The degree of similarity in economic progress between Italian and Mexican immigrants is striking (figures 3.10 and 3.11). It is important to note, however, that by raising their average occupation score from 20 to 24, the Italian immigrants of the early twentieth century were closing much of the gap between their group and urban-dwelling natives. The nearly identical trend among more recent immigrants from Mexico represents a much smaller improvement in relative terms. Labor force participation rates for Italian immigrants were remarkably high, dampened only by the onset of the depression in 1930. Both trends for Italian immigrants also display a strong similarity to the trends for the immigrant population as a whole. Recalling that Italians were considered to be remarkably uneducated and unskilled at their time of

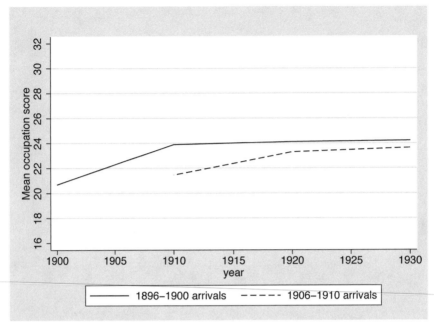

**FIGURE 3.10**
**Occupation Score of Italian Arrivals over Time**

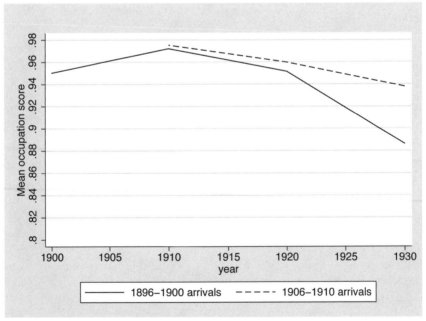

**FIGURE 3.11**
**Labor Force Participation of Italian Arrivals over Time**

immigration, and that many immigrants from more developed portions of Europe arrived in the same cohorts, this similarity is quite striking.

## Across-Generation Economic Assimilation

Traditionally, the assimilation of immigrant groups is considered to take place both within and between generations. The evidence shown to this point tracks *within-generation* assimilation: the tendency for immigrants arriving as adults to close the economic gap with the native-born majority as they spend more time in the United States. Prior research has also tracked the extent of economic assimilation across generations—that is, the tendency for the children of foreign-born immigrants to erase a significant portion of the gap between their parents and the native-born.[43]

In the IPUMS data, it is not always possible to tell which individuals are the children of immigrants. Data on parents' birthplace is available in the early twentieth century, for example, but not in the years since 1980. As an alternative to studying native-born children of immigrants, studies of between-generation assimilation often focus on foreign-born individuals who were brought to the United States at a young age by their parents. These members of "Generation one-and-a-half," or 1.5 for short, bear much resemblance to their native-born siblings. They were educated in American schools, and exposed to various American cultural influences.

Table 3.4 reports labor market outcomes, including both the occupation score and labor force participation rates, for "Generation 1.5" male immigrants at three different points in time, and by nationality. Here, Generation 1.5 members are defined as individuals born abroad who arrived in the United States by age five. The labor outcomes are reported for members of this generation at the time they are between thirty and forty years old.

Just as prior evidence has shown that adult immigrants were advantaged relative to the native-born in the late nineteenth and early twentieth centuries, the foreign-born children of immigrants themselves show an advantage over the native-born in 1900 and 1930. The sole exception among groups listed here pertains to the children of Scandinavian immigrants observed in 1900, who were slightly disadvantaged in terms of occupation score. This most likely reflects the rural distribution, and consequent employment as farm labor, among Scandinavians in the late nineteenth century.

In 2007, immigrants born between 1967 and 1977 and brought to the United States by the age of five also exhibit an advantage, on average, relative to their native-born counterparts. Just as was the case for their parents, however, the average masks important differences across groups. Mexican

**TABLE 3.4**
**Economic Standing of Generation 1.5 Immigrants, 1900–2007**

|  | Mean Occupation Score | Labor Force Participation Rate |
|---|---|---|
| 1900 | | |
| All Generation 1.5 | 23.9 | 95.4 |
| Irish | 25.3 | 93.5 |
| German | 22.8 | 95.2 |
| Scandinavian | 21.8 | 96.3 |
| Native-Born | 22.7 | 96.3 |
| 1930 | | |
| All Generation 1.5 | 27.9 | 96.9 |
| Italian | 27.5 | 98.6 |
| Russian | 30.1 | 97.8 |
| Native-Born | 25.3 | 96.3 |
| 2007 | | |
| All Generation 1.5 | 32.2 | 90.1 |
| Mexican | 27.9 | 90.2 |
| Filipino | 32.3 | 84.8 |
| Korean | 35.6 | 86.9 |
| Vietnamese | 36.0 | 85.5 |
| Native-Born | 30.9 | 88.2 |

*Note:* Sample consists of adult males born abroad, arriving in the United States by the age of five, between the ages of thirty and forty at time of enumeration.

immigrants belonging to Generation 1.5 are disadvantaged relative to the native-born majority. Other prominent groups, including migrants from Korea and Vietnam, are more advantaged than the average would suggest.

In all years, members of Generation 1.5 show evidence of doing slightly better than their parents' generation. In 1930, for example, the average occupation score among all immigrants arriving between 1896 and 1900, or between 1906 and 1910, was around 25 or 26. This compares with an average of 28 for selected Generation 1.5 members in this year. In 2007, the overall immigrant occupation score for late 1970s arrivals was just under 30; for selected Generation 1.5 members around the same time the comparable average is 32. Restricting attention to Mexicans, the overall first generation average occupation score among late 1970s arrivals was just over 24 in 2007; the corresponding Generation 1.5 average was closer to 28.

## Summary

From the mid-nineteenth century to the early twenty-first, immigrants to the United States have managed to improve their economic position as they spend time—generally no more than a decade—in the American workforce. There is little evidence that the process has fundamentally changed over time, or operates very differently for immigrants facing varying circumstances. First-generation immigrants experience modest progress. Trips from the mailroom to the executive boardroom are exceedingly rare, vastly outnumbered by relatively modest moves up the occupational ladder. The children of immigrants, both historically and presently, tend to attain moderately higher occupational status than their parents. In most historical examples, both immigrants and their children have outperformed the native-born average, largely because immigrants more rapidly took advantage of superior economic opportunities available in the growing cities of the late nineteenth and early twentieth centuries.

Perhaps the most striking change in the economic status of immigrants has been the profound increase in the variability of starting points across groups. The Irish immigrants of the mid-nineteenth century worked in a set of occupations quite similar to those of their British contemporaries. Similarly, the work of early twentieth-century immigrants was not highly stratified by country of origin. In these earlier times, when the United States was an industrializing nation with a nearly insatiable demand for manufacturing labor, a similar set of opportunities drew migrants from many nations.

In the late twentieth century, with manufacturing on the wane and the postindustrial economy generating a combination of "knowledge sector" jobs requiring high training and service sector jobs requiring virtually none, migrants from different nations have witnessed a much wider degree of stratification. The improvements that any single immigrant experiences over decades in the American labor market are dwarfed by the stark differences in work performed by highly skilled and less-skilled immigrants. On the whole, the skill composition of the immigrant population has fallen behind that of the native population, but the outliers are in many ways more interesting than the norm.

This heterogeneity is one critically important point of departure when comparing the modern debate over immigration policy to historical debates. When immigration quotas were first debated in the early twentieth century, immigrants from various nations competed with natives for the same set of industrial jobs. A century later, the nation faces a more multifaceted form of immigration, with large influxes of immigrants at the extremes of the skill distribution. In some sense, the greater complementarity of immigrant and native labor market skills portends a more favorable net impact of immigration in the twenty-first century relative to earlier periods. In another sense, however, the concentration of immigrants in certain skill groups introduces both variability in the impact of immigration and complexity to the political problem of immigration reform.

# 4

# Fitting In Linguistically

In the first place, as it concerns our means of living, we must, above and beyond all, *rely upon a knowledge of the English language*, and the progress that we make therein has the most important and propitious influence upon our welfare.

—Frederick W. Bogen (1851), *The German in America* (italics in original)

WHILE THE ECONOMIC IMPACTS of immigration have attracted much scholarly attention, public debates commonly focus on perceived threats to native culture—most specifically, to the status of English as the common language of professional and personal interaction in the United States.[1] About half of the immigrants currently residing in the United States, nearly twenty million people, were born in Spanish-speaking nations. The dispersal of the Latin American immigrant population from its traditional centers in Florida and the Southwest to urban and rural areas throughout the country has introduced the challenges of bilingualism to regions with no recent history of immigration.

In response to the rise of Spanish as a de facto second language, interest groups have arisen to promote the official use of English. A majority of states have passed statutes, referenda, or constitutional amendments declaring English the official language of government. While pro-English interest groups often state a desire to promote the assimilation of immigrants as one of their principal motivations, opponents of the movement argue that its message is a thinly veiled attack on immigrants in general.[2] It is difficult to quantify the cultural impact of immigration in a traditional cost-benefit framework, but it is clear that for many concerned citizens, cultural considerations weigh much more heavily than economic ones.

In the United States, the inability to speak English has commonly been the most obvious sign that a resident was born abroad. Walking the streets of any American city, it is virtually impossible to tell whether the passersby are gainfully employed or citizens of the country. In the world's modern developed societies, it is impossible to tell a person's birthplace just by observing their outward appearance. Should that person open their mouth and speak a foreign language, the clearest possible external clue to their nationality appears. Virtually every person born in the United States, or taught in American schools, speaks English as their primary language. When an adult speaks a foreign language in public it is reasonable, if not always accurate, to presume that they were born in a different country.

Perhaps for this reason, the debate over whether immigrants to the United States should be encouraged or required to speak English has often attained a higher pitch than comparable debates over citizenship or eligibility for public services. Benjamin Franklin's 1751 diatribe against "Palatine Boors" mentioned in chapter 2 worried not about the labor market impacts of immigration, or whether the migrants would show allegiance to the colonies, but rather their "[l]anguage and [m]anners," not to mention their "swarthy [c]omplexion."[3] In the early twentieth-century wave of immigration, Theodore Roosevelt went on the record repeatedly with statements such as "Every immigrant who comes here should be required within five years to learn English or to leave the country."[4]

While many state and local authorities have passed ordinances mandating that government business be conducted in English over the past thirty years, organized efforts to promote or require English language acquisition date to much earlier eras. Frederick Bogen's 1851 primer, quoted in the epigraph to this chapter, was written in both German and English and provided readers with bibliographic and price information for eight different reference texts as well as a bilingual Bible. Congress made knowledge of English a requirement for immigrants seeking to become naturalized citizens in 1906.[5] The Daughters of the American Revolution, in their 1911 guide for Italian immigrants, offered two pages' worth of advice about how to learn English—written only in English.[6] Other groups such as the Emergency Committee on the Education of Non-English Speaking Women were established to reach out to immigrants of the early twentieth century.[7]

The modern debate over English language skills is seldom undertaken seriously, because both sides have a tendency to dismiss the other rather than directly address salient points of contention. To the pro-English community, the opposition can be caricatured as a group of ivory tower types with little grounding in reality. The English-only crowd can itself be stereotyped as a group of monolinguistic xenophobes who lament the fact that automatic telephone scripts prompt them to select their language before offering them additional menu choices. It may come as some surprise to stalwart members of either camp, then, that there are serious economic arguments regarding whether individuals can be trusted to make the right decisions about language acquisition on their own.

The basic argument, elaborated below, begins with the basic model of assimilation as an investment introduced in chapter 1.[8] Learning English is costly; the time spent in class could be devoted to other activities, and the money spent on instruction could purchase other goods or services. The benefits to learning English accrue over time. Following the logic of the basic model, immigrants will choose to make this investment if the expected returns exceed the upfront costs. Those who expect to leave the country soon face less of an incentive to acquire English skills, as do those who find that they are able to get by economically as members of a linguistic minority.

What makes the language decision different is that the immigrant him or herself is not the only one who stands to benefit. A simple example will help to illustrate this point. Suppose a vendor at a farmer's market faces the possibility that produce will rot if not sold that day. Towards the end of the market, such a producer may be willing to sell for a reduced price, but may also be reluctant to advertise that fact if she expects that consumers willing to pay full price may soon stop by. In this case, the crucial information that the price of the produce is negotiable can only be conveyed through language. A potential buyer who does not speak the same language as the seller cannot learn that the potential for a mutually beneficial transaction exists. Commonality in language, at least in theory, produces gains to society. Below, we will learn that basic evidence confirms this theory, and introduces additional reasons to stress the importance of commonality.

This chapter analyzes information on English language ability collected by the U.S. Census Bureau, in the decennial censuses of 1900, 1910, 1920, 1930, 1980, 1990, and 2000. Since 2000, comparable information has been collected annually in the American Community Survey. We will learn that immigrants to America are actually more conversant in English than they were a century ago, but also that the rate of English language learning is slower now than it was then. Continued immigration to the United States can therefore be expected to perpetuate the existence of linguistic minority groups. The children of immigrants, by contrast, speak English almost universally. Were immigration to cease, then, those linguistic minority groups now present in American society would gradually decline over time—a pattern quite similar to the one that took hold at the end of the last major wave of immigration to the United States.

The evidence presented here complements a significant amount of prior scholarship on the subject of immigrant language acquisition. Prior studies have focused primarily on recent samples of immigrants, examining the basic reasons why some immigrants appear to learn English more rapidly than others. Economist Barry Chiswick has documented several basic findings using data from the United States and other countries. More educated immigrants and those arriving at earlier ages are more likely to learn new languages, and language proficiency increases with time spent in the host country.[9] Alejandro Portes, Ruben Rumbout, and other sociologists have noted similar patterns in their studies of recent Latin American immigrants.[10] This chapter both corroborates these basic patterns and provides a basis for historical comparison over more than a century.

## Why Language Matters

Those of us raised in the United States take the ubiquity of English for granted. In fact, the supremacy of a single language and the tendency for immigrants to rapidly adopt that language is quite exceptional.[11] Throughout the world, there are numerous cases of linguistic minorities persisting across generations. About one-fifth of the Canadian population speaks French, in spite of the fact that France ceded Quebec to Britain nearly 250 years ago. By comparison, most of the states of Texas and California were under unquestioned Spanish rule until the Mexican war of independence began in 1810, and remained Mexican possessions for at least a decade after the conclusion of that war. Much smaller linguistic minorities have also survived over generations, sometimes in spite of official persecution. The number of native Basque speakers in Spain, for example, amounts to no more than 2 percent of the nation's population.

The twin examples of Francophones in Canada and Basques in Spain intimate that linguistic diversity may have its pitfalls. A simmering separatist movement in Quebec has introduced periodic threats of secession since confederation in 1867. The Basque separatist movement in Spain has for forty years been associated with the violent ETA paramilitary group. One could easily argue, though, that the violence and disharmony associated with these movements would be unlikely to take root in the United States. French Canadians and Basques can both claim that the heritage of their ancestral homeland was oppressed by government authority; most immigrants in the United States have left their ancestral homeland behind. Further study, however, reveals that problems have a tendency to arise even in nations where differing language groups peaceably coexist.

In the developing world, many countries have an incredible array of languages and dialects spoken by small groups in society. In the 1960s, Soviet researchers developed a measure known as "ethno-linguistic fractionalization." This simple numeric index measures the likelihood that two residents of a country drawn randomly from the population speak different languages. In three African nations—Tanzania, Uganda, and Zaire—this likelihood is 90 percent or greater. Linguistic fractionalization tends to be high in sub-Saharan African nations, and is also very high in India.[12]

In the mid-1990s, economists and political scientists began noticing that nations with a plethora of native languages tended to have more political conflict, and less economic development, than nations with one dominant language. A prominent study following up on the international patterns found that even across counties in the United States, areas with more ethnic or racial divisions tended to make fewer investments in their infrastructure.[13] When asked basic questions about the degree to which they trust others, residents of racially or economically heterogeneous communities are more likely to invoke suspicious attitudes.[14] Ethnic diversity appears to influence even the most basic of civic decisions, such as the choice of whether to fill out and mail a census form.[15]

Do the documented relationships between linguistic or cultural heterogeneity and negative outcomes demonstrate a universal truth—does division automatically lead to conflict and economic struggle? There are clear arguments supporting an answer of "yes" to that question. On a grand scale, societies benefit from cooperation rather than competition among groups. To state an obvious example, nations that descend into civil war on a regular basis will find it difficult to establish and maintain the physical infrastructure needed to spur economic growth.

On a more human scale, the lack of a common language impedes business transactions between individuals, whether they be in an open-air marketplace or an office building. This basic story, invoked in the introduction to this chapter, was initially argued by economist Edward Lazear.[16] Many of the theoretical arguments in this chapter are rooted in Lazear's work, and the empirical evidence presented below confirms many of his original hypotheses.

The academic debate over the purported negative effects of diversity, as in many cases, hinges on a number of technical questions over measurement and the proper interpretation of ambiguous patterns in the available data.[17] And if linguistic diversity is the road to economic ruin, there are clearly alternate paths: Haiti, one of the world's poorest countries, is also one of the most homogenous from a linguistic perspective. Let's set aside these two concerns for a moment and consider the implications of the findings if they are true.

When an immigrant chooses to learn English, he or she reaps personal benefits. New opportunities for work and consumption arise, and the capacity to participate in American society increases as well. Society itself benefits as well—those of us who do not speak the immigrant's native language gain the opportunity to communicate with an additional person. Economists have a term, *positive externality*, for a scenario where one person's actions create benefits for others, but the others have no way to compensate that person. Positive externalities are nice things to have, but they present a challenge for public policy. A rational person, who engages in activities when their own private benefit exceeds their own private cost, will engage in too little of an activity when positive externalities are involved. In this case, the implication is that immigrants to the United States do not take sufficient steps to learn English, because there is no mechanism for society to compensate that individual for the benefit they bestow upon others.

The idealized solution to this problem would be to create a mechanism whereby society could repay some of its benefits back to the individual. It isn't difficult to imagine such a policy; in fact there are two basic strategies for accomplishing it. The first would be a program of subsidy for English language learners. The argument for subsidies is straightforward: society as a whole shares the benefits when an immigrant learns English, society as a whole should share in the costs as well, by paying taxes to support the activity. The argument against subsidies is a pragmatic one—they are expensive, and though they support a good cause there may be even better causes competing for scarce government resources.

The second basic strategy, less compassionate than the first but also cheaper in the long run, would be to penalize the inability to speak English. The most direct form of penalty would be a fine. The use of financial penalties for immigrants without appropriate language skills is not unprecedented; the Australian government effectively penalizes non-English speakers by charging them higher fees for permanent visas.[18] A milder form of penalty would be to take steps such as those already taken in jurisdictions that have established English as their official language: to render it more difficult to live the life of a non-English speaker in America.

Either penalty or subsidy would have the impact of encouraging immigrants to learn English. They would have differential impacts, however, on the overall attractiveness of the United States to prospective immigrants. A subsidy, by lowering the costs of assimilation, would encourage immigration. Penalties, which raise costs, would have the opposite effect.

The federal government employs some modest forms of encouragement for immigrants to learn English. Upon becoming a permanent resident, an immigrant is offered a pamphlet titled "Welcome to the United States: A Guide for New Immigrants."[19] It advises immigrants interested in learning English to check their local phone book for listings of school districts, community colleges, or private language schools. Although the pamphlet is available in a dozen languages besides English, it is not clear that this basic advice, which presupposes English skills sufficient to understand the organization of a phone book, and to hold a meaningful conversation with the party that answers the phone, actually accomplishes anything. Among other things, it ignores copious resources for language learning available electronically—many for free—via the Internet. Frederick Bogen's 1851 primer provided more valuable information than the U.S. Department of Homeland Security's 2007 publication. It is not hard to imagine that the federal government could take more useful steps to ease the path of language learning at little cost to taxpayers.[20]

Should we think of the United States as a nation at linguistic peril? Or as a place experiencing only transitory fluctuations in language, as waves of immigration come and go? Is there a strong case to be made for policy intervention, or are the decisions of private citizens and residents providing society with the full extent of potential benefits from linguistic commonality? These questions are ultimately empirical. Fortunately, the Census Bureau has collected enough data through the years to allow a critical examination of the state of linguistic assimilation among immigrants to America.

### The Census and Language

In 1900, the U.S. Census Bureau sent enumerators from door to door with forms that look like the predecessors to the modern spreadsheet. At the top of each form, enumerators wrote the name of the state, county, township, and city they were working in, their own name, and the date the form was filled out. The remainder of the form consists of a table with twenty-eight columns and many rows. At each home, the enumerator took down each person's name, personal information including month and year of birth, sex, race, marital status, and birthplace. Toward the end of the row, under a broad heading of "education," enumerators recorded whether an individual attended school, could read, could write, and could speak English. This marked the first time in American history that the census asked specifically about the ability to speak English. The question was undoubtedly inserted as a consequence of official concern about the rising immigrant population of the time. The 1900 census was to count ten million foreign-born residents in the population, nearly twice the number enumerated just thirty years before.

Enumerators were provided with few instructions as to what rules should be used to determine English-speaking ability. The 1900 booklet of instructions had a checklist of sixty-six items for recording individuals' occupation, but for determining English ability offered only this advice: "Write 'Yes' for all persons ten years of age and over who can speak English, and 'No' for all other persons of that age who can not speak English. For persons under ten years, leave the column blank."

Were enumerators to assess the ability to speak English themselves? If an Italian immigrant answered affirmatively, but in Italian, how should that be recorded? If a husband answered affirmatively for his wife, but the wife herself said nothing, what was to be done? The census contained no provisions for proving respondents' ability to read or write, so it is possible that enumerators similarly relied on respondents to assess their English ability truthfully. The possibility remains, though, that enumerators took matters into their own hands when assessing the ability to speak English.

One hundred and seven years later, more than a million households received a questionnaire in the mail. The American Community Survey asked residents of these households to fill out a twenty-four page questionnaire—the successor to the decennial census of old. The increased complexity and scope of the response form mirrors the growth of government itself. In the midst of a survey that asked about educational attainment, commuting patterns, military service, and disabilities, every member of the household was asked a three-part question about language, with what survey designers call a "skip pattern" in the middle. The first question pertained to the language spoken at home. If an individual reported speaking English at home, they were permitted to skip the second two questions. The second question provided a blank line to list the actual language spoken at home, and the third asked respondents to check one of four boxes to describe their ability to speak English. The response categories ranged from "Very well" to "Not at all."

One might ask the obvious question, if a respondent were unable to read English, how would they fill out the form in the first place? The solution, for Spanish-speakers at least, can be found on the form's first page:

Necesita Ayuda? Si usted habla espanol y necesita ayuda para completar su cuestionario, llame sin cargo alguno al 1-877-833-5624. Usted tambien puede pedir un cuestionario en espanol o completar su entrevista por telefono con un entrevistador que habla espanol.

Even if Spanish-speaking respondents had the option of completing a phone interview in Spanish, or requesting a Spanish-language questionnaire, one might further wonder whether contacted households of any sort would bother responding, given the barrage of unsolicited mail arriving daily at the typical twenty-first-century address. Response to the ACS, and other Census Bureau questionnaires, is mandated by law, and households that do not respond are contacted directly via phone or in person. For those respondents who escape all attempts at contact, the Census Bureau has a proprietary protocol of statistical methods to address "nonresponse," to ensure that the information collected in the survey is reasonably close to being representative of the nation as a whole.

The census and the ACS provide the best possible opportunity to compare and contrast the English language skills of immigrants across more than a century. This "best" opportunity is by no means perfect, however, for the reasons described above. Responses in the early period—through 1960, the last year census enumerators went door-to-door to interview each household—were filtered by an interviewer. Although this interviewer's training and instructions may have been limited, the force of experience could provide a guide as to whether a respondent was overoptimistically reporting his or her English skills. Respondents in the later period, beginning in 1980, were afforded an opportunity to elaborate on their English skills, rather than merely report whether they had any. This opportunity came hand-in-hand, however, with a chance to overreport. These caveats must be born in mind when reviewing the evidence culled from these sources.

## Basic Evidence on Immigrant Language Skills

Figure 4.1 presents information on the English language ability of immigrants over the period between 1980 and 2007, a period when census and ACS respondents faced identical questions and enumeration methods. For this and all figures in the chapter, immigrants from nations where the

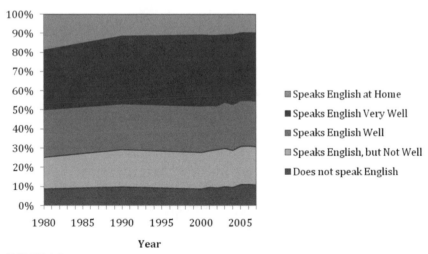

**FIGURE 4.1**
**Immigrant English Ability, 1980–2007**

predominant spoken language is English are excluded from the analysis.[21] The figure shows some evidence of a decline in English skills between 1980 and 1990, relative stability through the 1990s, and another slight decline since 2000. Between 2000 and 2006, the proportion of immigrants speaking no English rose from 9 to 11 percent, and the proportion speaking English poorly rose from 19 to 20 percent.

These slight trends are perfectly understandable in light of two facts: first, the immigrant population was growing rapidly over this time period, which implies that at any given point in time a high proportion of immigrants were recent arrivals. Second, English ability is generally weakest among the most recent arrivals.[22] In spite of these slight trends, the clearest vision in figure 4.1 is one of stability. During a period of time when the immigrant population tripled, the proportion of immigrants from non-English-speaking nations who either speak English at home or speak English "very well" held steady at around 50 percent.

How do these patterns compare to the early twentieth century? Figure 4.2 provides the best information available for this period, tracking census enumerators' reports of whether the immigrants they interviewed could speak English. Once again, immigrants born in nations where the predominant language is English are excluded from the analysis. The proportion of non-English-speaking immigrants appears to have been larger in this earlier era, with a pronounced spike in 1910, when nearly a third of the immigrant population lacked the ability to speak English. Not coincidentally, the 1910 census was taken at the close of the period of heaviest immigration in American

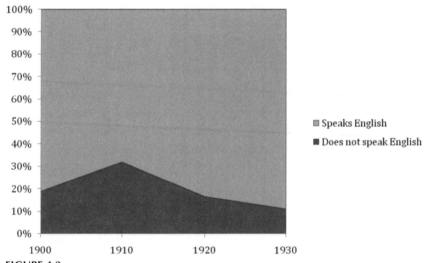

FIGURE 4.2
Immigrant English Ability, 1900–1930

history, at a point when immigrants formed the largest share of the American population between 1850 and the present. As World War I and legal restrictions cut off the flow of new immigrants into the country, the linguistic skills of immigrants improved; by 1930 the proportion of non-English-speaking immigrants approaches its modern value of around 10 percent.

It is difficult to compare these two sets of information, collected using very different methods. At face value, the English-speaking ability of the non-Anglophone immigrant population appears to be considerably better than it was a century ago. It is also possible, however, that many of the immigrants who report themselves to be poor English speakers would have been labeled as nonspeakers by census enumerators. Nonetheless, to this point we have uncovered no indication that the English language skills of the immigrant population have deteriorated rapidly.

### Linguistic Assimilation

Figure 4.3 presents information on the progress in English language acquisition for four cohorts of immigrants—groups arriving in the late 1970s, late 1980s, late 1990s, and first few years of the twenty-first century. Like the

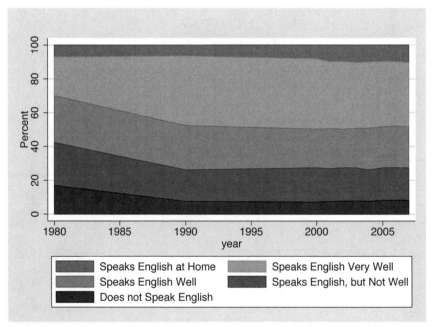

**FIGURE 4.3A**
**English Ability of 1975–1980 Arrivals over Time**

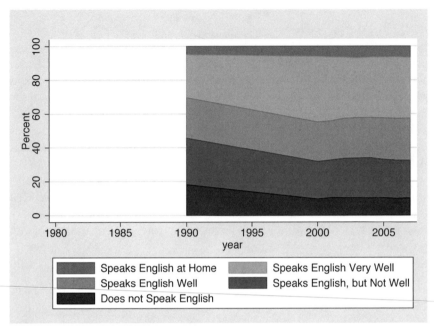

**FIGURE 4.3B**
English Ability of 1986–1990 Arrivals over Time

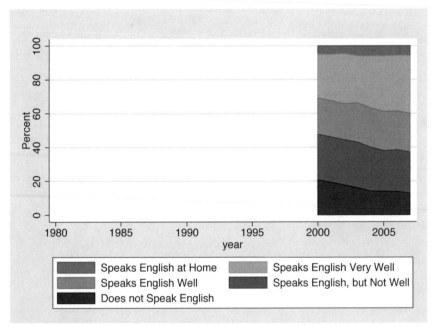

**FIGURE 4.3C**
English Ability of 1996–2000 Arrivals over Time

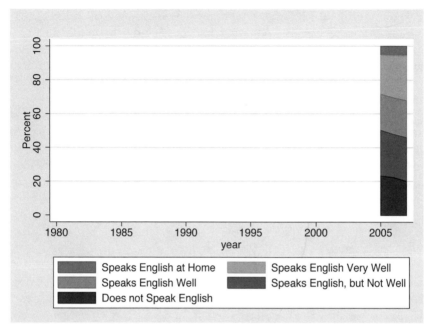

**FIGURE 4.3D**
**English Ability of 2001–2005 Arrivals over Time**

analysis of economic assimilation in the preceding chapter, this evidence is based on repeated cross-section analysis, and is thus subject to the caveat that trends may reflect either true assimilation or the selective exit of immigrants with poor English skills.

Each cohort of immigrants, whether arriving in the late 1970s, early 2000s, or any point in between, shows some evidence of language acquisition over time. For the older cohorts, progress is most evident in the first decade, where the proportion of immigrants with no or limited English skills declines, and the proportion with very good English ability increases. Few immigrants, even after multiple decades in residence in the United States, adopt English as the language they speak at home.

There is some evidence in this graph that the most recent cohorts of immigrants arrived with poorer English skills than their predecessors. The proportion of immigrants arriving without the ability to speak English has increased over time, from 17 percent in the late 1970s cohort to 22 percent in the early 2000s cohort. In this most recent cohort, nearly half of all immigrants from non-Anglophone nations arrive with at most poor English skills; this is an increase of five percentage points since the late 1970s cohort.

Figure 4.4 repeats the strategy of figure 4.3, following the linguistic progress of immigrant cohorts over time, but focusing on the immigrants of a century ago. Once again, these charts omit information on immigrants born in countries where English is the predominant language. Like figure 4.2, it is restricted to analyzing only whether census enumerators coded individuals as speakers or nonspeakers.

In this earlier era, the English language skills of newly arrived immigrants appear to be much worse than over the past few decades. Less than half of non-Anglophone immigrants arriving between 1896 and 1900 spoke English in 1900, and less than 40 percent of such immigrants arriving between 1906 and 1910 spoke English in 1910. Even admitting that many immigrants who now report that they speak English poorly would have been classified as nonspeakers if interviewed by an enumerator, the figures still support the conclusion that the English skills of newly arrived immigrants are better now than they were a century ago.

Equally striking, however, is the rate at which members of these cohorts made progress as they spent more time in the United States. In 1920, 80 percent of the 1906–1910 arrival cohort and 85 percent of the 1896–1900 cohort were coded as speaking English. To be fair, this process may not entirely re-

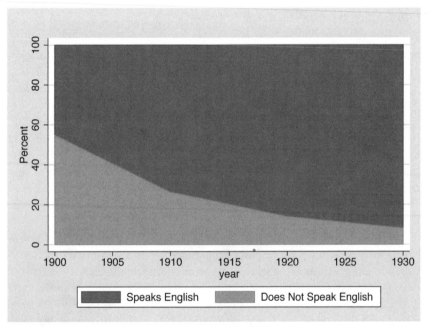

**FIGURE 4.4A**
**English Ability of 1896–1900 Arrivals over Time**

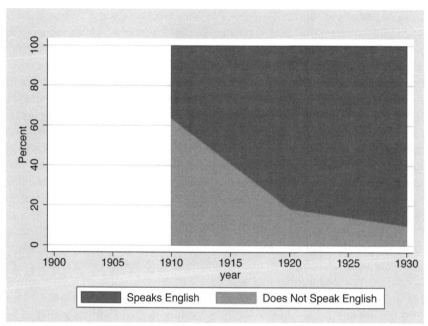

**FIGURE 4.4B**
**English Ability of 1906–1910 Arrivals over Time**

flect immigrant progress—non-English speakers may have been more likely to return to their homeland before 1920.[23] Nonetheless, the rapid transformation of these cohorts is remarkable. Forgetting about the return migration concern for a moment, these statistics indicate that about three-quarters of the non-English speakers in the 1896–1900 cohort acquired English skills within twenty years. In more recent times, the proportion of non-English-speaking members of the 1975–1980 cohort who acquired the ability to speak English over the next twenty years (once again setting return migration concerns aside for a moment) was lower, at 58 percent.

How does the potential for return migration change this picture? As discussed in chapter 2, return migration was much costlier for the immigrants from a century ago, who largely came from overseas and in some cases faced war or persecution upon their return home. The option of returning for those migrants who have difficulty assimilating is thus much more valuable in the present era. This implies that our image of immigrant progress is more likely to be skewed in the present rather than the past. Altogether, then, there is substantial evidence that immigrants of a century ago, in spite of arriving with poorer English skills, acquired them at a significantly more rapid rate.[24]

As a final note, figure 4.4 replicates the pattern observed among more recent immigrants, that those arriving later in the wave of immigration have poorer English skills than their immediate predecessors. This is an entirely logical pattern: the first immigrants from a particular origin country are those who anticipate fitting in rapidly with the native majority. Later cohorts can then benefit from ethnic group-specific networks set up by their predecessors. As immigration from one nation or linguistic group accelerates, the average English language skills of the group will tend to deteriorate. Continued growth in the immigrant population also reduces the pressure on preexisting immigrants to learn English, as linguistic enclaves develop around them. The more rapid growth in the immigrant population in recent decades, relative to the early twentieth-century wave, might explain why the rate of English language acquisition appears lower now than it was then.

These arguments can be easily recast in the framework of English learning as an investment decision. The returns to learning English are highest when there are very few potential trading partners who speak one's language of origin; hence those immigrants who arrive at the beginning of a wave either know the language already or learn it quickly. The returns are lower when immigrants face a high likelihood of returning to their home country. The argument above that easier return migration skews our image of linguistic progress in later years can be turned around: the ease of return migration is itself a cause of slower rates of English learning among more recent cohorts. The returns to learning English also decline with age—the older you are when you learn a language, the fewer years you will have to realize a return on your investment. This phenomenon, as much as any cognitive limitations to language learning that arise with age, can explain why the greatest rate of English learning occurs in the first years after migration.

Each of the arguments used to explain the variation in English language skills over time can also be applied to variation across groups at a point in time. We would expect immigrants with a stronger network of fellow language speakers to exhibit less rapid English language acquisition.[25]

Figure 4.5 presents information similar to that in figure 4.3, but focusing specifically on the English language skills of immigrants born in Mexico. In recent cohorts, Mexican immigrants have arrived in the United States with poorer English skills than the remainder of the non-Anglophone immigrant population.[26] In the earliest cohort, arriving in the late 1970s, more than a third of immigrants did not speak English, and another third spoke English poorly. This group reported some progress over time, to the point where more than half now report speaking English "well" or "very well." As is the case for the immigrant population as a whole, most of this progress occurred in the first decade of residence in the United States.

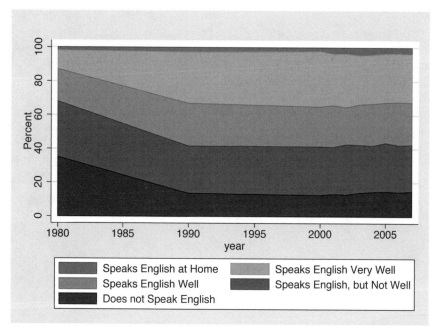

**FIGURE 4.5A**
**English Ability of 1975–1980 Arrivals from Mexico**

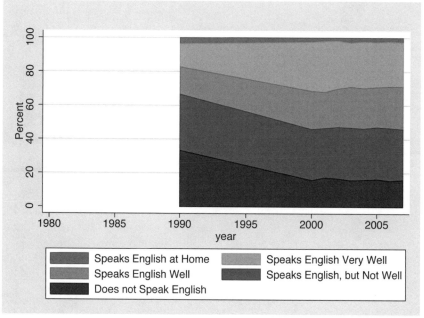

**FIGURE 4.5B**
**English Ability of 1986–1990 Arrivals from Mexico**

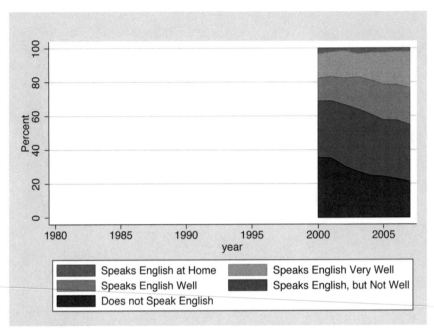

**FIGURE 4.5C**
**English Ability of 1996–2000 Arrivals from Mexico**

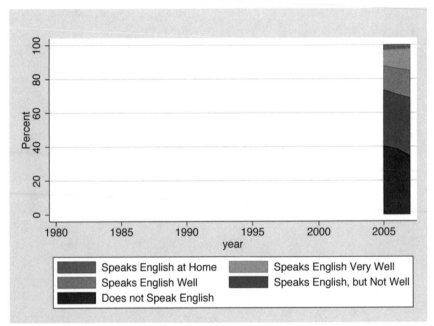

**FIGURE 4.5D**
**English Ability of 2001–2005 Arrivals from Mexico**

The cohorts of Mexican immigrants arriving in the late 1980s and late 1990s display trajectories similar to the first cohort, with roughly two-thirds of new arrivals having at most poor English skills, and some evidence of progress over the first decade. The English skills of the most recent cohort, arriving in 2001 or later, are worse than in earlier cohorts. Forty percent of this cohort arrived without the ability to speak English, and another third reported poor English skills. Between 2005 and 2007, this group shows evidence of progress at a rate comparable to earlier cohorts. The popular perception that the English language skills of the nation's largest foreign country-of-origin group have declined is thus supported by the data—and is consistent with the overall pattern of lower skills among immigrants who arrive later in a wave.

While the English skills of Mexican immigrants are lower than for other immigrant groups, their apparent rate of progress is higher. This is perhaps surprising, given our intuitive prediction that the presence of a strong network would retard language acquisition rates. Ignoring the issue of return migration, 63 percent of non-English speakers in the late 1970s birth cohort acquired the ability to speak English by 2000. For Mexican immigrants, though, the issue of return migration is particularly important, given the nation's proximity to the United States and the porousness of the border between the two nations. It is therefore difficult to ascertain whether the higher apparent rate of English language acquisition for Mexican immigrants is a function of rates of learning or of return migration.

Figure 4.6 examines the language acquisition of Vietnamese immigrants. The strong contrasts between Mexican and Vietnamese immigrants have been discussed before. For the purposes of studying language, it is worth emphasizing that the network of Vietnamese immigrants is much thinner, with ten Mexican-born residents for every one from Vietnam. Moreover, while the Vietnamese language overlaps with Cantonese to a small extent, it belongs to the relatively obscure Austro-Asiatic family of languages, of which it is the most commonly spoken. Each of these reasons implies that immigrants from Vietnam had stronger incentives to learn English and otherwise integrate themselves into the American mainstream.

In every arrival cohort, Vietnamese immigrants are more likely than their Mexican counterparts to speak English upon arrival in the United States. Although virtually no immigrants born in Vietnam speak English at home, the proportion with no knowledge of English upon arrival is never higher than one-quarter and is actually less than ten percent in the earliest cohort. Like other immigrant groups, individuals born in Vietnam show evidence of significant learning in their first decade in the United States. The proportion of late-1970s arrivals speaking English very well increased from 21 percent in 1980 to 47 percent in 2007. It makes little sense to track the progress

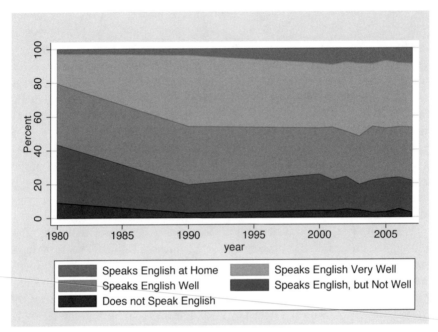

**FIGURE 4.6A**
English Ability of 1975–1980 Arrivals from Vietnam

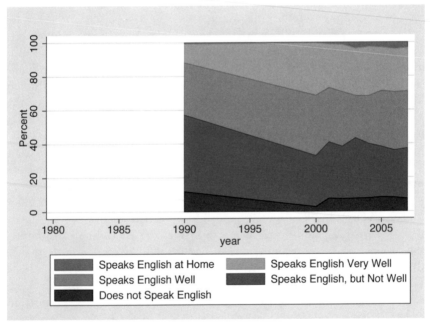

**FIGURE 4.6B**
English Ability of 1986–1990 Arrivals from Vietnam

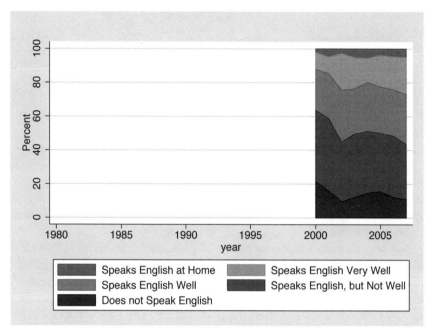

**FIGURE 4.6C**
English Ability of 1996–2000 Arrivals from Vietnam

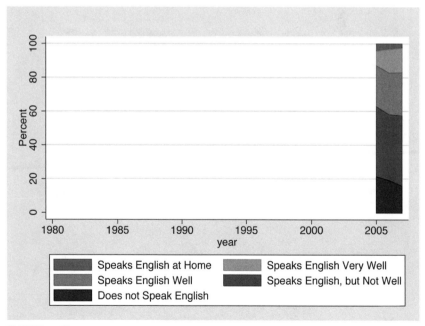

**FIGURE 4.6D**
English Ability of 2001–2005 Arrivals from Vietnam

of non-English speakers in this cohort since there were so few of them to begin with. Relative to Mexican immigrants, those from Vietnam arrived with a linguistic advantage and maintained that advantage over time. This confirms the basic intuition of the rational choice model, while indicating that the most important period of English language learning for many immigrants predates their arrival in the United States.

Also consistent with the rational choice model, the English skills of more recent Vietnamese cohorts are poorer than those of their predecessors. Whereas less than 10 percent of the late-1970s cohort arrived without knowing English, 21 percent of post-2000 arrivals reporting speaking no English in 2005. Across nationalities, then, the pioneers at the beginning of an immigration wave tend to have superior English skills relative to their followers.

Just as economic assimilation takes place across generations, the children of immigrants tend to exhibit English skills vastly superior to their parents. This can be seen in a study of "Generation 1.5" immigrants. Figure 4.7 presents information on the English language skills of adult immigrants as a function of their age upon arrival in the United States. The figure considers only those immigrants at least twenty-five years of age in 2007. The vast majority of "Generation 1.5" immigrants report speaking English very well as adults.

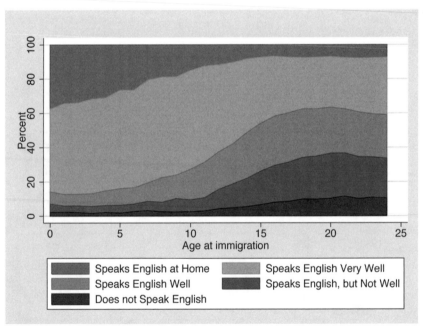

**FIGURE 4.7**
**English Fluency and Age at Immigration for Foreign-Born Adults in 2007**

Over 80 percent of immigrants arriving at age seven or below fall in this category. More than a quarter of immigrants arriving at age six or younger speak English at home as adults. Although their parents may have difficulty in learning English, the children of adult immigrants show much evidence of assimilating linguistically.

While the differences in English skills between immigrants who arrive as newborns and as seven-year-olds are minor, the differences between those who arrive as seven- and fourteen-year-olds are stark. Barely half of this latter group speaks English very well, and more than one in five speak either no or very little English. While consistent with the notion that younger children can acquire second language skills more easily, it might also reflect the fact that teenage immigrants to the United States have the opportunity to drop out of school before they learn much English. A considerable academic debate persists on the question of whether there is a "critical period" in second language adoption.[27] English-speaking skills are lowest for immigrants arriving in their late teens or early twenties; more than a third of immigrants arriving as twenty-one-year-olds, for example, speak either no or little English. Some portion of this trend may reflect the fact that adult immigrants who arrived as younger adults have had fewer years to learn English than those who arrived as children. Immigrants who arrive as older adults, although not depicted in this figure, have even poorer skills—nearly half of those immigrants arriving at age twenty-five or later speak little or no English. Once again, this may reflect the relatively more recent arrival of these individuals.

## Conclusion

This brief study of immigrant English language acquisition has identified points of similarity and difference in the experiences of varying groups over the past century. While changes in the measurement of English skills by the Census Bureau make long-term comparisons difficult, the contemporary immigrant population appears stronger in English, primarily because they are more likely to speak English upon arrival in the United States. The superior English skills of newly arrived immigrants may reflect improvements in the education systems of foreign countries over the last century, or a change in the composition of the group of individuals who choose to emigrate.

In spite of this initial advantage, the rate of English language learning among those immigrants who arrive without the ability to speak appears lower than it was a century ago. As discussed previously, the more rapid rate of growth in the immigrant population may contribute to this trend. The benefits of learning English are inherently tied to the economic advantage conferred by knowing that language. For immigrants residing in a large community of same-language speakers, the extra opportunity associated with acquiring English skills may be limited—jobs can easily be found within their existing linguistic network. Finally, it is also possible that in an age of mass media and communication, it is easier to get by in the United States without knowing English than it was a hundred years ago, regardless of the size of one's group network.

Finally, the English skills of Mexican immigrants are worse, on average, than the immigrant population as a whole, though there is some evidence that their rate of English language acquisition is higher.

If the statistics do not paint a picture of an English language crisis, why has there been so much popular concern over the use of other languages in the public sphere? The perception of a language problem most likely reflects the large number of recent immigrants in the population, and the wider distribution of those immigrants relative to earlier waves. In 2000, nearly a quarter of the 31 million immigrants counted in the census had been in the country fewer than five years. The proportion of recent arrivals in the immigrant population has been at or near this level since 1980, but the immigrant population itself doubled over these two decades. The immigrant population also expanded outward from traditional receiving states to "new destinations" in the 1990s, exposing many communities to their first significant foreign-born populations.[28]

Finally, to be fair, in characterizing the English skills of immigrants as "not a crisis," we are comparing them to a period of time when immigrant language skills were a grave national concern. Fear over immigrants' inability to speak English resulted in the imposition of a language requirement for naturalization in 1906, and fueled repeated attempts to adopt a literacy test for new immigrants, which finally came to fruition in 1917. It may therefore come as little surprise that modern political debates over immigrants and the English language offer so many parallels to this earlier era.

# 5

# Fitting In Officially

I don't want to belong to any club that will accept people like me as a member.

—Comedian and second-generation immigrant Groucho Marx, message to the Friar's Club of Beverly Hills, as reported in his autobiography

THE DECISION TO BECOME a naturalized citizen of the United States is in some ways the ultimate sign of assimilation. Unlike other aspects of integration, however, the process of naturalization is governed as much by official policy as by any individual desire to join the ranks of the citizenry. Whereas some assimilation decisions, such as the choice to learn English, are fundamentally unilateral, naturalization is effectively the outcome of a bilateral negotiation between immigrant and host country. Immigrants may opt not to naturalize because they feel it is not worth their while; in some cases, however, policy leaves them with no choice.

Would a liberalization of naturalization policy lead large numbers of immigrants to obtain citizenship? Has the propensity of aliens to become naturalized citizens increased or decreased over the past century? These are questions of considerable importance. While numerous empirical studies of naturalization behavior have been conducted by economists and sociologists over the past few decades, our insight as to the answer is surprisingly limited.[1] The limitations are generally rooted in study design: most analyze only a single cross-sectional dataset, or at best one cohort observed over time.[2] Most studies examine exactly one policy regime, making it impossible to infer what the effects of policy might be. There have been some cross-country studies, but these are generally limited to a small number of nations.[3] Opining that policy makes some difference should generate little controversy—it is easy to imagine draconian initiatives that would eliminate naturalization.[4] But we have little sense of the degree to which policy makes a difference.

Although the academic literature is limited in this way, there are many important patterns to be taken from it. Economist Barry Chiswick, cited repeatedly in chapter 4 for his study of English language acquisition among immigrants, along with coauthor Paul Miller, studied naturalization patterns in the 2000 census and came to the conclusion that the decision to become a citizen is governed largely by perceived costs and benefits.[5] This pattern is entirely consistent with the rational choice framework presented in chapter 1. It has also been corroborated by studies of other time periods and of other nations. A widely cited study by sociologist Guillermina Jasso and economist Mark Rosenzweig, which analyzed immigrants who arrived in the United States in 1971, found that immigrants were more likely to naturalize when the option of returning to their home country was less attractive—either because that country was physically distant, or because living standards in that nation were low.[6] Some evidence also shows that refugees and asylees, who would presumably face negative consequences upon return to their home country, naturalize at elevated rates.[7] Chiswick and Miller's analysis identified factors including indices of political rights, civil liberties, and economic freedom as measures of the attractiveness of an immigrant's return option. These factors are all quite sensible in the context of a rational choice model of immigrant assimilation.[8] Questions remain, however, regarding the importance of host country policy rather than individual and origin country characteristics.

This chapter presents a long-run analysis of immigrant naturalization in the United States, which can answer both the basic question of what has happened over time and the more fundamental question of the impact of policy. In the United States, naturalization policy has undergone significant and complex change over time. The barriers to citizenship have been lowered for some groups and raised for others. In 1900, a non-English-speaking, unskilled European immigrant could become a citizen but a skilled professional born in an Asian country could not. A hundred years later, the opposite was true.[9] In spite of these differences, there has been little change in the overall rates of naturalization over the past century. Figure 5.1 shows the naturalization progress of six immigrant cohorts, the earliest arriving between 1896 and 1900, the latest between 2001 and 2005. Each cohort begins with very low naturalization rates—a completely unsurprising phenomenon, since American policy has always imposed some form of waiting period for most immigrants. By the time a cohort has spent twenty to twenty-five years in the United States, somewhere between 60 and 70 percent of its members have become naturalized citizens.

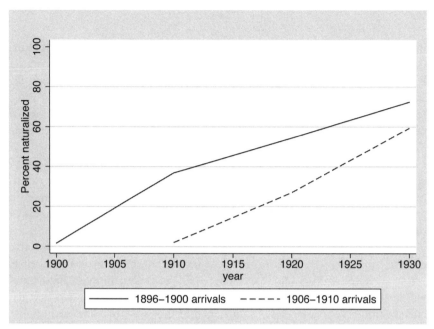

**FIGURE 5.1A**
Naturalization of Immigrant Cohorts, 1900–1930

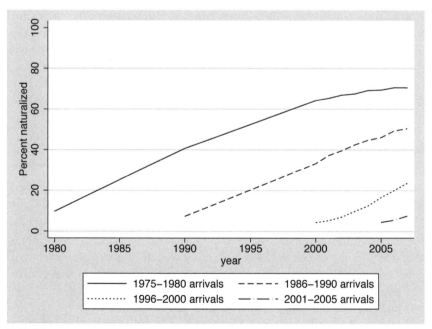

**FIGURE 5.1B**
Naturalization of Immigrant Cohorts, 1980–2007

This quick glance at the data might tempt an observer to conclude that official policy plays little role in the naturalization process. Further inspection will radically alter this conclusion. Immigrants from Mexico, for example, naturalize at very low rates—not necessarily because they attach little value to American citizenship, but because so many hold only temporary visas, or reside in the country illegally.[10] Recent immigrants from Somalia, who are likely to be refugees or asylees, naturalize at higher rates in part because their status places them squarely on a path to citizenship. A change in official policy could well alter these patterns—and quite likely alter the raw number of immigrants entering the country as well. The behavior of some other immigrant groups, particularly those from wealthy nations, indicates that anything short of a draconian change to naturalization policy would have little effect. Importantly, the role of the English language requirement for most prospective citizens appears to be little impediment for those who desire to naturalize. There are some immigrants who value American citizenship very highly and will bear substantial costs to obtain it. There are others who could become citizens under very favorable circumstances if they so chose, and decline.

These patterns highlight an essential tension in naturalization policy: those immigrants we would most like to admit as permanent members of society are not always the ones who place the highest value on the offer. In the spirit of this chapter's epigraph, one might term this the Groucho Marx paradox. Naturalization policy can be tailored either to attract a certain type of immigrant from abroad or to reward those immigrants who place a high value on citizenship in the United States. In certain circumstances, these two goals might not be in conflict, but in early twenty-first century America they may well be. Naturalization policy debates thus encapsulate much of the more general debates on immigration policy: should government adopt a selective or inclusive policy toward immigration?

### The Evolution of Naturalization Policy in the United States

In some respects, naturalization policy has changed little through American history; in others it has shifted radically. Since the first federal law on naturalization was passed in 1790, citizenship has been reserved for aliens who have met a minimum residency requirement, who have displayed "good moral character," and who can pass a test covering aspects of American history and government.[11] Through the years, racial restrictions on citizenship have fallen, an English language mandate has been imposed and then relaxed, and intermediate steps on the road to naturalization have been altered.

Table 5.1 tracks the evolution of naturalization policy in the United States from the colonial period to the twenty-first century.[12] In the colonial era, the

**TABLE 5.1**
**The Evolution of Naturalization Policy in the United States**

| Year | Event |
|------|-------|
| 1666 | Maryland Assembly passes an act naturalizing one family; "private" naturalizations common in the colonial era. |
| 1683 | First naturalization statutes passed by New York and Pennsylvania. |
| 1740 | British parliament establishes a naturalization law for all colonies. |
| 1783 | Under the Articles of Confederation, states establish naturalization statutes |
| 1790 | Under the Constitution, Naturalization Act signed by George Washington. Requirements include two years' residence, one year's residence in the same state, "good moral character," oath of support. Eligibility restricted to free whites. |
| 1795 | Naturalization Act introduces declaration of intent requirement, three year "waiting period" after declaration, five years' total residence. |
| 1798 | Naturalization Act (one of the four Alien and Sedition acts) increases waiting period to five years and total residence requirement to fourteen years. |
| 1802 | The Naturalization Act of 1798 is repealed; rules of 1795 act reinstated, with some legal clarifications. |
| 1828 | Waiting period between declaration of intent and naturalization reduced to two years. |
| 1855 | Wife and children become citizens upon the naturalization of the husband/father. Automatic naturalization by marriage discontinued in 1922; at that point women must undergo the naturalization process individually. |
| 1862 | Declaration of intent waived for applicants with an honorable discharge from the U.S. Army. Privilege extended to Naval veterans in 1894; residency requirement waived for veterans with three or more years of service in 1918. Naturalization preferences for military personnel and veterans continue to exist. |
| 1870 | Naturalization Act extends privilege to immigrants of African origin. |
| 1882 | Chinese Exclusion Act affirms ineligibility of Chinese for naturalization while simultaneously prohibiting new immigration from China. Act was temporary, but renewed in 1892 and made permanent in 1902. |
| 1898 | Supreme Court, in *United States v. Wong Kim Ark* (169 U.S. 649) rules that children born in the United States to foreign-born parents are citizens except when the parents are in the country temporarily, are diplomats, or are members of a hostile occupying force. |
| 1906 | Basic Naturalization Act establishes the Bureau of Immigration and Naturalization, which has the authority to investigate petitions for citizenship, ensuring a greater degree of consistency across various courts. Candidates for citizenship must produce statements from witnesses. Requirement that candidate speak English introduced; other requirements generally maintained. |
| 1913 | Bureau of Naturalization becomes separate entity when the Department of Commerce and Labor is reorganized into separate Departments. |
| 1933 | Executive order creates the Immigration and Naturalization Service within the Department of Labor. |

*(continued)*

**TABLE 5.1**
**(*continued*)**

| Year | Event |
|------|-------|
| 1940 | The INS is relocated to the Department of Justice. |
| 1943 | Magnuson Act permits the naturalization of immigrants from China, while maintaining strict quotas on new entry. |
| 1946 | Luce-Celler Act extends right to naturalize to natives of India and the Philippines, while maintaining strict quotas on new entry. Natives of the Philippines had been considered U.S. nationals between 1898 and 1934. |
| 1952 | Immigration and Nationality (or McCarran-Walter) Act removes all remaining racial barriers to naturalization; removes declaration of intent requirement. Immigrants over fifty who have resided in the U.S. for twenty years exempted from English requirement. State residency requirement reduced to six months. Establishes framework for legal permanent residence and temporary visas. |
| 1965 | Hart-Celler Act, best known for eliminating national origin quotas, alters preferences for legal permanent residence, improving standing of aliens seeking permanent residence through family relationships. |
| 1990 | Immigration Act extends English exemption to immigrants over fifty-five who have resided in the United States for fifteen years; reduces state residency requirement to three months. |
| 1995 | State department conducts first "diversity lottery" for green cards. |
| 2003 | U.S. Citizenship and Immigration Service established within the Department of Homeland Security; INS ceases to exist. |

question of granting citizenship was often undertaken on a case-by-case basis. Under the Articles of Confederation, each state had the authority to establish its own naturalization policy. Article I, section 8 of the Constitution transferred this authority to the federal government. In the dozen years after the ratification of the Constitution, Congress passed four different laws governing naturalization. While each law tinkered with the specifics of the naturalization process, the basic structure of the policy—a waiting period, a moral character clause, and an oath of loyalty—was established in 1790.

Over time, the barriers to citizenship embodied in naturalization law have ebbed and flowed with opinions toward immigration in general. The most restrictive naturalization law in American history was ushered in with the wave of Francophobia that spawned the Alien and Sedition acts in 1798; the law was repealed four years later. The requirement that immigrants speak English, introduced in 1906, was an early foray into immigration restriction that culminated in the quota system of the 1920s. Exemptions to this requirement were introduced in 1952 and 1990. For eighty years, the privilege of naturalization was restricted to whites only; racial restrictions were not completely abolished until the McCarran-Walter Act in 1952.

Since 1906, the overriding tendency over time has been to relax citizenship requirements. State residency requirements have been relaxed twice, racial barriers have been eliminated, and a system of exemptions from the English language requirement instituted. Special privileges for members or veterans of the armed forces, present in some form since the Civil War, have been extended.

Although naturalization policy has been consistently relaxed for over a century, a secondary set of restrictions has always been in place. A system of national origin quotas for new immigrants remained in place until 1965. While the McCarran-Walter Act did remove some of the most odious barriers to citizenship, it also introduced the concept of legal permanent residence, making it a prerequisite for citizenship. Legal permanent residence, commonly referred to as obtaining a "green card," is a completely insurmountable barrier for certain immigrants.

The path to a green card is direct and uncomplicated for some—the spouse and young children of a citizen, highly skilled professionals, and asylum seekers.[13] Some other eligible immigrants face quotas that effectively introduce waiting periods of a decade or more, after which time they will be a mere five years from citizenship.[14] For an unskilled worker who is neither the child nor spouse of a citizen or permanent resident, nor the sibling of a citizen, there is no path to legal permanent residence or citizenship, with one exception. Immigrants born in relatively obscure foreign countries—ones that do not send a large number of emigrants to the United States—are eligible to participate in the "diversity lottery" for green cards. More than 6.4 million persons entered the 2008 diversity lottery, vying for fifty thousand permanent resident visas.[15] More than 98 percent of these entrants would go away empty-handed.[16] Entrants in the diversity lottery would be ten times more likely to win a prize if they bought an ordinary scratch-off ticket at an American gas station.[17] Especially when we factor in the obstacles to legal permanent residence, it is clear that between the early twentieth and early twenty-first century, the road to citizenship became much easier for some immigrants and much more difficult for others.

## What Is the Goal of Naturalization Policy?

Understanding an immigrant's rationale for pursuing naturalization is straightforward. When government grants citizenship, it forgoes the right to deport an individual. From the immigrant's perspective, this is a valuable concession. What's more, several other rights of civic participation are bundled in. In theory, an immigrant must renounce his or her prior citizenship when taking the oath of loyalty to the United States. In practice, foreign governments do not necessarily recognize this renunciation and dual citizenship is accepted, if not exactly encouraged, under current American policy.[18] Thus, in the absence of real barriers we might expect all immigrants to pursue citizenship in the United States.

How exactly does granting citizenship serve the government's purposes? In exchange for giving up the right of deportation, the government is guaranteed little if anything. There is no requirement that citizens vote, work, or even reside in the United States. Legal permanent residents are liable for the same taxes as citizens, so there is no automatic fiscal benefit. Indeed, under the Personal Responsibility and Work Opportunity Reconciliation Act of 1996, citizens are eligible for certain public assistance programs while legal permanent residents are not. From a political perspective, granting citizenship threatens to dilute the power of the native-born. Concerns of this nature have driven previous efforts to impose more stringent naturalization requirements. If there is so little in the way of direct tangible benefit from naturalization, why does government permit it to happen?

One possible response to this question is that native-born Americans receive an intangible "warm glow" from extending offers of citizenship. While the nation's legacy of welcoming foreigners to its shores is undoubtedly a source of civic pride for many, there is an additional class of indirect but tangible benefits stemming from the use of naturalization as an incentive. By holding out the promise of naturalization, we encourage some immigrants to do things they might not otherwise do.

The government rationale for extending offers of citizenship is thus analogous to the use of frequent-flier loyalty programs. Airlines gain nothing through the actual exchange of seats for earned miles. They do, however, gain by encouraging travelers to alter their behavior, favoring one carrier over another (and possibly paying higher prices in the process) simply to accrue miles. Similarly, government and existing citizens benefit not from naturalization itself, but from the behaviors it encourages. The most obvious exhibit in this argument is the use of accelerated pathways to citizenship to encourage legal permanent residents—and in some cases, even nonpermanent visa holders—to serve in the armed forces. Less obviously, but more importantly, the offer of citizenship encourages an immigrant to come to the United States and remain on a narrow pathway of approved behavior—to exhibit the "good moral character" that has been a hallmark of naturalization policy since the beginning. Were immigrants permitted to enter the country, but prohibited from participating in the nation's civic life, one might worry that a wide range of subversive behaviors would ensue.

Government can use naturalization policy to encourage certain types of immigrants to come to America, while discouraging others. At no point in our nation's history has the United States been willing to accept any foreign-born human being as a citizen. The nature of the selection process has changed over time. Early naturalization policy emphasized race and national origin. More recent naturalization policy continues to place some emphasis on national origin, for example in restricting the set of immigrants eligible for the diversity lottery, but places a much greater emphasis on economic priorities. Naturalization law is now designed to encourage skilled workers and entrepreneurs who are in short supply, or who hold out the promise of bringing jobs for locals along with them, to become permanent residents of the United States. Similar preferences can be found in other developed nations.[19]

These changes in naturalization policy over time offer, at least in theory, an opportunity to infer the role of policy in promoting or restricting immigrant decisions to become citizens. As already noted, however, there has been remarkably little change in the average propensity for immigrants to naturalize, dating back a century or more. It is conceivable that official policy has little impact on naturalization patterns—some immigrants may be willing to bear any burden in order to achieve citizenship, and others may be unwilling, perhaps because they are loathe to sacrifice their allegiance to their home country. It is also possible that the tracking of naturalization patterns over time is flawed in some technical sense. Finally, it is possible that this picture of long-term stability in the rate of naturalization masks important underlying trends. As we will soon learn, there is more to the story than figure 5.1 might indicate.

## Does Naturalization Policy Matter?

Before poring over current and historical naturalization patterns in greater depth, it is worth assessing the just-raised concerns about data limitations. In chapter 4, we learned that changes in the way the Census Bureau collects information about language ability threaten the validity of long-run comparisons. These concerns are less obvious in the study of citizenship. Census enumerations began inquiring about respondents' citizenship in 1870. In that year, citizenship information was only collected for those with the potential right to vote: males over the age of twenty-one. Information on the citizenship of all foreign-born individuals was not collected until 1920. Until the passage of the McCarran-Walter Act in 1952, naturalization was a two-step process, the first step being a declaration of intent, with a waiting period imposed before a final hearing. Between 1900 and 1940, the Census Bureau separately coded those foreign-born persons who had declared intent but not yet completed the naturalization process. At no point were enumerators ever instructed to verify whether a respondent could properly document his or her naturalization. In the modern era of mailed census questionnaires, respondents are directly instructed to indicate whether they, and members of their household, are citizens of the United States.

The recording of citizenship status in the immigrant population appears quite consistent over time, in contrast to the collection of information regarding English-speaking ability. There may be some tendency to misreport citizenship status; immigrants may intentionally misrepresent their citizenship status, or might misunderstand the nature of the naturalization process. The nature of the distinction between legal permanent residency and citizenship may be obscure to some, for example. It is unclear whether the rate of misrepresentation would be higher in the interview era or the mail survey era. On the one hand, lying to a person is a more egregious act than checking the wrong box on a form. On the other hand, the incentive to misrepresent may be higher when facing a representative of the United States government. In any event, our confidence in the consistency of citizenship data is almost certainly stronger than our confidence in the consistency of measurement for economic status or English language ability.

Ruling out shifts in census methodology as an explanation for the patterns in figure 5.1, we are left with the question of why major shifts in naturalization policy did not alter basic naturalization patterns. A first partial answer to this apparent puzzle is that some changes to naturalization policy have had little practical impact. Many of the racial restrictions on naturalization in the early twentieth century were of little relevance, since they were trumped by restrictions on immigration in the first place. Government refusal to grant citizenship to natives of China, for example, had little impact on overall naturalization patterns because the Chinese Exclusion Act reduced the number of immigrants from China to near zero.

A second response to the puzzle is that basic naturalization patterns, covering all immigrants in an arrival cohort, do not adequately convey the variation in experiences of members of varying groups. Previous literature on the determinants of naturalization has established a number of important sources of variation across nationalities. Figure 5.2 displays one of the more prominent patterns, using data on immigrants from the 2007 American Community Survey. This scatterplot compares the naturalization rate for immigrants arriving in the United States between 1995 and 1999 to the economic standard of living in an immigrant's country of birth, as measured by GDP per capita.[20]

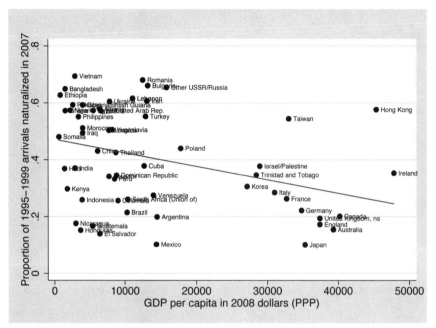

**FIGURE 5.2**
**Birth Country and Naturalization Rate, 2007**

As previous studies have documented, there is a noticeable negative relationship between home country living standards and naturalization rates.[21] The straight line superimposed on the chart is derived from an ordinary least squares regression, and is the line that statistically best represents the relationship between the two factors. It indicates that on average, naturalization rates drop 5 percent with every $5,000 increase in home country GDP per capita. Immigrants from developed nations, including the United Kingdom, Canada, Japan, Australia, and Germany, are unlikely to become naturalized citizens. At the other end of the spectrum, immigrants from poor countries such as Somalia, Ethiopia, and Bangladesh are much more likely to naturalize. The inverse relationship between home country living standards and naturalization in the United States makes sense from a rational choice perspective. Citizenship eliminates the threat of being sent back to one's home country. The economic cost associated with this threat is strongest when the home country is poor.

The role of policy forces can be most easily seen in the exceptions to the economic rule. Figure 5.3 replicates the image of the preceding plot, superimposing a "cross-hair" that neatly divides the data points into four quadrants.

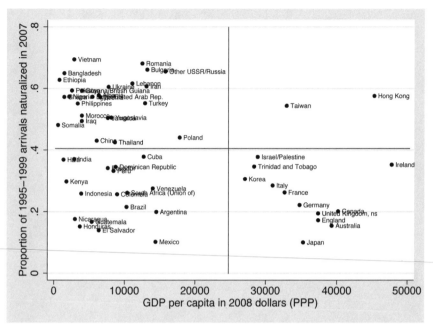

**FIGURE 5.3**
**GDP and Naturalization Rate, 2007**

Most of the data points lie in the upper left and lower right quadrants: poor origin countries with high naturalization rates and wealthy origin countries with low naturalization rates. There are only two nations in the upper right quadrant, wealthy countries of origin with high naturalization rates: Taiwan and Hong Kong. These two nations face a common source of uncertainty rooted in their nation's status relative to China. A political risk, the likelihood that living standards in their home nations will converge to the levels of mainland China, might explain these elevated naturalization rates.

The lower left quadrant is populated with a number of important immigrant-sending nations, including Mexico, a relatively poor nation with a naturalization rate at the very low end of the spectrum. Four Central American nations, Nicaragua, Guatemala, Honduras, and El Salvador, are also noteworthy for their low naturalization rates. Five South American and three Caribbean origin countries also lie in this quadrant. Why is there so much heterogeneity in naturalization rates among immigrants from poor countries?

There are several answers to this question. In February 2009, the Department of Homeland Security released a report on the unauthorized immigrant population of the United States.[22] The report lists the ten most common countries of origin for illegal immigrants; seven of them appear in the lower left quadrant of figure 5.3. Two more (China and Korea) are just over the border. For many immigrants from these countries of origin, citizenship is not an option. Were an official amnesty to offer a path to legal permanent residency and citizenship, it is reasonable to think that naturalization rates for these immigrants would rise considerably. Following a general amnesty that offered illegal immigrants a route to citizenship, we might expect the nations in the lower left quadrant to ascend.

A second explanation for the disparity in naturalization between, say, Colombian and Ukrainian immigrants is the "wild card" route to citizenship: the diversity lottery for legal permanent residency, for which only the latter group is eligible. Among the eighteen countries of origin in the lower left quadrant, one-third were ineligible for the lottery as of 1999. Among the countries in the upper left, less than one-fifth are ineligible. While the number of green cards issued through the lottery is limited, the existence of family preferences for relatives of green card holders magnifies the effect of victory.[23] Thus, even in the absence of illegal immigration, restricted access to this special avenue to permanent residency and citizenship would lead to disparities.

Third, migrants from some relatively poor nations constitute the economic elite of their home country, while migrants from other nations do not. Mexico, Argentina, and Bulgaria have comparable living standards as measured by per capita GDP. Fewer than one in twenty Mexicans in the 2007 ACS has a college degree; by contrast nearly a third of the Argentines and more than half of the Bulgarians are college graduates. Higher education levels imply a greater likelihood of qualifying for legal permanent residence on the basis of occupational skills; prior studies of naturalization in the United States and other countries have identified educational attainment as an important predictor of citizenship.[24]

A fourth explanation for the differences in naturalization rates among immigrants from poor countries points toward the special status awarded refugees (who apply for residence while outside the United States) and asylees (who apply when already in the United States). Eight nations had more than five hundred accepted applications for asylum during fiscal 1999; six of those appear in the upper left quadrant of figure 5.3. The exceptions are Indonesia, in the lower left quadrant, and Liberia, which is not depicted in the figure but would have appeared in the lower left.[25] In theory, the number of admitted refugees is subject to an annual cap, but in recent years the number of admissions has remained well below the cap.[26]

All of these arguments point to the conclusion that naturalization rates among immigrants from Mexico and similar nations would rise dramatically if an amnesty policy opened a legal route to citizenship. It is also true, though, that many of the nations in the lower left quadrant are proximate to the United States. Thus, it may be possible that low naturalization rates are not entirely reflective of the lack of a legal option to become a citizen, but rather a lower willingness to take that option.

While this last argument is entirely plausible, one can find compelling rebuttals elsewhere on the chart. Presumably the distance argument would also apply to immigrants from Canada. While the naturalization rate of Canadian immigrants is low in an absolute sense, it is actually higher than the rates of naturalization for immigrants born in either the United Kingdom or Australia, two comparably wealthy and predominantly English-speaking nations at much greater distances from the United States. Given advances in transportation and communication technology, distance is likely much less of a barrier to migration than it once was.

The various rationalizations for the differences in naturalization rates across poor countries all point to the importance of policy. Restrictions on access to citizenship not only influence naturalization rates; they in part determine the number of immigrants who choose to locate in the United States. Were restrictions on naturalization to be dropped, the naturalization rates of many nations in the lower left quadrant of figure 5.3 would likely rise at least to some extent. What is more, the raw number of immigrants from nations in the upper left quadrant would likely also rise. For every winner of the State Department's green card diversity lottery, there are at least ninety-nine losers, individuals who would come to America and join the path to citizenship if given the chance. Some of them will come anyway, using temporary visas or entering the country without the authorization to stay or work, foregoing the path to citizenship but reaping economic rewards. The illegal route to residence and employment in the United States is easier to pursue from a proximate starting point.

## Naturalization Among the Children of Immigrants

With one noteworthy exception, the naturalization rates of "Generation 1.5" immigrants, born abroad but raised in the United States, have been high for more than a century. Table 5.2 shows that the overall rate of naturalization for the middle-aged males born abroad but raised in the United States studied in chapter 3 ranges between 87 percent in 1900 to 76 percent in 2007. If we exclude Mexican-born immigrants from the 2007 sample, the overall naturalization rate climbs to 84 percent; Mexicans themselves have only a 60 percent naturalization rate, presumably because a high proportion of them came to the United States illegally as children. For other prominent nationali-

**TABLE 5.2**
**Naturalization Rates for Generation 1.5, 1900–2007**

| Year/Group | Naturalization Rate |
|---|---|
| 1900 | |
| Overall | 86.7 |
| Irish | 87.7 |
| German | 90.5 |
| Scandinavian | 87.8 |
| 1930 | |
| Overall | 80.6 |
| Italian | 81.9 |
| Russian | 88.2 |
| 2007 | |
| Overall | 75.7 |
| All nationalities except Mexico | 83.5 |
| Mexican | 59.6 |
| Filipino | 91.2 |
| Korean | 94.5 |
| Vietnamese | 92.9 |

*Note:* Sample consists of adult males born abroad, arriving in the United States by the age of five, between the ages of thirty and forty at time of enumeration.

ties within today's Generation 1.5, naturalization rates are high by historical standards, above 90 percent.

## What Is the Impact of the English Language Requirement?

While the above analysis indicates that naturalization law imposes restrictions that limit both access to citizenship and rates of immigration for some emigrants, it does not directly address one of the most controversial aspects of current policy. Immigrants over the age of fifty who have lived in the United States for at least twenty years, or those over fifty-five who have lived in the US for fifteen years, may apply to take the required civics examination in their native language. On the one hand, this does permit foreign-born individuals with absolutely no knowledge of the English language to become citizens—provided that they are permanent residents and otherwise meet the requirements of citizenship. On the other hand, it is not clear that a large number of older immigrants both desire to become citizens and do not understand English.

There are several empirical methods of assessing the importance of the English language exemptions. Among those immigrants who arrived in the United States at least twenty years ago, is there a noticeable upward tick in citizenship rates among those who qualify for the English exemption at ages fifty and higher? Among those immigrants fifty to fifty-four years of age, is the rate of citizenship higher for those who arrived more than twenty years ago? Figure 5.4 shows the answer to the first question, plotting the naturalization rates among immigrants with twenty years' or more residence in the United States, by age. Immigrants over fifty clearly have higher citizenship rates on average, but there is also an overall tendency toward higher citizenship at older ages, even for those immigrants age forty-nine and lower. There is no evidence of an upward spike in citizenship for those who reach age fifty.

Figure 5.5 addresses the second empirical question, showing the naturalization rates of fifty- to fifty-four-year-old immigrants in 2007, by year of arrival. Those arriving in 1987 or earlier would be eligible to take citizenship tests in their native language. There is a clear tendency for immigrants arriving in earlier years to display higher naturalization rates, consistent with evidence presented earlier in this chapter and in much prior work on the subject, but no distinct uptick for those who arrived in 1987 or earlier. Among those age fifty to fifty-four, the naturalization rate among those with nineteen years in the United States is just about equal to the rate for those with twenty to twenty-three years in the United States. Seen either way, there is little evidence

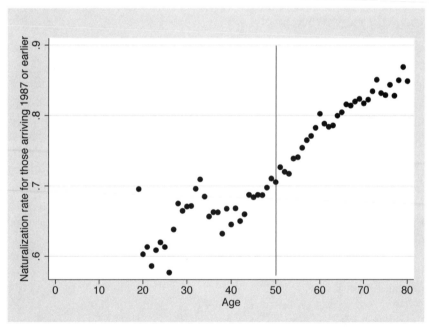

**FIGURE 5.4**
**Age and Naturalization Rate, 2007**

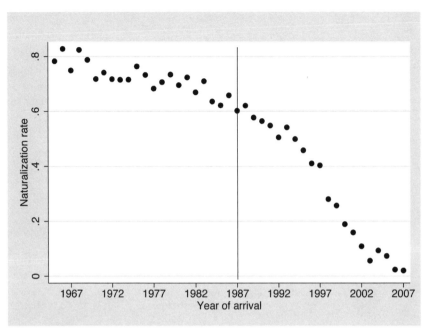

**FIGURE 5.5**
Naturalization Rate of Fifty- to Fifty-Four-Year-Old Immigrants, 2007

of a mass of non-English-speaking immigrants waiting to qualify for an exemption on the citizenship exam.

The English requirement was imposed in 1906. Coupled with the five-year residency requirement, this implies that non-English-speaking immigrants seeking citizenship who arrived in 1902 or later were at a distinct disadvantage relative to those who arrived in 1900 or earlier. Figure 5.6 provides one more check of the importance of the English requirement, plotting the naturalization rates of Italian immigrants in 1920 by year of arrival. Once again, there is clear evidence that naturalization is more likely among those immigrants with longer tenure in the United States, but no evidence of a discrete drop in naturalization rates for those immigrants subjected to the English language requirement. A relatively smooth downward-sloping line could be drawn through the points on the graph.

In summary, the evidence on the importance of English language requirements is rendered difficult to interpret by the simple fact that naturalization takes time, and older immigrants or those with more time in the United States will tend to have higher citizenship rates under all circumstances. Bearing this caveat in mind, there is little to suggest that substantial numbers of immigrants hope to gain citizen status without learning English.

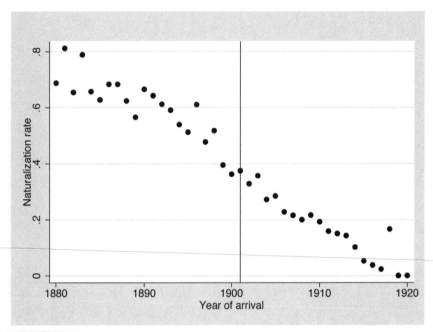

**FIGURE 5.6**
**Naturalization of Italian Immigrants by Year of Arrival, 1920**

## What Have We Learned?

As becoming a citizen is a costly process, the willingness of legal residents to undergo the process mirrors the value that immigrants place on citizenship. Over a period of time, if the costs of naturalization remain roughly constant, declines in naturalization rates imply a declining valuation of citizenship. Conversely, increased naturalization rates suggest that immigrants' valuation of citizenship is increasing.

Have the costs of naturalization remained constant over time? For a native of China in 1900, the cost was effectively infinite; for prospective immigrants facing racial barriers, the costs have clearly fallen. If we restrict our attention, though, to those immigrants legally permitted to enter the United States at any given point in time, the overriding trend in the costs of citizenship has been upward. The avenues to legal permanent residence have been both narrowed and lengthened. Many immigrants would jump at the offer of a green card if given the chance; a relaxation of the restrictions on their availability would undoubtedly result in a substantial increase in the net inflow of migrants to the United States.

The costs have increased, yet overall the rate of naturalization in the immigrant population has remained relatively steady over the past century. The logical conclusion from this pattern is that the valuation of American citizenship has increased over the past hundred years. This reflects both the value of guaranteed access to the American labor market, and access to the less tangible qualities of life in the United States that remain scarce in other parts of the world.[27]

# 6

# Fitting Into the Neighborhood

S INCE THE COLONIAL ERA, immigrants to the United States have elected to settle in close proximity to members of their own ethnic or linguistic group. Immigration thus imbues an ethnic character on physical locations, and vestiges of that character can persist for centuries. A neighborhood in the northwest portion of Philadelphia is called Germantown, in spite of the fact that less than 4 percent of the population reported German ancestry in the 2000 census.[1] A section of lower Manhattan is still referred to as Little Italy, even though barely a tenth of its population claimed Italian heritage in 2000.[2]

The observation that newly arrived immigrants tend to form ethnic enclaves, and then gradually abandon them as they enter the mainstream, dates back at least as far as the work of sociologists Robert E. Park and Edward Burgess in the 1920s.[3] Working in a city, Chicago, which had witnessed an immigration-driven population boom dating to the late nineteenth century, Park and Burgess integrated a model of immigrant residential progress into their broader theories of urban organization. They noted a tendency for immigrants to first gravitate towards older neighborhoods, with cheaper and lower-quality housing, close to the city's center. Over time, the economic ascent of these immigrants and their descendants permitted them to relocate to the newer, more attractive communities at the city's periphery.

Implicit in this model of the residential progress of immigrants is a fairly standard rational choice framework for decision making.[4] The decision to reside in an enclave neighborhood entails both benefits and costs. Immigrants residing in enclaves benefit from access to a social network that can be the key to employment opportunities and to overcoming linguistic barriers that might otherwise prevent them from satisfying the basic necessities of life. Isolation from the remainder of the population can impose costs, however. Expanding one's social network beyond one's ethnic group, for immigrants themselves or for their children, will tend to bring additional economic opportunity, and residential isolation impedes this expansion.[5]

As the importance of capitalizing on social networks and overcoming linguistic barriers is greatest for newly arrived immigrants, it is only natural to expect them to exhibit the greatest degree of residential clustering. Over time, immigrants assimilate linguistically and in the workplace, which reduces the benefits associated with enclave residence. The costs of isolation from the native-born majority, in turn, may become more onerous over time.

Both immigrant enclaves and the progress individuals make in exiting them have been the subject of much study since the time of Park and Burgess. Significant pieces of scholarship have studied specific neighborhoods at specific points in time: Herbert Gans examined Italian immigrants in Boston's West End; Nathaniel Glazer and Daniel Patrick Moynihan studied several groups in New York City; Olivier Zunz analyzed immigrants to Detroit.[6] From a broader perspective, sociologist Stanley Lieberson's 1980 book *A Piece of the Pie* presents a comprehensive analysis of immigrant segregation in the period between 1910 and 1920.[7] In more recent years, the work of sociologist Douglas Massey has renewed an emphasis on the measurement of segregation as an outgrowth and indicator of assimilation.[8]

Has the tendency for immigrants to form enclave communities changed over time? Are the immigrants of the early twenty-first century just as likely as their predecessors to move to more integrated surroundings as they spend more time in the United States? This chapter presents basic evidence on trends in immigrant segregation over time, and more detailed analysis of the tendency for specific cohorts of immigrants to become less residentially isolated over time.

The basic evidence is consistent with the Park/Burgess model: when there are many newly arrived immigrants, segregation is high; when immigrant inflows are low segregation is also low. More detailed data, however, show important and remarkable differences between the immigrants of the early and late twentieth century. In census data for the period between 1900 and 1930, there is a clear tendency for immigrants to begin their residency in ethnically isolated neighborhoods, then experience greater integration as they spend more time in the United States. This pattern is much less evident at the end of the twentieth century; while immigrants tend to be less isolated upon arrival, they appear less likely to integrate over time.

It should come as no surprise that there are significant caveats to these conclusions. Census neighborhood statistics have changed in important ways over time, and the analysis of segregation of the foreign-born is complicated by the fact that immigrants can appear more integrated simply by having children after they arrive in the United States.[9] Nonetheless, the data clearly point to the conclusion that the process of residential assimilation works differently than it once did.

## Summarizing Segregation

Most people with any amount of experience residing in or visiting major cities in the United States probably have an intuitive sense for what an immigrant or ethnic enclave looks like. And through the documentary work of past generations of authors and photographers, we have some idea of what these enclaves looked like a century or more in the past.[10] These various qualitative and interpretative works provide us only a few clues as to the degree of similarity or difference between modern and historic ethnic neighborhoods. Quantitative measures offer at least some hope of a more systematic comparison.

The degree of separation between two groups in a population is typically measured using a so-called segregation index. There are numerous different methods of measuring segregation, but these methods share some fundamental common features.[11] A segregation index classifies a group along a scale from "perfectly integrated" to "perfectly segregated." A perfectly integrated group is spread evenly through the larger population. If the group represents 10 percent of the population as a whole, perfect integration would imply that in every single neighborhood, 10 percent of the residents are members of the group. The typical segregation index assigns a value of 0, the least possible segregation, to such a hypothetical group.

A perfectly segregated group is concentrated exclusively within a small number of neighborhoods, where they comprise 100 percent of the population, and entirely absent from others. The typical segregation index assigns a value of 1, or 100 percent, to such a group. While perfect segregation might seem an abstraction, like the Galilean frictionless plane, human society has come quite close to it at various points in history.[12]

Where segregation indices differ is in their treatment of intermediate cases. What should qualify as a scenario "halfway" between the two extremes? The methods of description in most cases boil down to mathematical formulas, which in some cases have intuitive explanations, and in others not.

One of the most common measures of segregation is the *dissimilarity index*, introduced to the sociology literature by Julius Jahn, Calvin Schmid, and Clarence Schrag in 1947.[13] It is generally interpreted as the proportion of a group that would have to switch neighborhoods in order to attain perfect integration. Figure 6.1 offers a simple example of its construction. Suppose that a city consists of two neighborhoods, 1 and 2, both with a population of one thousand. Group A comprises 10 percent of the overall population, but resides entirely in neighborhood 1. Let's think about what it would take to perfectly integrate this group. As a rough approximation, we can begin by moving half of them (one hundred) to neighborhood 2. The ratio of group A to others is then 100:800 in neighborhood 1 and 100:1,000 in neighborhood 2. That's not quite even. If we move another eleven, the proportions become 89:800 and 111:1,000. Group A is now evenly distributed, comprising just about 10 percent of the population in both neighborhoods. We had to move 111 out of 200, or about 55.5 percent, of the group in order to achieve this, which makes the dissimilarity index 55.5 percent or 0.555.

Figure 6.1 conveniently illustrates one of the main criticisms of the dissimilarity index. In its initial state, group A was concentrated in neighborhood 1. Even in that neighborhood, though, the group comprised only a fifth of the population, implying that members probably had numerous opportunities to interact with individuals outside their group. They were segregated, to be sure, but they were not isolated.

There are alternative measures of segregation designed to specifically capture isolation, defined as a scenario when members of a group have few opportunities to interact with members of other groups in their home neighborhood. The *isolation index* attempts to capture this type of situation by basing its computation on the composition of the neighborhood occupied by the typical group member.[14] In the case of figure 6.1, the "typical" group A member lives in a neighborhood where 20 percent of the residents are fellow group members; this is ten percentage points higher than what we'd expect in a perfectly integrated city. The isolation index takes this ten percentage-point differential and applies a correction factor to ensure that it returns a value of 100 percent under perfect segregation. Applying the correction factor in the example of figure 6.1 yields an index equal to 11.1 percent or 0.111. This is substantially lower than the equivalent dissimilarity index for the same hypothetical scenario, consistent with the perception that the minority group in this case, although confined to one neighborhood, is not really isolated in that neighborhood.

|         | Neighborhood 1 | Neighborhood 2 |
|---------|----------------|----------------|
| Group A | 200            | 0              |
| Others  | 800            | 1000           |

**FIGURE 6.1**
**Dissimilarity Index**

There are many other ways to calculate segregation indices. Dissimilarity and isolation are summary measures for application to a single group; there are other measures that summarize the total amount of segregation across all groups when there are more than two in the population.[15] Since we are interested in using segregation as a measure of assimilation for members of individual groups, we'll steer away from these multigroup measures, although they are highly appealing in certain applications. In some cases, segregation indices incorporate information not just on the population of ethnic enclaves, but their physical proximity to more integrated areas.[16] This information on the geographic arrangement of neighborhoods is generally lacking in historical census data collected prior to 1980.

With segregation indices in hand, all we need in order to start comparing and contrasting immigrant enclaves is systematic information on the distribution of foreign-born residents across neighborhoods in cities past and present. This, as it turns out, is not as easy as it might sound. While the Census Bureau has published tabulations of the foreign-born population by neighborhood since 1910, the definition of a neighborhood has changed, as has the definition of a city itself.

Before 1940, the census reported statistics for wards—political units used as city council districts, or for purposes of tabulating votes in general elections. The trouble with wards is that their shape and size varies from city to city. In the early twentieth century, for example, Detroit drew up its wards by drawing a series of parallel lines on a map. Each ward measured only a few blocks from east to west, but miles from north to south. In large cities, a ward might contain one hundred thousand inhabitants; in smaller cities the number might be less than five thousand.

To see why the number, shape, and size of wards matters, consider figure 6.2, which presents a graphical depiction of the information in figure 6.1. The specific area occupied by Group A is shaded. If the city is divided into two neighborhoods, as in the original example, segregation takes on an intermediate level. This scenario is represented by the heavily marked line in the figure.

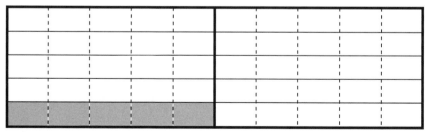

**FIGURE 6.2**
**Graphical Depiction of Neighborhoods**

Suppose instead that the city is divided into ten wards of equal population. Consider first the solid lines, which place all of Group A into a single ward. Group A will now appear perfectly segregated, but only because we have used a different method of dividing the city into units. Now consider the dashed lines, which split Group A into five of the city's ten wards. Dissimilarity and isolation in this case will be exactly the same as in the initial case. The degree of segregation can be manipulated by choosing the size and shape of wards. Remembering that wards are drawn for political purposes; there may be clear motivations to concentrate groups in some cases, or divide them in others.

No counts of the foreign-born population by sub-city area are available at all in published census data between 1930 and 1960.[17] Starting in 1970, though, the census reports foreign-born statistics at the level of the census tract. Tracts are units drawn expressly for the purpose of the census, although certain federal programs are targeted based on census statistics reported at the tract level.[18] They are intended to correspond roughly to neighborhoods, and to contain a consistent number of inhabitants—about four thousand, though the actual number varies considerably. Because tracts are smaller, on average, than wards, tract-level segregation measures tend to be higher.[19] The next generation of segregation indices uses even finer geographic information, down to the level of the city block.[20] For purposes of historical comparison, the ward and the tract offer the best, albeit limited, measurement opportunity.

As wards are creatures of cities, the city serves as a natural "unit of observation" for the early twentieth century. In the postwar era, however, rapid suburbanization increased the distinction between the political and economic conceptions of cities. From a political perspective, a municipality ends at the city limits. From an economic perspective though, city limits do not necessarily mark a significant boundary. The Census Bureau recognized the impact of suburbanization in the 1960s by introducing the concept of Standard Metropolitan Statistical Areas, groups of counties thought to have relatively integrated economies. Census tracts, originally confined to the political boundaries of cities, were gradually delineated in broader areas, until the boundary-drawing process completed for the 1990 census.

If immigrants are concentrated in cities and underrepresented in suburbs, as the Park/Burgess model would suggest, then the failure to incorporate suburbs when computing segregation indices will lead to understatement.[21] Over time, then, the tendency to include more suburbs in census tract enumeration will make segregation appear to increase even if the population is remaining in place. Of course, if immigrants are in fact equally represented in cities and suburbs, no such concern arises.

A final technical concern with measuring the segregation of the foreign-born in the United States is that immigrants might appear to integrate themselves with the native-born not by moving but rather by having native-born children. A natural way to deal with this problem would be to exclude the native-born children of immigrants from computation of a segregation index. Such a strategy is complicated by the fact that ward- or tract-level counts of second-generation immigrants are generally unavailable in the census. The Census Bureau stopped asking questions about parents' birthplace entirely after the 1970 enumeration.

David Cutler, Edward Glaeser, and I attempted to infer the extent to which immigrant segregation is understated by a tendency to cohabitate with native-born children, using a version of the 1990 census microdata unavailable to the public but accessible through special arrangement with the Census Bureau.[22] We computed an alternative version of both the dissimilarity and isolation indices, treating native-born residents who cohabitated with immigrants as if they did not exist. We concluded that immigrant childbearing does lead to an understatement of segregation, but that the degree of understatement is generally modest. In the case of the dissimilarity index, the understatement is effectively imperceptible. The isolation index is understated by about one percentage point, on average.

Having completed our crash course in the measurement of segregation, we're finally ready to start examining the evidence.

## The Decline and Rise of the Immigrant Ghetto

The immigrant enclave, in the Park/Burgess view, can be likened to a bathtub. At any one point in time, the number of immigrants in the enclave is a function of new migrant inflows and outflows of families joining the residential mainstream. With this analogy in mind, the evidence in figure 6.3, which tracks the dissimilarity and isolation of immigrant communities over the course of the twentieth century, has an easy explanation.[23] Immigration restrictions adopted in the 1920s shut off the flow of new migrants to ethnic enclaves. As a consequence, these enclaves dissipated after 1910, just as the level of water in a tub declines when the faucet is shut off and the drain left open. This trend is most obvious in the isolation index; dissimilarity actually posts an increase between 1920 and 1940. This is most likely an artifact of the switch from ward to tract data. Even so, the relative stasis between 1910 and 1950 is a strong contrast with the next forty years.

The figurative flood of new immigrants arriving after the relaxation of restrictions in 1965 contributed to the production of new immigrant enclaves. The dissimilarity of immigrants in the United States rose dramatically between 1950 and 1990. Isolation remained low until 1970, but rose

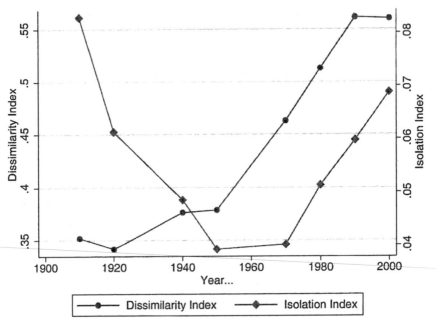

**FIGURE 6.3**
Dissimilarity Index and Isolation Index Compared

substantially in the period of intense immigration after that date. Immigrant dissimilarity in 2000 appears to be substantially higher than it was in 1910. It's impossible to say, however, how much of this apparent increase is real and how much is attributable to the switch from ward to tract data in 1940, or from the incorporation of suburbs into the analysis after 1950. By any measure, isolation was higher in 2000 than it was a generation before, but the 1910 index value remains the historic high-water mark, even without an adjustment for the switch from ward to tract. In spite of this high relative isolation level, in absolute terms immigrant segregation is modest. The isolation index indicates that the typical foreign-born immigrant resides in a census tract where his group's population share exceeds the citywide average by about seven percentage points.

A more direct comparison between the isolation of early and late twentieth century immigrant groups appears in figures 6.4A and 6.4B.[24] Focusing exclusively on the isolation index, the top panel shows that Eastern and Southern European immigrants began the century with average isolation index values as high as 12 percent, but then exhibited steady reductions in subsequent decades. The lower panel shows that in more recent years, the isolation of some new groups falls in a comparable range. Mexican and Dominican immigrants

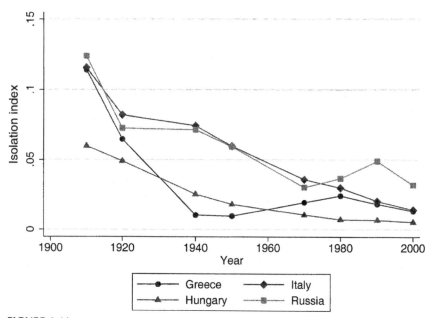

FIGURE 6.4A
Isolation Index, Major Groups of the Early Twentieth Century

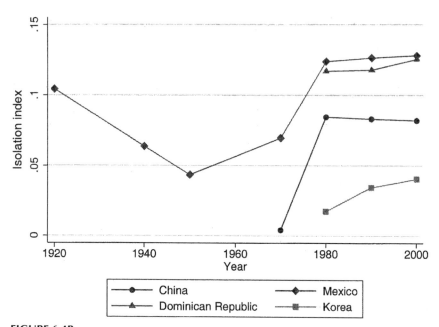

FIGURE 6.4B
Isolation Index, Major Groups of the Late Twentieth Century

in 2000 display tract-level isolation very similar to the ward-level isolation of Russian and Italian immigrants in 1910.

Surprisingly, figure 6.4 shows little evidence that the rapid increase in the immigrant population has been associated with strong increases in isolation. The population of Mexican immigrants more than tripled between 1980 and 2000, but isolation inched up only slightly. The population of immigrants from China and the Dominican Republic grew at the same rate or higher, yet these groups also display little change in isolation. Among the four groups depicted here, only immigrants from Korea, who grew at a comparatively slow rate between 1980 and 2000, show an increase in segregation over this time period.

How can increasing segregation for the immigrant population overall be consistent with the evidence that segregation did not increase rapidly for most groups after 1980? The answer harkens back to figure 1.1, which showed that the rise of immigration after 1970 was accompanied by a significant shift in the composition of the immigrant population. The population shifted away from permanently less-segregated European groups toward permanently more-segregated Asian and Latin American groups.

The simple Park/Burgess prediction that immigrant enclaves rise with inflows of immigrants and fall as immigrants assimilate thus doesn't really capture all of the story. The Park/Burgess vision of new immigrants crowding into existing enclaves, making them substantially more ethnically concentrated, isn't consistent with the facts. Such a pattern would lead to higher levels of immigrant segregation for individual groups. Instead, the evidence is more consistent with a pattern whereby new immigrants create new enclaves, rather than crowd into the existing ones. Immigrants on the whole continue to live in conditions of modest concentration, but the monolithic ethnic ghettos of the earlier era are not being replicated.

Why is the Park/Burgess model failing to the extent that it is? There are two easy explanations. First, the concentric ring model of urban development imagined a world where manufacturing and office employment was centered in a downtown, surrounded by older and somewhat dilapidated housing stock. Immigrants concentrated in part because that made life easier for them, but also because they needed to find cheap housing that was close to their workplace.

That may be a reasonable way to think about a city in the 1920s, but it is quite a stretch to apply the concentric ring model to a postindustrial, suburbanized economy.[25] Both employment and population are now centered in suburbs.[26] Immigrants may still desire inexpensive housing close to where they work. But workplaces are scattered these days, and the cheapest housing might not necessarily be close to downtown. A combination of urban redevelopment and severe land use regulations has made some central cities quite expensive relative to their furthest-flung suburbs.[27]

Second, the concentration of immigrant groups in ethnic ghettos may have been spurred on by explicit discrimination in housing markets. The history of housing discrimination against African Americans is well known; discriminatory acts against members of specific ethnic or national origin groups were also committed in the early twentieth century.[28] Restrictive covenants, which prohibited property owners from selling or renting their homes to members of specific groups, at times mentioned ethnic groups.[29] Less formalized methods of discrimination may have also contributed to the ghettoization of earlier immigrant groups.[30]

These average statistics, of course, obscure much detail about the existence of specific examples of immigrant-dominated neighborhoods. According to the 2000 census, 93 percent of the population of tract 867 in Flushing, Queens, was born outside the United States. Census tract 120, in Bay Ridge, Brooklyn, was 87 percent foreign-born. In the modern-day United States, these neighborhoods are the exception rather than the rule. Over 90 percent of the nation's sixty-five thousand census tracts were at least two-thirds native-born in 2000, and the overwhelming majority of the nation's immigrants lived in such neighborhoods.[31]

The differences in ethnic segregation between the early and late twentieth century can be seen in figures 6.5 and 6.6, which track the ethnic concentration experienced by immigrants belonging to different arrival cohorts between 1900 and 1930, and again between 1990 and 2000. The first figure uses IPUMS data, which reports each individual's city ward of residence for the period between 1900 and 1930.[32] The second is not based on individual-level data, but relies instead on tract-level counts of the foreign-born population, by year of arrival, in 1990 and 2000. Sadly, these detailed neighborhood-level statistics will never be available again after the 2000 census, and the American Community Survey interviews too small a sample to provide comparably detailed information at the neighborhood level.

In 1900 and 1910, urban immigrants who had arrived in the United States within the past five years lived in city wards where about 40 percent of the population, on average, was foreign-born.[33] Native-born city dwellers, by contrast, lived in wards where about 20 percent of the population was foreign-born. Both figures seem high when considering that the entire nation was only between 13 and 15 percent foreign-born in this era, but bear in mind that only city dwellers could live in wards. In 1900, two-thirds of the U.S. population resided in rural areas or in cities so small (population under 25,000) that the census did not bother enumerating them by ward. In these areas, over 90 percent of the population was native-born.

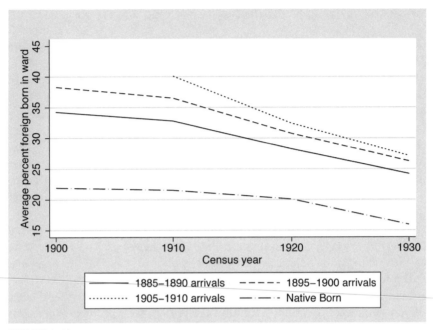

**FIGURE 6.5A**
**Neighborhood Concentration, 1900–1930: All Cities**

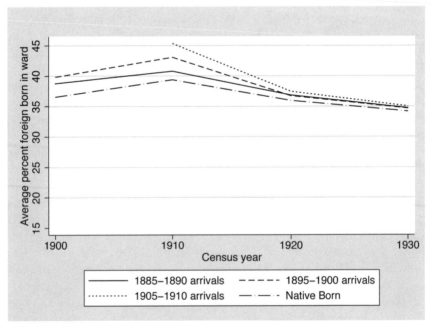

**FIGURE 6.5B**
**Neighborhood Concentration, 1900–1930: New York**

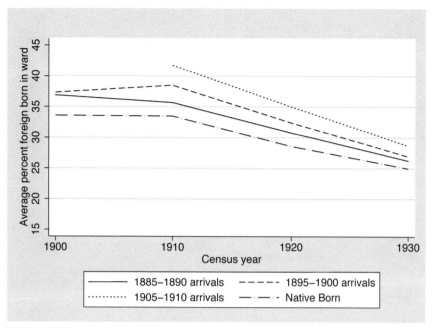

**FIGURE 6.5C**
**Neighborhood Concentration, 1900–1930: Chicago**

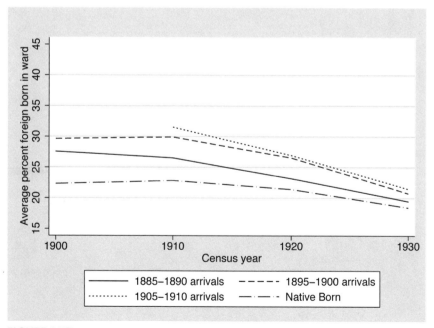

**FIGURE 6.5D**
**Neighborhood Concentration, 1900–1930: Philadelphia**

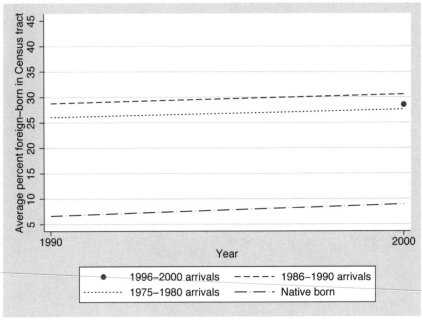

**FIGURE 6.6A**
Neighborhood Concentration, 1900–1930: United States

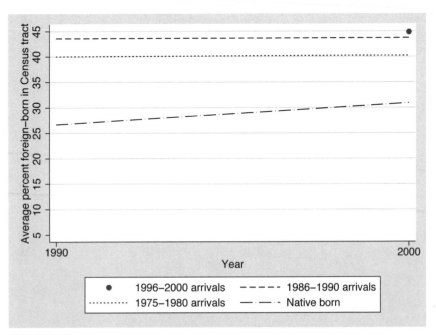

**FIGURE 6.6B**
Neighborhood Concentration, 1900–1930: Los Angeles MSA

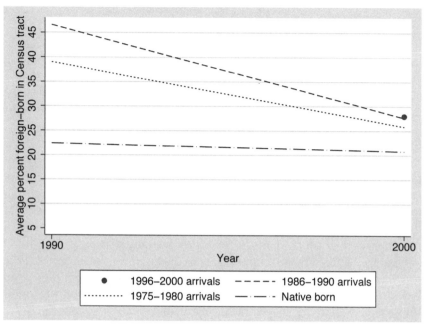

**FIGURE 6.6C**
Neighborhood Concentration, 1900–1930: Miami MSA

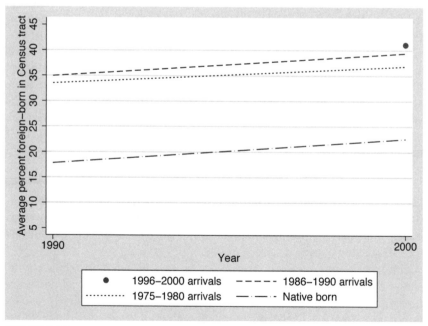

**FIGURE 6.6D**
Neighborhood Concentration, 1900–1930: New York MSA

The first panel of figure 6.6, which incorporates the entire U.S. population and not only urban areas, shows that the typical newly arrived immigrant of the late twentieth century resided in a census tract that was between 25 and 30 percent foreign-born. By contrast, the average native-born American lived in a neighborhood where less than 10 percent of the population was foreign-born. At both endpoints of the century, then, there is a clear contrast between the experiences of the native- and foreign-born. Immigrants have always been more likely to congregate with other immigrants. But the degree of congregation has fallen sharply over time. Recall that city wards tend to be larger than census tracts, and it is reasonable to think that their boundaries were drawn to limit the political power of certain groups. With this in mind, the fact that the new immigrants of 1910 have nearly twice the proportion of foreign-born neighbors as their counterparts in 2000 is all the more striking.

Figure 6.1 showed that the immigrants of 2000 were less isolated than those of 1910, even without applying corrections that would boost up the earlier index value, and the basic statistics in figures 6.5 and 6.6 support the point. Immigrants were more concentrated then than they are now. But figure 6.1 also showed that the dissimilarity index—which tracks the degree of separation between immigrants and natives—is quite a bit higher than its 1910 value. In 1910, isolation was high but dissimilarity low; in 2000 the opposite is true.

The key to explaining this puzzle lies in figures 6.5 and 6.6 as well. Isolation is high when immigrants form a large share of their neighborhood population; for dissimilarity to be low under these circumstances, natives must also experience a relatively high level of exposure to immigrants—just not quite as high as the immigrants themselves. Looking at the three largest immigrant destinations of 1910, New York, Chicago, and Philadelphia, we can see some evidence to this effect. In New York, newly arrived immigrants lived in wards where 40 to 45 percent of the population was foreign-born. Native-born residents of the city also had a high proportion of immigrants among their neighbors—between 36 and 38 percent in the first decade of the twentieth century. Once the flow of immigrants slowed during and after World War I, New York City became remarkably integrated by national origin. Immigrants and natives alike occupied wards that were on average 36 percent foreign-born in 1920, and just under 35 percent foreign-born in 1930. The city was clearly a magnet for immigrants, but within the city itself there came to be little distinction among neighborhoods.[34]

Similar, if less dramatic, stories apply to Chicago and Philadelphia. Native-born Chicagoans lived in wards where a third of their neighbors were foreign-born, on average, in both 1900 and 1910. Thus while newly arrived immigrants were relatively concentrated, with an average ward share above 40 percent in 1910, the contrast with the native-born residing in the same city was modest. There is some evidence of neighborhood convergence between 1910 and 1930. Finally, the contrast between native- and foreign-born in Philadelphia is also modest, in this case because newly arrived immigrants experienced relatively low levels of residential concentration in 1900 and 1910. Post-1910 convergence between native and foreign-born neighborhoods occurs in Philadelphia as well.

In the late twentieth century, dissimilarity is unprecedentedly high, while isolation is not. Intuitively, this must imply that the residential arrangements of the native- and foreign-born differ, on average, but in spite of these differences immigrants are not very concentrated in absolute terms. A study of the three largest immigrant destination areas in 2000, shown in figure 6.6, confirms this intuition.

In the New York City metropolitan area, which in this case includes not only the five boroughs but also suburban Long Island, the three southernmost upstate counties, a dozen counties in New Jersey, and one county in Pennsylvania, recent immigrants on average live in census tracts where 35 to 40 percent of their neighbors are also foreign-born.[35] Especially considering the smaller size of tracts relative to wards, the absolute concentration of immigrants in New York area neighborhoods declined somewhat over the twentieth century. The contrast with the native-born population in New York, however, is stronger than it once was. In 2000, the average native-born resident lived in a neighborhood where fewer than one-quarter of the residents were born abroad.

Immigrants are even more concentrated, in absolute terms, in the Los Angeles metropolitan area, comprising Los Angeles and Orange counties. Newly arrived immigrants tend to live in neighborhoods where nearly half of the residents were born abroad. Native-born residents of Los Angeles count three foreign-born neighbors in every ten, on average. Once again, the high residential concentration of new immigrants has a historical precedent, but the disparity between the native-born and foreign-born does not.

The Miami metropolitan area, which includes Dade, Broward, and Palm Beach counties, shows hints of the convergence shown by earlier immigrant centers. We'll make more of that contrast in trends in a moment. The newly arrived immigrants of the late 1980s, like their counterparts in Los Angeles, resided in tracts where over 45 percent of the residents were born abroad. Natives, by contrast, counted fewer than one immigrant in four among their neighbors.

Across the board, then, immigrants of the late twentieth century were found in ethnic enclaves that appear relatively integrated by historic standards. At the same time, though, they lived in metropolitan areas dotted with neighborhoods in which few immigrants lived. This created a contrast in the experiences of the native- and foreign-born urban population that did not exist in the early twentieth century.

The key word in the preceding sentence is "urban." Perhaps the most useful way to think about the change in immigrants' residential experiences over time is as reflective of change in the structure of cities and metropolitan regions. In the early twentieth century, immigrants flocked to cities, where they formed a large share of the population. In most every ward of every city, a reasonable number of foreign-born residents could be found. The majority of the native-born population lived in smaller towns and rural areas, where there were comparatively few immigrants. Measures of immigrant segregation, which focus only on the large cities, highlight the high concentration but relatively even spread of the foreign-born.

In the late twentieth century, most of the population lives in metropolitan areas, with more in the suburbs than in central cities themselves. Immigrants continue to flock to cities, and are less likely to form dense enclaves within them, but these cities lie within metropolitan areas that have agglomerations of lower-density communities at their periphery. Immigrant segregation, measured now at the metropolitan level, captures the contrast between urban ethnic enclave and suburban homogeny. Put simply, the native population has suburbanized more rapidly than the immigrant population.[36]

## Residential Assimilation

As the preceding discussion indicates, figures 6.5 and 6.6 encapsulate a wealth of information about the residential concentration of immigrant groups at two points in history. At a very basic level, though, each mirrors charts that we have previously examined while discussing immigrant economic, linguistic, and civic progress.[37] The only exception in this case is that assimilation implies a relative decline in neighborhood immigrant concentration, rather than an increase as we've seen with other indicators. So, apart from the other things we've learned, what do these graphs tell us about the residential assimilation of immigrants, both past and present?

The story here is in fact quite similar to the analysis of immigrant language patterns in chapter 5. There, we learned that contemporary immigrants possess superior language skills, as best as we can tell, relative to their counterparts of a century ago. Over time, though, the rate of progress for today's immigrants is slower than it was for those of the early twentieth century.

Here, we see that newly arrived immigrants of the late 1980s and late 1990s reside in neighborhoods that are less residentially concentrated than those of the late 1890s and late 1900s. This pattern occurs in spite of the fact that a "neighborhood" in the early period was a ward—large, and possibly drawn in order to minimize the voting strength of particular ethnic groups. Over time, and especially after 1910, residential concentration for the three depicted cohorts declined. By 1930, the new immigrants of 1910 had witnessed a drop in ward-level concentration from 40 percent to just under 30 percent. Substantial declines are seen in each of the three depicted cities.

By contrast, the period between 1990 and 2000 witnessed no decline in residential concentration for the immigrants of the late 1970s or late 1980s. Trends in the New York and Los Angeles areas mirror the national pattern. It is only in Miami, where the convergence has been previously noted, where trends appear comparable to the earlier period.

Tellingly, Miami is also the only metropolitan area depicted in the later era where the neighborhood-level immigrant concentration declines for the native-born. Across the nation, and in New York and Los Angeles particularly, the stagnant ethnic concentration of longer-term immigrants associates with a period of overall increase in the immigrant population. So perhaps the failure to residentially assimilate reflects the continued arrival of large numbers of new immigrants—a factor that was not present in the period between 1910 and 1930. Older cohorts of immigrants may find that newer arrivals flock to them wherever they are—implying that their movements out of enclaves may be offset to some extent by the development of enclaves around them.

A fairer comparison, then, should focus attention on the experience of pre-1900 immigrants in the decade between 1900 and 1910, when the immigrant population grew in absolute and relative terms. Even in this decade, there is some evidence that immigrants, particularly those arriving prior to 1890, are converging to native neighborhood conditions even as the foreign-born population grows. Nationally, both cohorts exhibit a downward trend. In the three large cities, the 1885–1890 cohort manages to exhibit either a downward absolute trend (in Chicago and Philadelphia), or a convergence toward a native trend that is itself increasing (in New York). The 1895–1900 cohort tracks parallel to the native-born in New York and Philadelphia, while diverging slightly in Chicago. In a direct comparison of growth decade to growth decade, the rate of residential assimilation thus appears higher in the early twentieth century.

The similarity in conclusions for residential and linguistic assimilation may not be coincidental. Immigrants' superior English skills upon entry in the modern era may explain why they are less likely, on average, to gravitate toward enclave neighborhoods. The slow rate of assimilation along one dimension could in part cause the slow rate of assimilation in the other. It's not clear which way causality runs in this case. Immigrants' slow progress in learning English could be reinforcing their ties to enclave neighborhoods. On the other hand, a continued desire to reside in an enclave could retard the process of learning English for some immigrants. Both processes could occur simultaneously. And both processes themselves could reflect some other underlying factor; the benefits of assimilation along either dimension may be limited, or the costs greater, in the later time period relative to the earlier.

There is one final discrepancy in the experiences of early and late twentieth century immigrants worth noting. In the early twentieth century, successive waves of immigrants consistently and predictably experience more residential isolation than their immediate predecessors, both nationwide and in specific cities. We have seen already that newly arrived immigrants are less assimilated along a number of dimensions, and residential location is no exception. Moreover, as noted previously in our analysis of language acquisition, the later participants in a migration wave tend to be less assimilated than their predecessors on arrival. The pioneering migrants in a wave must be prepared to enter a society where few speak their language; followers need not be so prepared.

This systematic pattern fails to appear in the 1990s. The newly arrived immigrants of the late 1990s were actually more residentially integrated in 2000 than immigrants who arrived a decade earlier. This is reflective of a widely noted trend during the 1990s, and on into the following decade, of immigrants moving to "new destinations" outside of the traditional metropolitan centers of immigration.[38] The reversal of the traditional pattern, whereby immigrants first move to enclaves and then disperse, coupled with the relative decline of enclaves in general, might help explain changes in attitudes toward immigration in the general population over time. Relative to an earlier era, where newly arrived immigrants were concentrated in urban ghettos and the native-born population was predominantly rural, the average American-born citizen comes into closer contact with less-assimilated migrants.

The move toward "new destinations" also stands to tell us something about the costs and benefits of assimilation themselves. As argued above, immigrants are drawn to enclave neighborhoods because they allow residents to avoid some of the costs of assimilation. The broad decline of enclave neighborhoods and establishment of immigrant communities in new destinations suggests that immigrants are less concerned with the costs of assimilation than they once were. The reduced rate of integration over time, however, suggests that those immigrants who do reside in enclaves face lower incentives to leave them as time goes on—either because they are not assimilating over time, or they aren't concerned that continued residence in the enclave will retard their progress toward the American mainstream.

# 7

# Joining the Family

I N THE PAST FOUR CHAPTERS of this book, we have considered a series of assimilation decisions, arguing that each can be thought of as an investment choice—whether to incur costs in the present in exchange for benefits in the future. For many, inserting the marriage decision into this framework seems awkward or unnatural. It is an act imbued with sacred and intangible character, and might seem inappropriate to translate into the mundane language of costs and benefits. Yet the scientific study of marriage decisions by sociologists and economists boasts a long history, and the decision to marry outside one's ethnic, religious, or socioeconomic class has garnered an outsized portion of that research effort over the years.[1]

Marriage, aside from being a symbol of love, personal commitment, and other ethereal things, is a legal contract. It entitles the two participants to certain rights and protections under the law that are not otherwise available to any ordinary pair of individuals. Particularly for a foreign-born individual in post-1965 America, the potential rights and privileges obtained from marriage are substantial. Marriage to a citizen of the United States offers instant access to legal permanent resident status, from which the path to citizenship is relatively straight and uncomplicated. Marriage to a foreign-born legal permanent resident does not entitle a temporary visa holder to an instant green card, but does place him or her in a relatively modest queue.[2] So, beyond the traditional romantic incentives to pursue marriage, the incentives to acquire legal permanent residency and citizenship discussed in chapter 6 can come into play when an immigrant selects a spouse.

In a certain sense, intermarriage can also be interpreted as a clear sign of commitment to life outside an immigrant's origin country, perhaps even more significant than the decision to become a naturalized citizen. By choosing to marry an individual with a tangible bond to the United States, and without such a bond to one's origin country, an immigrant tacitly or explicitly accepts the bond him or herself. The children of such a union will be more explicitly tied to the United States, and have a relatively weak connection to the immigrant's home country.[3]

What the evidence presented in this chapter will show us, however, is that these hypothetical demonstrations of allegiance through intermarriage are in fact rare, and that the policy-induced incentives to intermarry are mere tinkering around the edges compared to cultural constraints and preferences governing one's choice of spouse. Among foreign-born adults in the 2007 American Community Survey, only 14 percent of males and 16 percent of females were married to native-born spouses (see figure 7.1).[4] Even these statistics overstate the rate of true ethnic intermarriage, however. For example, 94 percent of American natives married to Mexican-born spouses claim Mexican—not just Hispanic, but specifically Mexican—origin. Only one in

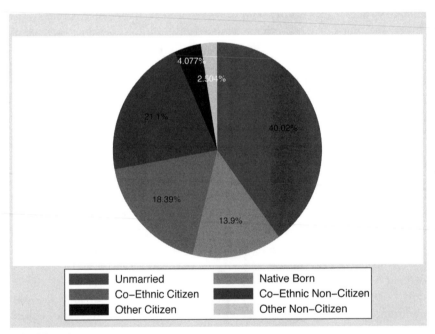

**FIGURE 7.1A**
**Spouses of Foreign-Born Adult Males, 2007**

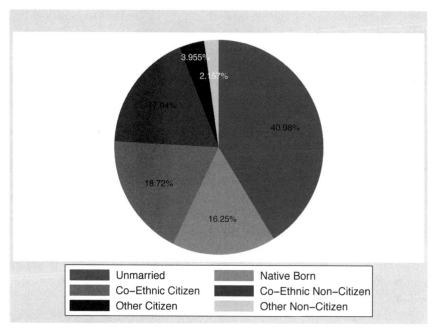

**FIGURE 7.1B**
**Spouses of Foreign-Born Adult Females, 2007**

five hundred Mexican-born adults residing in the United States is married to a non-Hispanic native-born spouse.

Marriage across ethnic groups among first-generation immigrants is in most cases exceedingly rare, and essentially always has been. Even among second-generation immigrants, or the "Generation 1.5" immigrants born abroad but raised in the United States, the overwhelming tendency is to marry within one's own ethnic group. The exceptions to this generality occur when the cultural distinctions between an immigrant group and the native-born majority are minimal. About 40 percent of Canadian- or British-born adults living in the United States, for example, have native-born spouses.

Ultimately, then, since intermarriage is so rare within the first generation, it is really too early to judge the marital assimilation of the newest immigrants in historical context. The information embodied in intermarriage rates—some groups, it is true, are more likely to marry native-born spouses, or citizen spouses—is to a large extent merely reflective of assimilation evidence we've reviewed already. For example, immigrants that naturalize at a high rate are quite logically more likely to marry citizen spouses—even though most of those citizen spouses are in fact foreign-born. Overall, the most reasonable conclusion is that there has been no dramatic change in the propensity of immigrants to intermarry over the past century or more.

## The Constraints on Intermarriage

Sociologists have extensively documented the low intermarriage rates of immigrants past and present. Perhaps the most ambitious early documentary effort was exerted by Julius Drachsler, an economist and sociologist at Smith college who collected and categorized information on one hundred thousand marriages in New York City covering the years 1908 through 1912.[5] The results, published in 1920, show incredibly small rates of marriage between immigrants and natives. Of the nearly sixty-five thousand foreign-born grooms in the marriage database, less than one in ten married a bride born in the United States to American-born parents.[6] The overwhelming majority of marriages were to first- or second-generation immigrants of the same nationality. Immigrants were much more likely to marry immigrants of other nationalities than natives of native parentage.[7]

Drachsler's analysis has been confirmed by more modern analysts using historical data, and replicated in analyses of more recent immigrants to the United States. Sociologists Deanna Pagnini and S. Philip Morgan similarly show low intermarriage rates using both Drachsler's New York City data and national records from the 1910 census.[8] The 1910 data show, for example, that only one in twenty-five Italian-born grooms had married a bride born to a native-born mother. Zhenchao Qian and Daniel Lichter, using 1990 census data, document low intermarriage rates among more recent migrants to the United States.[9]

An untrained observer might write off the tendency for immigrants to marry members of their own group as a consequence of individuals choosing to migrate after they had married. Drachsler's statistics, however, show that even those immigrants marrying after arrival in the United States show an overwhelming propensity to choose spouses of the same ethnic group. Why, given the menu of alternative spouses available in the host country, do immigrants exhibit such a preference for members of their own group? The rational choice perspective offers several insights into the answer.

The original economic treatise on the "marriage market" was published by Nobel laureate Gary S. Becker in 1973.[10] Becker's conceptualization of the marriage market comes directly out of the labor economics tradition. Individuals divide their time between working for pay and housework, otherwise known as "household production." A traditional marriage involves a division of labor between these two spheres, and spouses select one another for the same reason that two nations might choose to trade different goods with one another. Each party to the transaction has a comparative advantage in one aspect of production. Importantly, Becker did not assume that one gender or the other would specialize in household production, but instead presumed that comparative advantage would dictate patterns in marriage market equilibrium. Becker argued that his model could explain a number of empirical phenomena, most importantly the tendency toward assortative mating along various economic dimensions.

How can a marriage market model based on division of labor explain the tendency for immigrants to marry within their own group? Group members might have common preferences for the types of goods they wish to have produced in their household. These "goods" might range from meals to household decorations to investments in the human capital of children. Parents of a common ethnicity are more likely to share preferences to have their children speak a specific language at home, or to adopt particular cultural norms or behaviors.

The preferences likely to be shared by members of the same ethnic group could very well extend beyond the household. Spouses of common ethnicity may value the same types of leisure pursuits, for example. They may share common opinions about important issues, and may benefit from a shared base of knowledge derived from an upbringing in similar households or school systems. The rationalization of within-group marriage as a function of common tastes and preferences is consistent with social psychological theories of attraction, which emphasize the role of potential shared activities and the minimization of sources of conflict.[11] As sociologist Matthijs Kalmijn wrote in his 1998 survey of the literature on intermarriage, the tendency to select a spouse from one's own group may be the "unintended by-product of individual preferences."[12]

To this point, our explanation of within-group marriage has had a distinctively free market flavor. The tendency to marry spouses of similar ethnic heritage could be the product of unrestricted rational choices by informed consumers. To extend the analogy, however, homogamy could be the product of regulations and restrictions on individual behavior. There are a number of external forces that might restrict free choice of spouses in the marriage market. Individuals may face familial or cultural pressure to choose a spouse of a particular ethnicity. These pressures might originate out of a desire to preserve a religious heritage, or in some cases for more blatantly racist reasons. The tendency for immigrants to reside in enclave neighborhoods, documented in the preceding chapter, might further restrict immigrants' choice of spouse.[13]

Not all external pressures on marriage decisions work to encourage homogamy. In some cases, the ratio of eligible males to eligible females may be significantly unbalanced for an ethnic group, in which case one gender may find it must consider potential spouses outside the group. In practice, immigrant groups with gender imbalance may exhibit low rates of marriage rather than high rates of intermarriage.[14]

From a social scientific perspective, then, the big question is whether immigrants tend to marry within their group because they want to, or because they have no choice. In more purely economic terms, do potential spouses of the same ethnicity offer greater benefits, or does marrying outside one's group impose higher costs?

From a more purely pragmatic perspective, these questions are entirely academic. Regardless of the rationale for low intermarriage rates, the implication is that intermarriage itself is a lagging indicator of assimilation. Intermarriage occurs only after other cultural or economic differences between groups have eased to a significant extent. When these differences dissipate, external pressure to marry within a group declines, and the prospect of finding a spouse of different ethnic heritage but similar preferences, opinions, and background improves.

One might conclude from this discussion that it isn't even worth reviewing the evidence on intermarriage. There are, however, a couple of points of intrigue worth examining. For one, there has been a substantial shift in the incentives to marry citizens of the United States between the early and late twentieth century. Between 1855 and 1922, foreign-born women became citizens only if they married a citizen; foreign-born men by contrast attained no advantage from marrying a citizen. In the post-1965 immigration wave, the benefits of marrying a citizen became equal for both genders. We might expect, therefore, that the intermarriage rates of men have increased relative to those of women. And even though the intermarriage rate is small overall, small differences over time might help illuminate changes in the degree of cultural difference between natives and immigrants over time, or changes in the willingness of spouses to bridge cultural differences.

## Immigrant Intermarriage Today

We've already reviewed some basic statistics on the frequency of intermarriage for immigrants in the 2007 ACS. Roughly 60 percent of foreign-born adults residing in the United States are married, and among those currently married, about a quarter have a spouse born in the United States. This leaves somewhere around 45 percent of the adult immigrant population with a fellow-immigrant spouse. In most cases, both members of these dyads were born in the same country. About half of the foreign-born spouses are naturalized citizens.

**TABLE 7.1**
**Hispanic Ethnicity of Native-Born Spouses, Selected Nationalities**

| Nationality of Immigrant | Native-Born Spouse's Ethnicity | | |
| --- | --- | --- | --- |
| | Identical | Other Hispanic | Non-Hispanic |
| Mexico | 94.3% | 3.4% | 2.3% |
| El Salvador | 77.6% | 19.2% | 3.2% |
| Guatemala | 76.7% | 16.2% | 7.1% |
| Honduras | 74.7% | 15.1% | 10.2% |
| Nicaragua | 77.2% | 16.9% | 5.9% |
| Cuba | 90.3% | 2.2% | 7.5% |
| Dominican Republic | 88.9% | 8.1% | 3.0% |

Exactly which of these marriages should we consider to be "intermarriages?" As we've already noted, there are many immigrant-to-native unions that fall strictly within ethnic lines, as when a first-generation immigrant marries a native-born second-generation immigrant. The ACS lacks information on parents' birthplace, which makes a complete analysis of first-to-second-generation marriages impossible. But information on ancestry and Hispanic origin enables some assessment. We noted above, for example, that 94 percent of native-born spouses of Mexican-born adults report Mexican ancestry. Table 7.1 shows that this high proportion of across-generation but within-ethnicity marriages applies to several other groups. The listed groups account for 22 percent of all immigrants married to native-born spouses, and the overwhelming majority of these marriages are within ethnicity.

There certainly are examples of what we might call "true" intermarriages, defined as those matching immigrants of a specific nationality with native-born spouses having no specific affiliation with the same nation. Figure 7.2 shows that a plurality of Canadian-born males residing in the United States, and a near-plurality of Canadian-born females, have American-born spouses. Intermarriage rates are similarly high among immigrants from other developed countries, including most of Europe, Japan, Australia, and New Zealand. While only 15 percent of all adult immigrants were born in these nations, they account for 40 percent of all intermarriages.[15] The cultural distinctions among residents of developed nations are in many cases small, hence the concordance of tastes and opinions between potential spouses is high, and the cultural barriers to intermarriage are low. High intermarriage rates for immigrants from developed nations are thus not so much an independent indicator of assimilation as a reflection of cultural assimilation along other dimensions.

So far, we have described two major categories of marriage between natives and immigrants. Two-fifths of such marriages involve a foreign-born

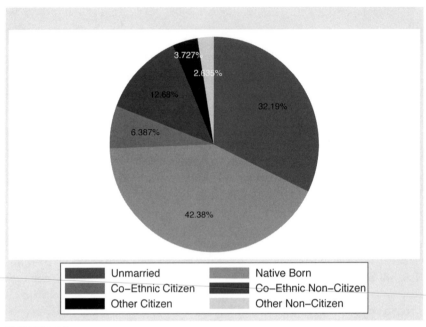

FIGURE 7.2A
Spouses of Canadian-Born Adult Males, 2007

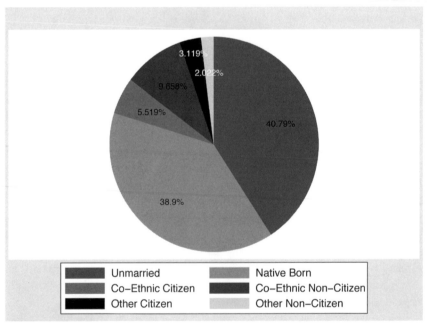

FIGURE 7.2B
Spouses of Canadian-Born Adult Females, 2007

spouse from a developed nation, reflective of the cultural similarity across such nations in the twenty-first century. Another quarter involve a foreign-born spouse from a nearby nation in Central America or the Caribbean, and the overwhelming majority of these are within-ethnic group but across-immigrant generation marriages.[16] The remaining third of intermarriages can be divided into two more groups.

Immigrants born in a set of eight Asian nations—China, India, the Philippines, Korea, Vietnam, Thailand, Iran, and Israel—account for about half of the remaining intermarriages. For most of these groups, the likelihood of intermarriage is small: only 5 percent of immigrants born in mainland China, and 4 percent of immigrants born in India, have native-born spouses. What intermarriages do occur for members of these groups, however, appear relatively likely to be "true" across-ethnicity pairings.[17] In many cases, intermarriages involve Generation 1.5 immigrants born abroad but raised in the United States. Among adult immigrants brought to the United States before age fourteen, the intermarriage rate is about 50 percent higher than for the immigrant population as a whole. In other cases, intermarriage appears to have been driven by American nationals returning from service abroad. Figure 7.3 shows marriage patterns for adult Vietnamese immigrants in 2007. Intermarriage rates are much higher among females than males.[18]

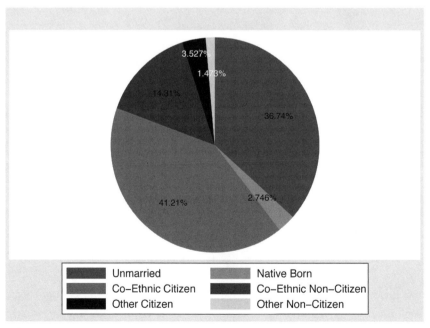

**FIGURE 7.3A**
**Spouses of Vietnamese-Born Adult Males, 2007**

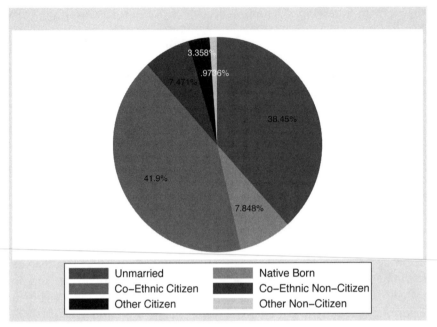

**FIGURE 7.3B**
**Spouses of Vietnamese-Born Adult Females, 2007**

The remaining one-sixth of all native-to-immigrant marriages in 2007 incorporate foreign-born spouses from a vast array of smaller nations, from Latin America to Eastern Europe to Africa and Asia. These are by their nature difficult to catalogue, and undoubtedly reflect some combination of "true" interethnic pairings and within-ethnicity but across-generation marriages. To a first approximation, then, among the 15 percent of foreign-born residents of the United States married to native-born spouses, between a quarter and a third share the same ethnicity as their spouse. "Truly" intermarried immigrants thus account for perhaps 10 percent of the foreign-born adult population, and a disproportionate number of these individuals either arrived in the United States as children or were born in the developed world.

## Immigrant Intermarriage through the Ages

The intermarriage rates of earlier immigrant waves to the United States have been thoroughly analyzed by early researchers. It is worth taking a moment, however, to apply metrics similar to what we've just used with the 2007 immigrant population, to see whether there has been any significant trend in the propensity for immigrants to intermarry over time.

There is one significant advantage to studying intermarriage with historical data: in earlier census years, including 1880 and 1910, the questionnaire collected information about the birthplace of respondents' parents. It is thus possible to distinguish a second-generation immigrant from an individual whose parents were born in the United States. Whereas we have limited opportunity to assess across-generation but within-ethnicity marriage in the American Community Survey, first-to-second-generation marriages are easily identified in the historical census data.

In 2007, we concluded that somewhere around a tenth of all foreign-born adults living in the United States participated in what might be called "true," or interethnic, intermarriages. In both 1880, near the peak of immigration from Germany and Ireland, and in 1910, the high point of immigration from Southern and Eastern Europe, the equivalently calculated proportion is actually quite similar. In 1880, about one in eight first-generation immigrants was married to a spouse whose parents were both born in the United States (see figure 7.4).

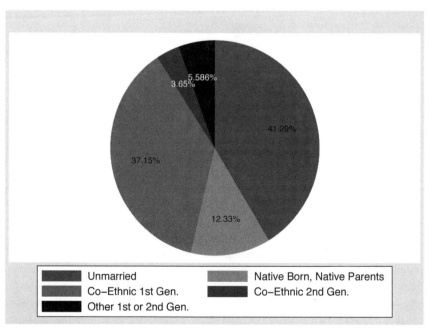

**FIGURE 7.4A**
**Spouses of Foreign-Born Adult Males, 1880**

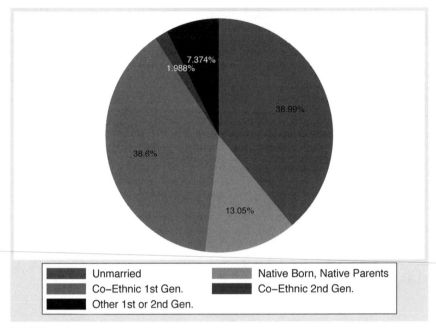

**FIGURE 7.4B**
**Spouses of Foreign-Born Adult Females, 1880**

In 1910, this proportion was about one in ten (figure 7.5). In both years, about 38 percent of foreign-born adults were married to spouses born in the same country, and another 2 to 3 percent were married to native-born spouses with at least one parent born in their origin country. The proportion of unmarried immigrants has changed very little over time, hovering around 40 percent in 1880, 1910, and 2007.

The heterogeneity in intermarriage rates across ethnicities, demonstrated with the comparison of Vietnamese and Canadian immigrants above, is also evident in the earlier data. Irish immigrants in 1880 were significantly less likely to be intermarried than the immigrant population as a whole (figure 7.6). The likelihood of marriage to a native-born spouse with native-born parents for this group is comparable to the rate observed for Vietnamese-born men in 2007. Figure 7.7 echoes the earlier work of Drachsler, Pagnini, and Morgan by charting the marriage patterns of Italian-born immigrants in 1910. Consistent with this earlier work, less than 1 percent of Italian-born men were married to spouses with native-born parents in this year.[19] The rate for Italian-born women, who are remarkably likely to be married overall, is on the order of one in a thousand.

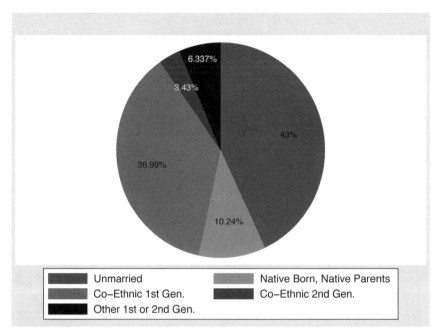

**FIGURE 7.5A**
Spouses of Foreign-Born Adult Males, 1910

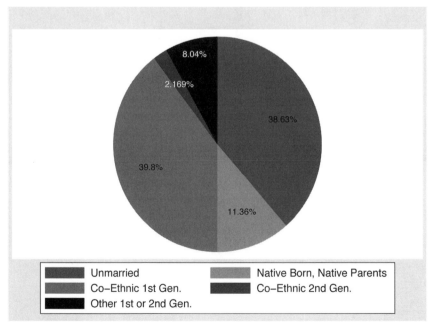

**FIGURE 7.5B**
Spouses of Foreign-Born Adult Females, 1910

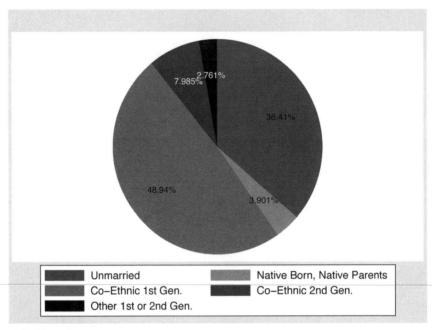

**FIGURE 7.6A**
**Spouses of Irish-Born Adult Males, 1880**

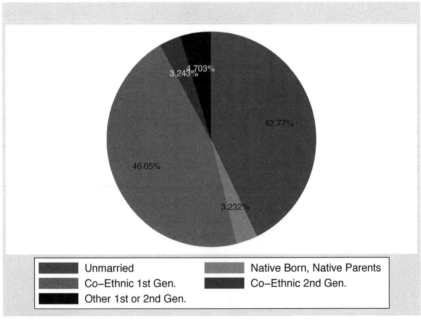

**FIGURE 7.6B**
**Spouses of Irish-Born Adult Females, 1880**

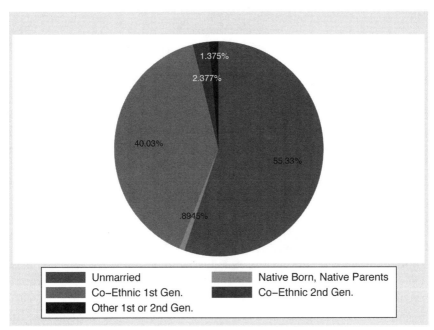

**FIGURE 7.7A**
**Spouses of Italian-Born Adult Males, 1910**

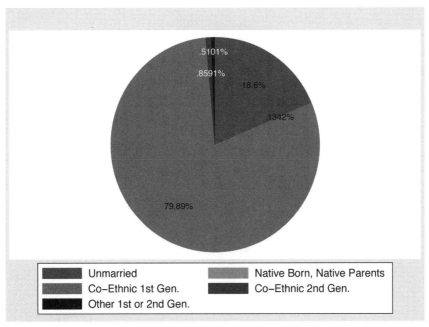

**FIGURE 7.7B**
**Spouses of Italian-Born Adult Females, 1910**

As a final note, recall that the incentives to marry a citizen increased for men relative to women between 1910 and 2007. It is interesting, then, that there is little evidence of a broad increase in intermarriage rates of men relative to women over time. Between 1910 and 2007, the overall intermarriage rate for men increased about four percentage points, from 10 to 14 percent. The rate for women increased from 11 to 16 percent over the same time period. Thus, to the extent that offers of citizenship or legal permanent residence influence the choice of spouses, that influence must be minor relative to other cultural factors that changed over the intervening century.

Recall the argument above that intermarriage is not so much an independent mark of assimilation as a reflection of assimilation along other dimensions. From this perspective, the evidence presented here shows that there has been little change overall in the basic patterns of immigrant assimilation. In each period, it is possible to identify groups that virtually never intermarry, but the overall rate of intermarriage across all groups remains comparable. Over long periods of time, the barriers to intermarriage fall. Whereas Italian immigrants virtually never intermarried in 1910, immigrants born in that nation had an intermarriage rate comparable to the high European average in 2007.

Does this imply that today's Mexican immigrants will experience the same path of assimilation across generations? Not necessarily. If intermarriage is a reflection of assimilation along other dimensions, the evolution of those other dimensions will be a critical determinant. If linguistic, geographic, and economic differences persist, the prospects for marital assimilation may be weak in the long run.

# 8

# Conclusion

It was the best of times, it was the worst of times.

—Charles Dickens (1859), *A Tale of Two Cities*

DICKENS BEGAN HIS FAMOUS historical novel with a paradoxical description of the atmosphere in London and Paris in 1775. A similarly juxtapositional set of conclusions describes the state of immigrant assimilation in the United States at the beginning of the twenty-first century. Along some dimensions, the modern immigrants compare favorably to prior generations of foreign-born residents of the United States. On average, modern immigrants have superior English language skills. For some groups, progress toward naturalization is rapid and nearly universal. Immigrants have integrated themselves more fully in a geographic sense, and some groups find themselves enjoying economic success that exceeds the native-born average. And finally, some groups, particularly those from more developed origin countries, have found few cultural barriers in their way, going so far as to intermarry at high rates.

At the other end of the spectrum, the picture is not so rosy. For the first time in history, America is home to immigrant groups with economic fortunes well below the national average. Naturalization is not an option for many immigrants, both legal and illegal, and in many other cases the option exists but is not taken. The strong average English skills and high degree of residential integration mask persistent cultural differences for subsets of the immigrant population. Four of every ten adult Canadian immigrants in the United States are married to a native-born spouse, but only one in five hundred adult Mexicans is married to a native of non-Hispanic heritage.

## Bringing the Evidence to the Policy Debate

These basic facts and patterns serve as a backdrop to the modern immigration policy debate. Virtually no serious observer of current immigration policy is satisfied with the status quo. The steady flow of what some would call illegal immigrants, and others undocumented workers, is the principal objection. There isn't really a "pro–illegal immigration" or "pro–undocumented worker" lobby in the United States. While some groups advocate for the preservation of certain basic human rights for immigrants working in the country illegally, none would argue that the immigration policy status quo is desirable. Setting aside the potential labor market, fiscal and cultural impacts discussed above, and even ignoring the costs of immigration law enforcement, illegal immigration creates problems for society. To successfully live and work in a society where they lack the official right to do either, undocumented immigrants must take risks that put themselves and others in harm's way.

For example, in a nation where the vast majority of workers get to work by driving their own car, many undocumented immigrants face restrictions preventing them from obtaining a driver's license. At least some choose to drive without a license, and therefore without the benefit of education regarding the basic rules of the road.

The real policy debate, then, is not whether illegal immigration is good or bad, but rather what should be done about it. While arguments can go back and forth regarding the virtue of upholding the law as written, the debate ultimately centers on the question of whether immigration itself should be encouraged or discouraged. There are many observers who argue that the flow of *legal* immigrants to the United States is too large and should be curtailed.[1] Others argue that the supply of legal permits to live and work in the United States should be expanded to more closely match demand.

The two sides of the immigration debate reflect two opposing views regarding the long-run impact of immigration on American society. At one end of the spectrum, the arrival of more Americans could produce a nation that is more populous and productive, basically a larger version of its current self, or alternatively of the self that existed in 1965. At the other end of the spectrum, immigration threatens to drag society down, to gradually erase the differential in living standards that the United States has long enjoyed, while introducing new forms of social strife and cultural bifurcation. In the popular imagination, at least, there are also concerns that immigration, whether legal or illegal, could threaten the territorial integrity of the United States.[2]

These competing attitudes toward immigration do not divide neatly along traditional partisan lines. The more negative viewpoint is most readily associated with economic populists and social conservatives. Television commentator Lou Dobbs and congressman Tom Tancredo are perhaps the most notorious representatives of this view, but it would be incorrect to conclude that the dystopian camp is dominated by rhetoric rather than evidence. The writings of Mark Krikorian, executive director of the Center for Immigration Studies, make reasoned arguments for placing new restrictions on immigration, placing modern immigration in historical context and bringing data to bear on the question.[3] For these observers, the evidence on the low rates of assimilation among immigrants from Mexico and Latin America are sure to confirm at least some fears.

The more positive vision has been adopted by a range of public personae and institutions. Conservatives of a more libertarian, or "free-market," orientation often view restrictions on immigration as an impediment to economic efficiency. *Wall Street Journal* editorial page writer Jason Riley has forcefully argued for a policy of open and unrestricted legal immigration.[4] At the more liberal end of the political spectrum, support for the relaxation of immigration restrictions is more widespread. The Obama administration's official agenda involves increasing opportunities for legal immigration to the United States—a stance that many in the more dystopian camp would oppose. The principal labor unions in the United States also advocate broader avenues of legal immigration. For advocates of less-restricted immigration, the evidence on the more successful experiences of the majority of modern immigrants to the United States will be most heartening.

A cynic might argue that these views are motivated less by a long-range utopian vision of immigration in America but rather by more immediate political considerations: unions would prefer to substitute legal immigrants who can be organized for illegal ones who cannot; both Democratic and Republican strategists may be courting a large and growing bloc of voters whose political allegiance might be in play. Setting these accusations of ulterior motives aside, there are a number of significant issues brought up in the debates between camps.

### The Goal of Immigration Policy

In theory, immigration policy can serve numerous objectives, not all of which can be satisfied simultaneously. It can serve to protect the rights and privileges of those born into a nation, the value of which is in many cases tied to the exclusivity of access. An unskilled worker born in the United States, by virtue of his place of birth, can expect to enjoy living standards superior to those enjoyed by workers of comparable skill born elsewhere in the world. Standard economic theory predicts that an unfettered flow of migrants would eventually erode that advantage of birth. Immigration policy can preserve it, at least to some extent. When employers have the right and ability to move their production abroad, however, these advantages can erode even in the absence of immigration. Moreover, the preservation of living standards for some workers comes at a clear cost to other native-born members of society, in the form of higher prices for consumer goods and lower shareholder returns.

Alternatively, immigration policy can be used to allow certain domestic firms to arbitrage international differences in living standards. Advocates of expanded legal immigration often argue that immigrants perform duties that native-born workers are simply not willing to do, whether that involves working in sweatshops, in fields, or in slaughterhouses. In the restricted immigration era between 1920 and 1965, however, these industries did not lie dormant. Rather, they paid higher wages to entice participation on the part of native workers. Immigration policy can permit workers to lower their wage bill, passing on the savings to customers in the form of lower prices or to shareholders in the form of higher dividends.

Rather than serve the narrow interests of domestic workers or domestic firms, immigration policy can also be used as a tool to influence the behavior of immigrants themselves, both in their decisions to emigrate to the United States and in the decisions they make upon arrival. Stating that policy can be used as a tool to influence behavior is not equivalent to claiming that society has a case for steering behavior in one particular direction. It isn't difficult to make such a case, however.

From a pure economic efficiency perspective, immigration policy could be used to resolve conflicts between the best interests of individual immigrants and society at large. Recall the discussion of the consequences of linguistic fractionalization in chapter 5. Using Edward Lazear's formulation, the benefits that any individual attains by learning to speak the dominant language in an economy accrue in part to that person but also to the remainder of society. There is a social return to language skill that an individual cannot be expected to consider when weighing the costs and benefits of skill acquisition. As such, immigrants will have a tendency to underinvest in language skill. Government policy could offset this tendency with various incentives to learn English. Some such incentives are present today—for most immigrants, learning English is a prerequisite for citizenship. Policy could be used to enhance these incentives.

There may be situations where society wishes to encourage certain behaviors or discourage others, even if there are no specific economic gains at stake. Immigration policy can be, and has been, used to encourage certain types of individuals to come to the United States, and to discourage others. It can be used to encourage or discourage specific behaviors among immigrants after their arrival.

The immigration policy debate is often boiled down to a simple question of whether immigration itself should be encouraged or discouraged. While this is certainly an important question, it overlooks the role that immigration policy plays in shaping the behavior of immigrants, and thereby the effect of immigration at any numeric level on the host society. The discussion of specific policy alternatives in this chapter will thus focus less on the basic question of whether they might lead to more or less immigration, and more squarely on the question of whether the policies encourage assimilation by decreasing costs or increasing benefits.

## Guest Worker Programs and Assimilation

At a first glance, a guest worker problem appears to be a "silver bullet" solution to the problem of illegal or undocumented immigration to the United States. By admitting workers legally, but temporarily, a guest worker program would permit foreign nationals to take advantage of superior opportunities in the American labor market. Domestic firms would also benefit from an expanded supply of labor. The temporary nature of the program would, in theory, permit the government to more tightly regulate the flow of immigrants into the United States, effectively lowering the size of the domestic workforce if conditions warranted.

Before we even discuss the ramifications of guest worker programs for immigrant assimilation, there are more basic questions as to whether such a program would work as well in practice as it might in theory. The forerunner of any new guest worker program in the United States would be the Bracero program, initiated as a means of alleviating labor shortages during World War II, and extended through the mid-1960s. The Bracero program brought as many as four hundred thousand Mexican laborers into the United States at any one point in time, for periods of up to six months.[5] Rather than receive credit as a program that forestalled illegal immigration by providing a legal alternative, scholars have actually blamed the program for causing illegal immigration.[6] European guest worker programs of the 1960s and 1970s have similarly been blamed for a range of unintended consequences.[7]

How could a guest worker program itself encourage illegal immigration? There are several mechanisms. Given the existence of pronounced wage differentials between countries, it is in any individual migrant's best interests to stay longer in the high-wage nation even when the legal work period has expired.[8] The availability of cheap labor might also cause employers to make long-term investments in more labor-intensive production technology, which effectively perpetuates demand.[9] The legal participants in a guest worker program might also ease the path of entry for illegal nonparticipants by initiating or extending a cross-border flow of information regarding employment opportunities.

Let's set aside these serious concerns for a moment and suppose that a guest worker program could potentially work as advertised. In other words, we'll presume that there exists a large pool of potential immigrants who would be willing to come work legally for a limited period of time in the United States, instead of coming over the border to work without authorization. When their temporary permission to work expired, these immigrants would return without incident to their home country.

It is barely even worth discussing the impact that such a program would have on the incentives of immigrants to assimilate, or the average level of assimilation among foreign-born residents in the United States. Guest workers, unless offered some chance of an avenue to more permanent residence, would have virtually no incentive to engage in any assimilative behavior, along any dimension. A guest worker program would boldly assert that assimilation is not the objective of immigration policy; rather, the goal would be to allow firms to take advantage of workers willing to accept a lower wage, passing the savings along to consumers and shareholders. A secondary goal would be to more directly control the flow of migrants to the United States—though experience suggests that such control would be largely illusory. The temporary residence of workers with little incentive to speak English, to participate in civic activities, or even to obey basic laws, would be accepted as a necessary cost of accomplishing these goals.

Should society be willing to accept the presence of "second-class residents," coming to the United States solely for the purpose of exploiting arbitrage opportunities, in order to reap some savings as consumers and some degree of higher returns as shareholders? It isn't our purpose here to make an argument one way or the other. Thinking back over the history of immigration to the United States, however, it seems clear that a preference for "job-seeking" immigrants over and above "home-seekers" is incongruent with the values that have traditionally driven immigration policy debates in the United States. From the Chinese Exclusion Act to the immigration quotas of the 1920s, restrictionary immigration policy has more commonly been used as a mechanism to keep the "job-seekers" away, not recruit them.

### Amnesty and Assimilation

Many of the most controversial immigration reform proposals involve some form of amnesty for aliens living and working in the United States without legal authorization. Many of the arguments in favor of amnesty relate to assimilation. A grant of legal status opens up a pathway to citizenship and civic participation, and may provide immigrants with stronger incentives for cultural assimilation as well. The opponents of amnesty proposals commonly argue that grants of legal status set precedents that encourage further illegal immigration. They also implicitly devalue the efforts of legal immigrants to obey the letter of the law, which compounds the effect of precedent by lowering the expected return to future efforts to comply with immigration policy.

Just as the Bracero program has been used as a case study in the impacts of a guest worker program, the Immigration Reform and Control Act (IRCA), signed into law in 1986, offers some insight as to the impact of amnesty. The IRCA granted temporary legal residency to illegal immigrants who had entered the country before 1982, as well as to immigrants who had worked illegally in the agriculture industry for a specified number of years. Amnesty applicants under both programs were presented a pathway to legal permanent residency. Over 3 million applications for amnesty were filed in 1987 and 1988, and nearly 90 percent of these applications were accepted.[10]

Scholarly evaluations of the IRCA have commonly focused on the question of whether the act led to a reduction in illegal immigration.[11] Evaluation of the effect of amnesty itself is complicated by the fact that the IRCA contained several related provisions, mandating that employers verify employees' eligibility to work, establishing penalties for knowingly hiring an undocumented worker, and stepping up border enforcement. Even if the amnesty itself encouraged further illegal immigration, these other provisions may have acted to stem the tide. Analysis is further complicated by the fact that there are no reliable statistics on the number of illegal immigrants entering the United States at any one point in time. Some studies have examined surveys such as the census and concluded that the amnesty had little effect on illegal immigration.[12] Others have used the number of apprehensions of illegal immigrants by the U.S. Border Patrol as a measure of the flow of illegal immigrants; these studies tend to find a reduction in illegal immigration immediately after IRCA was passed, but less evidence of a sustained impact over time.[13]

Did immigrants who qualified for amnesty under the IRCA assimilate more rapidly than they otherwise would have? This question relates to a key issue underlying the evidence of slow assimilation for Mexican immigrants in recent years. Immigrants from Mexico might naturalize at low rates, for example, because as illegal immigrants they are not eligible to do so. Alternatively, like immigrants from many developed nations they might place low value on the grant of citizenship.

The IRCA offers an opportunity to infer the impact of amnesty, because it is possible, in theory at least, to distinguish eligible from ineligible immigrants. In this case, an illegal Mexican immigrant who arrived in December 1981 became eligible for a pathway to citizenship after the passage of IRCA, but an immigrant who arrived in January 1982 did not. So, in later data, are the 1981 arrivals much more assimilated than the 1982 arrivals?[14]

Figures 8.1 and 8.2 address this question, using data on Mexican-born immigrants at least twenty-five years of age in the 2007 ACS. The leftmost vertical line separates those immigrants who report arriving in 1981 from those who report arriving in 1982. While there is a gradual increase in naturalization rates, and a gradual improvement in English skills, among immigrants who arrived at an earlier point in time, there is only slight evidence that the 1981 arrivals were more likely to naturalize relative to 1982 arrivals, and no evidence of an uptick in English skills.

The right-hand vertical line in figure 8.1 separates immigrants who arrived in 1988, a year in which applications for amnesty were accepted, from those who arrived after the expiration of the amnesty offer. Interestingly, there is a significant jump in citizenship rates for 1988 arrivals relative to those who arrived one or two years later. This is in spite of the fact that true 1988 arrivals

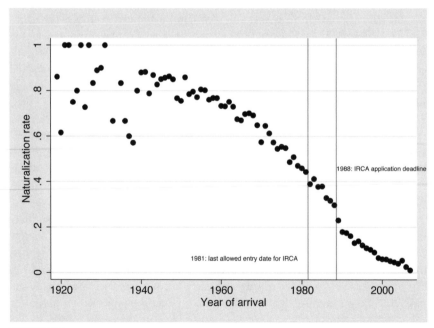

**FIGURE 8.1**
**Naturalization Rates of Mexican-Born Immigrants**

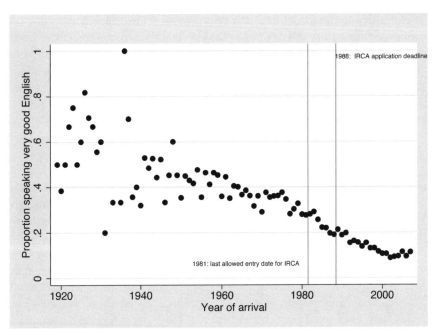

**FIGURE 8.2**
**English Ability of Mexican-Born Immigrants**

would not be eligible for amnesty. It is consistent, however, with allegations of widespread fraud in the application process.[15] Note that there is no comparable uptick in English-speaking rates between 1988 and 1989 arrivals.

Thus, one way to read the evidence is that amnesty led to higher rates of civic assimilation—the naturalization rates for immigrants who arrived while amnesty applications were accepted are about ten percentage points higher than for those who missed the cutoff by a year or two. It also appears, however, that much of this increase is associated with fraudulent activity: immigrants crossing the border to take advantage of the amnesty opportunity, and falsifying evidence of the duration of their residency. Two decades later, in responding to the ACS, many of these immigrants appear to reveal the truth about their date of arrival in the United States. Moreover, the opportunistic immigrants who took advantage of a chance to access the path to citizenship do not appear disproportionately likely to assimilate along other dimensions.

A reasonable evidence-based inference about the impact of amnesty on assimilation, then, is that it would have a modest impact on civic assimilation, by opening up an avenue to citizenship. Legalization also does not appear to drastically improve the incentives for immigrants to learn English.

The ultimate determination of whether amnesty is a good idea rests on value judgments beyond the scope of the evidence here. Past experience indicates, however, that a one-time amnesty by itself cannot be expected to eliminate future illegal immigration, and unless accompanied by other policy changes does not provide strong incentives for assimilation among newly legalized immigrants.

## Open Borders and Assimilation

For 130 years after the ratification of the Constitution, there were relatively few restrictions on immigration to the United States. Would a return to pre-1920s policy increase or decrease the rate of assimilation for immigrants in the modern era? On the one hand, a wholesale liberalization of immigration policy would reduce the costs associated with some forms of assimilation. Removing barriers to permanent residency and naturalization would presumably lead to at least some increase in applications. For some immigrants at least, a liberalization would increase the likelihood of remaining in the United States for an extended period, and hence increase the incentive to assimilate along other dimensions.

On the other hand, by liberalizing immigration policy the United States would forfeit the ability to select or encourage specific types of migrants. In the first era of relatively open borders, the simple economic barriers to migration ensured that only those migrants with the strongest incentives would elect to leave their home country. In the modern era, where transportation is cheaper and the flow of information across continents more reliable, the ratio of "job-seeking" to "home-seeking" migrants need not be similar to the earlier era.

We also have some evidence about the prospective impact of liberalizing immigration policy derived from the amnesty afforded to some immigrants as a result of the IRCA in 1986. In that case, there is little to suggest that a liberalization of immigration policy resulted in significant changes to immigrant behavior, with the exception that some proportion of immigrants newly eligible for citizenship accepted the offer. Liberalization might logically lead to a scenario where a higher proportion of foreign-born residents of the United States were sojourners, taking advantage of relatively short-term opportunities, with little sense of affiliation with the nation itself.

Once again, the case for open borders invokes values-based arguments that are beyond the scope of the evidence brought to bear here. But there are few assurances in theory or in practice that such a policy change would have the impact of increasing immigrants' demonstration of commitment to the United States.

## Strict Enforcement and Assimilation

In theory, strict enforcement of existing immigration law could dramatically increase the assimilation of immigrants across most measured dimensions. Much of the evidence presented here indicates that illegal immigrants are less assimilated along numerous dimensions, in some cases because they have no option to assimilate, and in others because they face only weak incentives. Logically, then, the removal of undocumented immigrants from the population would on net increase the average level of assimilation in the immigrant population.

The practical question, though, is whether strict enforcement could realistically be expected to reduce the population of undocumented immigrants to zero. Most calls for stricter enforcement involve some combination of increased border security and greater policing and punishment of firms that hire undocumented workers. So long as temporary visas are granted to some workers, students, and tourists, however, the risk remains that visitors will illegally overstay their visas after crossing the border legally. Moreover, so long as some employers are willing to hire workers "off the books," any mandatory background check will fail to prevent some individuals, whether native-born, legal immigrant, or illegal immigrant, from supporting themselves.

A policy dedicated to reducing the number of immigrants working illegally in the United States to zero would have to involve measures such as eliminating temporary visas, issuing ankle bracelets or comparable tracking devices to aliens on temporary visas, and ramping up enforcement of labor laws at even the smallest worksites. Enforcement teams would have to be periodically dispatched to construction sites and other small businesses. Such a policy would involve significant costs, and could potentially ensnare many otherwise law-abiding immigrants. Eliminating temporary visas, for example, would force hundreds of thousands of foreign-born students to seek education elsewhere.

A strict enforcement policy that fell short of completely eliminating undocumented immigrants could actually have a perverse effect on assimilation. Immigrants, both legal and illegal, base their decisions to assimilate on a comparison of costs and expected benefits. When the likelihood of deportation increases, the incentives for illegal immigrants to assimilate decline. Suppose that under current policy an undocumented worker faces a 10 percent chance of being deported in the next year. As there is a 90 percent chance that this worker will still be in the United States after a year, certain decisions such as learning to speak English might make sense from a rational perspective. Were the likelihood of deportation to increase to 50 percent, such decisions might no longer make sense.

So, in theory, strict enforcement sounds like a great way to enhance the average assimilation level of immigrants in the United States. In practice, a less-than-perfectly successful strict enforcement policy might have little net effect, or could conceivably lead to a net reduction in immigrant assimilation. And a "perfectly successful" policy would impose significant costs on many stakeholders in society—taxpayers, small business owners, educational institutions, and legal immigrants.

## An Alternative: The Assimilation Bond

The policies considered to this point have been discussed frequently in public debates, but none were formulated with the express goal of assimilation in mind. There are potential strategies for using immigration policy to encourage assimilation, and to selectively attract those immigrants interested in establishing themselves as long-term residents permanently committed to the United States. Such a policy would provide specific incentives for immigrants to take steps toward assimilation. It could incorporate incentives to learn and speak English, or to pursue naturalization. It might also create disincentives to migrate purely for short-term economic gain.

What kind of policy could accomplish these things? There's one easily described example, which one might call an "assimilation bond." Here's how it would work. Numerical limitations on the number of legal immigrants to the United States would be eased or dropped. The U.S. Customs and Immigration Service would adopt significantly higher fees for legal entry. These fees would be partly refundable, however, over time or in response to specific actions taken by an immigrant. Immigrants could recoup some portion of the fee as a credit against their federal income taxes.[16] Successful completion of an English language training course could lead to a partial refund of the fee. Naturalization could trigger a partial refund as well. Service in the armed forces could trigger an immediate refund, or accelerate the rate of repayment. Immigrants who take all these steps would, over time, receive a refund of virtually all of their entry fee. Immigrants who take very few of these steps would forfeit most or all of the fee. The higher entry fee could be seen as a subsidy for assimilation, or a tax on the failure to assimilate.

Let's put some hypothetical numbers on this to make it concrete. In 2009, an applicant for a temporary visa to the United States paid a processing fee of $131, and an applicant for legal permanent residence paid $400. Under an assimilation bond regime, there would cease to be a distinction between temporary and permanent visas, but the fee for legal entry would be significantly higher. For the sake of argument, let's set the fee at $10,000.

Immigrants would receive a schedule of potential reimbursements that might look as follows. Successful completion of an accredited English-language course might result in a refund of $2,000. Immigrants who speak English fluently upon arrival could receive an equivalent discount on the entry fee. Completion of the naturalization process could also result in a $2,000 rebate. Immigrants who paid the fee would be eligible to receive a credit against federal income taxes owed of up to $500 per year, until only $500 of the assimilation bond remained.

Under this policy regime, an immigrant who learns English, earns enough to face a federal income tax liability of at least $500 each year, and becomes a naturalized citizen could expect to receive 95 percent of their assimilation bond back within eleven years. The remaining $500 would be roughly equivalent to the nonrefundable fees immigrants currently face for legal permanent admission to the United States. By contrast, an immigrant who works "under the table" to avoid income taxes, and has no interest in either learning English or becoming a naturalized citizen would effectively forfeit the entire $10,000.

The principal objection to the assimilation bond proposal is that it might be seen as discriminating against potential immigrants with little or no wealth. The government could respond to such concerns by offering to sponsor a fixed number of immigrants—effectively loaning them money to post the assimilation bond. Sponsored immigrants would then work to pay off their debt over time, rather than to recoup their deposit. Nonprofit organizations such as churches or foundations could also enter into sponsorship agreements with individual immigrants.

Sponsors would face the risk of immigrants defaulting on their debt by leaving the country or otherwise not engaging in the activities that would ordinarily result in partial refunds. High default rates would discourage sponsors from participating in the marketplace, and thereby reduce the number of sponsored slots. This outcome may be acceptable, though, to those who would otherwise oppose an assimilation bond program. The assumption underlying the objection is that there exist many immigrants who would willingly participate in the assimilation bond system, but simply lack the funds. If that is true, then a sponsorship program would be sustainable in the long term. If not, the objections to the policy would be refuted, and sponsorship provisions could effectively sunset.

Now, while it does make some sense to offer a form of humanitarian assistance to extremely poor immigrants—the entry fee could be waived entirely for refugees, for example—bear in mind that the assimilation bond would be designed with the express purpose of discouraging some potential migrants from entering the United States. For the immigrant who was planning on being a lifetime resident, eventually learning English and becoming a naturalized citizen, this policy would be virtually costless. It's just requiring them to do something that they would have done anyway. For immigrants without these goals, there is a real cost involved. The policy therefore encourages the former and discourages the latter.

A second possible objection is that the cost to an immigrant of posting an assimilation bond is higher than the dollar amount of the entry fee, because the immigrant would forego accrued interest up until the point when the bond was fully refunded. The government could, of course, compute and repay interest on the bond, at a rate equivalent to that on other government-issued bonds. Alternatively, the interest on the bond could be transferred from the federal government to the state and local level, with the express goal of offsetting the costs of providing services to less-assimilated immigrants. These transfers could be targeted at the jurisdictions where immigrants actually reside. Were an assimilation bond of $10,000 to accrue interest at the rate of 5 percent per annum, the resulting $500 could be made available to defray the costs of offering English language courses, or other locally funded services for immigrants. As immigrants assimilated, reducing the value of the bond outstanding, the intergovernmental transfer would naturally decrease.

A final possible objection to an assimilation bond policy would be that the mere notion of charging an access fee to the world's most lucrative labor market is morally objectionable. This sort of argument goes beyond basic economics and would have to be resolved by the public or their elected representatives. It is worth noting, however, that the use of high fees, and fees that effectively create incentives to assimilate, is not unprecedented. Employer-sponsored permanent immigrants to Australia, for example, face basic fees of more than 2,400 Australian dollars—more than $1,700 at April 2009 exchange rates. Immigrants with "less than functional English" face a surcharge of 5,865 Australian dollars, or more than $4,000. The Australian visa pricing policy creates a strong incentive for prospective immigrants to learn English prior to application.

It is true that Australian visa application fees fall below the $10,000 level proposed above. Unlike the Australian regime, however, the fees paid under the assimilation bond program would be refundable, provided that immigrants take specific steps toward assimilation. Relative to the Australian model, the assimilation bond program would create stronger incentives for already-arrived migrants to study English, for example.

The policy proposal sketched here leaves many i's undotted and t's uncrossed. One would need to determine, for example, whether the spouse and children of an admitted immigrant would have to post their own bonds, or whether there might instead be "family pricing." The treatment of foreign students, many of whom expect to return to their home country immediately after receiving a degree, would have to be considered. One would also face the thorny issue of whether to permit illegal immigrants to post a bond and switch instantly to legal status. More fundamentally, society as represented by its legislators would have to decide whether the fundamental goal of immigration policy would be to add to future generations of Americans, or to accomplish some other goal.

## The United States One Generation from Now

The demographic transformation of the United States in the years since 1970 has clear historical precedent. The growth rate of the foreign-born population was similarly high in the late nineteenth century, and the proportion of American residents born abroad was slightly higher in the early twentieth century than in the early twenty-first. Immigration has triggered concerns about the cultural integrity of the United States since the colonial era, and motivated calls for reform of immigration policy periodically since then.

With the benefit of hindsight, we can see that Benjamin Franklin's worries about "Palatine Boors," the Know-Nothing fear of Irish Catholics, and concern over the "Italian dusk" dissipated over time. To the extent we can observe in historical data, these groups—or at least the members who chose to stay—diffused into native-dominated neighborhoods, learned to speak English, and became naturalized citizens. Although they exhibited a strong tendency to pick a spouse from the same ethnic group, their children became extremely difficult to distinguish from the children of the native-born. Why shouldn't we believe that a hundred years hence, we will add today's Latin American and Asian immigrants to the list of successful groups?

There are two reasons to doubt the relevance of past experience for predicting the future of today's immigrants. The first is rooted in immigration policy. The German, Irish, and Italian immigrants of a century or more ago had no concern about legal status. There was no barrier to legal entry, and mere presence in the United States placed one on the road to citizenship. The barriers to legal entry put in place in the 1920s have never been fully removed. The permeability of the nation's borders has contributed to the existence of an unprecedented class of immigrants in America, who persist in a less-assimilated state in part because barriers deny them the option, and in part because these barriers remove the incentive to assimilate.

Of course, we have uncovered evidence that even immigrants with the option and incentive to assimilate do not always exercise it. This reveals the second departure of present from past. In a world with more rapid and inexpensive travel, with a steadier devotion to free trade, and where commu- nication across the globe is instantaneous and nearly free, the significance of nationality has declined. The set of foreign-born residents with only tenuous attachment to the United States includes not only Latin Americans working in construction and service industries, but also highly educated Europeans and Asians working in finance, technology-related industries, and professional services. Ours is a nation where interest groups can, with a straight face, pro- test a proposed policy change by threatening to leave the country.

Increased immigration, and the decreased tendency for some immigrant groups to assimilate rapidly, can thus be seen as a symptom of the decreasing significance of national borders throughout the world, which in turn reflects the inexorable march of technological progress and international commit- ments to free trade. One can oppose immigration on the grounds that it poses a threat to native culture, or to the economic status of those born in the United States. But those who would imagine that immigration is the only threat to American culture and economic status, or even the predominant threat, possess a dangerously narrow vision of the modern world.

Although immigration policy alone cannot be viewed as an elixir for all forms of economic and cultural anxiety, sensible modifications hold the potential to ease the transition of immigrants to Americans, and to make the United States of 2050 more analogous to the United States of 1950. Ex- plicit curbs on legal immigration do not necessarily have to be part of such a policy modification. A policy that selects carefully among the millions of potential migrants who would jump at the chance for legal entry could simultaneously expand the legal immigrant population, reduce the number of illegal immigrants, and accelerate the process of economic, cultural, and civic integration into society.

# Notes

## Introduction

1. The 1990 census reports that 4 percent of the city's population was foreign-born, and just over 1 percent was of Hispanic origin. Durham is home to Duke University and is less than ten miles from the University of North Carolina at Chapel Hill.

2. Census estimates from the 2007 American Community Survey indicate that the city of Durham was 12 percent Hispanic, and 15 percent foreign-born, excluding those born abroad to American parents.

3. An article about the city's taco stands appeared in the September 2007 issue of *Gourmet* magazine.

4. Statistics drawn from the Central Intelligence Agency (2008), *The 2008 World Factbook*.

5. These terms originate in the work of Edward Alsworth Ross (1914), *The Old World in the New: The Significance of Past and Present Immigration to the American People*.

## Chapter 1

1. From a biblical perspective, the first migrant was Cain, banished from Eden in retaliation for his killing of Abel (Genesis 4:12; Adam and Eve were banished from the "garden" of Eden but not from Eden itself).

2. Central Intelligence Agency (2008). The specific counts of nations cited in the subsequent paragraph are derived from the same source.

3. Alfred Marshall (1890), *Principles of Economics*.

4. For a review of sociological theories of migration, see Douglas S. Massey, Joaquin Arango, Graeme Hugo, Ali Kouaouci, Adela Pellegrino, and J. Edward Taylor (1993), "Theories of International Migration: A Review and Appraisal."

5. A written transcript of the lecture was published as E. G. Ravenstein (1885), "The Laws of Migration."

6. See E. G. Ravenstein (1876), "Census of the British Isles, 1871; Birthplaces and Migration"; E. G. Ravenstein (1889), "The Laws of Migration," *Journal of the Statistical Society.*

7. For more recent assessments of Ravenstein's work, see D. B. Grig (1977), "E. G. Ravenstein and the 'Laws of Migration'"; Waldo Tobler (1995), "Migration: Ravenstein, Thornthwaite, and Beyond." Both of these assessments attempt to provide a complete enumeration of the laws, which vary somewhat across Ravenstein's writings.

8. Larry Sjaastad (1962), "The Costs and Returns of Human Migration." For further biographical information, see Kenneth W. Clements (2005), "Larry Sjaastad, the Last Chicagoan."

9. Sjaastad (1962), p. 83.

10. Sjaastad (1962), p. 85.

11. The gravity model, which in essence predicts that the flow of migrants between two regions decreases with the distance between them, has been subject to significant study since Ravenstein's initial formulation. See, for example, David K. Foot and William J. Milne (1984), "Net Migration Estimation in an Extended, Multiregional Gravity Model"; David Karemera, Victor I. Oguledo, and Bobby Davis (2000), "A Gravity Model Analysis of International Migration to North America."

12. For a formal model of the value of intangible characteristics of a local area, see Jennifer Roback (1982), "Wages, Rents, and the Quality of Life."

13. The notion that individuals with different skill sets might migrate in opposite directions is related to the theory of comparative advantage in international trade. The application of the theory of comparative advantage to migration is generally credited to A. D. Roy (1951), "Some Thoughts on the Distribution of Earnings."

14. For example, 2007 American Community Survey data indicate that about 40 percent of foreign-born citizens were college graduates in the Akron, Ohio, metropolitan area, in the heart of the Rust Belt. In Sun Belt centers such as Dallas and Houston, the corresponding percentage is less than a quarter.

15. Recent data show that Mexican migrants to the United States are generally less educated than the average among all Mexicans; see Pablo Ibarraran and Darren Lubotsky (2007), "Mexican Immigration and Self-Selection: New Evidence from the 2000 Mexican Census." At the same time, statistics from the 2000 Mexican census indicate that roughly 300,000 natives of the United States resided in that country. Recent census estimates from other Latin Americans indicate several thousand United States-born residents in Brazil, Chile, Colombia, and Costa Rica. These estimates are available through the IPUMS project, discussed later in the chapter.

16. For a discussion and review of evidence related to this life-cycle migration, see G. J. Lewis (1982), *Human Migration: A Geographical Perspective*, pp. 89–98.

17. For a formal economic model, supported by evidence, see William J. Carrington, Enrica Detragiache, and Tara Vishwanath (1996), "Migration with Endogenous Moving Costs."

18. In addition to Carrington et al. (1996), see J. Edward Taylor (1986), "Differential Migration, Networks, Information, and Risk"; Douglas T. Gurak and Fe Caces (1992), "Migration Networks and the Shaping of Migration Systems."

19. Immigration policy also contributes to the "wave" profile of immigration, by granting preferences for permanent residency to those with relatives who are already permanent residents or citizens themselves. For a discussion of this "multiplier effect" see Guillermina Jasso and Mark Rosenzweig (1986), "Family Reunification and the Immigration Multiplier: U.S. Immigration Law, Origin-Country Conditions, and the Reproduction of Immigrants." We will observe, however, that immigration waves can also be observed in the nineteenth century, an era of open immigration where policy was irrelevant.

20. For a review of estimates of the value of life, which typically measure the wage premium required to convince a worker to take a more dangerous job, see W. Kip Viscusi and Joseph E. Aldy (2003), "The Value of a Statistical Life: A Critical Review of Market Estimates Throughout the World."

21. Sjaastad (1962), pp. 83–91.

22. Prominent dissident or persecuted groups in the American colonies included the Puritans of the Massachusetts Bay Colony (members of which were themselves cast out and formed the colony of Rhode Island), the English Roman Catholics of Maryland, French Huguenots, Quakers, and Sephardic Jews.

23. To be more explicit, this migrant will be expected to move only if the improvement in economic circumstances is sufficiently large to completely offset the inferior intangibles. If the net intangible benefits of migrating are $-B$, then the tangible benefits must not only be greater than zero, they must be greater than B.

24. Robert Park (1926a), "Behind our Masks."

25. For a complete discussion of the Chicago School, see Richard D. Alba and Victor Nee (2003), *Remaking the American Mainstream: Assimilation and Contemporary Immigration*, pp. 18–23.

26. Milton M. Gordon (1964), *Assimilation in American Life: the Role of Race, Religion, and National Origins*.

27. See especially Nathan Glazer and Daniel P. Moynihan (1963), *Beyond the Melting Pot: The Negroes, Puerto Ricans, Jews, Italians and Irish of New York City*. For a more quantitatively oriented study, see Stanley Lieberson (1980), *A Piece of the Pie: Blacks and White Immigrants Since 1880*.

28. Edward Lazear (1999), "Culture and Language."

29. This evidence is reviewed in chapter 4.

30. For example, see Lazear (1999).

31. Alba and Nee (2003), p. 37.

32. In theory, citizenship can be revoked once granted. Under section 340 of the Immigration and Nationality Act, naturalization can be revoked if a candidate engaged in "concealment of a material fact" or "willful misrepresentation" in the application process. Under section 349 of the same law, both naturalized and native citizens can lose their citizenship under a number of conditions, such as serving in the armed forces of a nation "engaged in hostilities against the United States," committing an act of treason, or making a formal renunciation. These conditions are rare, however.

33. For detailed critiques of rational choice theory in various applications, see Donald Green and Ian Shapiro (1996), *Pathologies of Rational Choice Theory: A Critique of Applications in Political Science*; Dan Ariely (2008), *Predictably Irrational: The Hidden Forces that Shape our Decisions*; Daniel Kahneman, Paul Slovic, and Amos Tversky, eds. (1982), *Judgment Under Uncertainty: Heuristics and Biases.*

34. Philip Oreopoulos (2007), "Do Dropouts Drop Out Too Soon? Wealth, Health, and Happiness from Compulsory Schooling."

35. Ahmed Khwaja, Dan Silverman, and Frank Sloan (2006), "Time Preference, Time Discounting, and Smoking Decisions."

36. Brigitte C. Madrian and Dennis F. Shea (2001), "The Power of Suggestion: Inertia in 401(k) Participation and Savings Behavior."

37. The concept of bounded rationality is generally credited to Herbert A. Simon (1957), *Models of Man: Social and Rational.*

38. Recent theoretical work in economics has formalized the trade-off faced by minority group members when majority and minority group norms conflict. See David Austen-Smith and Roland G. Fryer Jr. (2005), "An Economic Analysis of 'Acting White.'"

39. This statistic is drawn from chapter 7.

40. As noted in chapter 5, the letter of American immigration law requires immigrants to renounce existing citizenship affilations upon naturalization, but in practice these renunciations are seldom required or recognized by foreign governments.

41. For example, Alba and Nee (2003) relate James Loewen's fieldwork examining Chinese immigrants in Mississippi, who placed an emphasis on assimilation so that the native white population would consider them as equivalent to fellow whites and not as "colored." See James Loewen (1971), *The Mississippi Chinese: Between Black and White.*

42. For example, the Australian government charges a higher fee to aliens applying for a permanent visa if they do not speak English.

43. For example, there are country-specific queues for permanent residency in some categories, and access to the State Department's "diversity lottery" for randomly distributed green cards is restricted by country of origin.

44. Park (1926a); Glazer and Moynihan (1963); Lieberson (1980); Alba and Nee (2003); Joel Perlmann (2005), *Italians Then, Mexicans Now: Immigrant Origins and Second-Generation Progress, 1890–2000.*

45. Steven Ruggles, Matthew Sobek, Trent Alexander, Catherine A. Fitch, Ronald Goeken, Patricia Kelly Hall, Miriam King, and Chad Ronnander (2008), *Integrated Public Use Microdata Series: Version 4.0.*

46. Counts of foreign-born by country of origin at the census tract level are not available in 2000 public-use data, but can be obtained from restricted-access versions of the census data available to employees and sworn agents of the Census Bureau.

47. The Pew Hispanic Center began conducting its National Survey of Latinos in 2002. Since that time it has fielded a variety of surveys on subjects related to immigration from Mexico and Latin America.

48. Specifically, the Census Bureau uses a system of weighting to resolve undercounting issues. If a certain population group, such as non-English-speaking Mexican natives residing in Los Angeles, is estimated to avoid being counted 50

percent of the time, for example, then the survey results of group members who actually complete the questionnaire will be counted twice for purposes of computing aggregate statistics.

49. See Paul M. Ong and Doug Houston (2002), "The 2000 Census Undercount in Los Angeles County."

50. Census Bureau undercount estimates for 1990, for example, amount to 1.6 percent for the population as a whole, and 5.0 percent for persons of Hispanic origin.

51. For a discussion of the misreporting of educational attainment, see Dan Black, Seth Sanders, and Lowell Taylor (2003), "Measurement of Higher Education in the Census and Current Population Survey."

## Chapter 2

1. The obvious analogy here is to Emma Lazarus's sonnet "The New Colossus," inscribed on a plaque at the Statue of Liberty.

2. Benjamin Franklin (1751), "Observations Concerning the Increase of Mankind."

3. Franklin (1751).

4. Kathleen Neils Conzen (1980), "Germans," in Stephan Thernstrom, ed. (1980), *Harvard Encyclopedia of American Ethnic Groups.*

5. A White Star Line advertisement from the May 25, 1887, edition of the *New York Times* lists the cost of transatlantic passage in steerage as $20, which translates to more than $400 in 2009 dollars. While this value would appear comparable to a discount one-way transatlantic airfare in the present day, incomes have grown much faster than the cost of living over time. Using economist Angus Madisson's estimate of GDP per capita for Germany, one of the primary origin countries for immigrants of the 1880s, the equivalent fare today in terms of ratio to per capita income would be over $2,000. Statistics on the relative safety of modern air travel and historic ocean liners are quite difficult to compute, but in the years since 2001 the number of passenger fatalities on commercial waterborne vessels in the United States has exceeded the number of air passenger fatalities (U.S. Bureau of Transportation Statistics [2007], *Transportation Statistics Annual Report*).

6. For a comprehensive history of immigrant groups through 1980, see Stephan Thernstrom, ed. (1980), *Harvard Encyclopedia of American Ethnic Groups.*

7. Arrival statistics need not coincide with census population statistics since some migrants return to their country of origin, while others arrive multiple times. For statistics on immigration from England, Ireland, and Germany, see Charlotte J. Erickson's entry on the English, Patrick J. Blessing's entry on the Irish, and Kathleen Neils Conzen's entry on the Germans in Thernstrom, ed. (1980).

8. Blessing, writing in Thernstrom, ed. (1980), estimates that nearly eight hundred thousand migrants moved from Ireland to the United States in the 1840s.

9. Carrington et al. (1996); Taylor (1986); Gurak and Caces (1992).

10. Conzen, writing in Thernstrom, ed. (1980), argues that few of the "forty-eighters" were actually fugitives from conflict in Germany. Rather, revolution was a hardship that compounded difficulties associated with industrialization and rural

dislocation. These factors will play a prominent role in motivating much migration from Europe through the early twentieth century.

11. John R. Mulkern (1990), *The Know-Nothing Party in Massachusetts: The Rise and Fall of a People's Movement.*

12. Letter of Abraham Lincoln to Joshua Speed, August 24, 1855. Roy P. Bassler, ed. (1953), *The Collected Works of Abraham Lincoln.*

13. Dora L. Costa and Matthew E. Kahn (2008), *Heroes and Cowards: The Social Face of War.*

14. H. M. Lai, writing in Thernstrom, ed. (1980), points out that the decline of the Chinese empire in the nineteenth century occasioned a migration from China to many nations.

15. O. Fritiof Ander (1979), "Reflections on the Causes of Emigration from Sweden."

16. Kendric Charles Babcock (1914), *The Scandinavian Element in the United States.*

17. See, for example, A. William Hoglund's entry "Finns" and Ulf Beijbom's entry "Swedes" in Thernstrom, ed. (1980).

18. Ander (1979).

19. Dorothy Burton Skardal, "Danes," in Thernstrom, ed. (1980).

20. See Bruno Ramirez (2001), *Crossing the 49th Parallel: Migration from Canada to the United States, 1900–1930.*

21. Philip T. Silvia Jr. (1979), "The 'Flint Affair': French-Canadian Struggle for 'Survivance'"; Damien-Claude Belanger (2000), "French Canadian Emigration to the United States, 1840–1930."

22. Charlotte J. Erickson, "English," in Thernstrom, ed. (1980).

23. William E. Van Vugt (1988), "Running from Ruin? The Emigration of British Farmers to the U.S.A. in the Wake of the Repeal of the Corn Laws."

24. William E. Van Vugt (1999), *Britain to America: Mid-Nineteenth-Century Immigrants to the United States.*

25. Stephen Constantine (2003), "British Emigration to the Empire-Commonweath since 1880: From Overseas Settlement to Diaspora?"

26. C. Erickson (1972), *Invisible Immigrants: The Adaptation of English and Scottish Immigrants in 19th Century America.*

27. There were relatively few Jewish residents in Russia itself at the time, owing to historic patterns of settlement and official Russian restrictions on legal residence. I. Michael Aronson (1992), "The Anti-Jewish Pogroms in Russia in 1881."

28. Arthur A. Goren, "Jews," in Thernstrom, ed. (1980).

29. See Ross (1914), pp. 164–67.

30. See James S. Pula (1995), *Polish Americans: An Ethnic Community*; Paul Fox (1922), *The Poles in America*; Victor Greene's "Poles" entry in Thernstrom, ed. (1980).

31. Pula (1995), p. 18.

32. See Robert Blobaum (1988), "The Revolution of 1905–1907 and the Crisis of Polish Catholicism."

33. Fox (1922), p. 59.

34. Ross (1914), p. 135.

35. Ross (1914), p. 95.

36. Ross (1914), p. 95.

37. Elsewhere in the volume, Ross showers much praise on the character of German immigrants and takes offense at the "slackness, unthrift, and irresponsibility" (p. 44) of the Irish.

38. Robert Franz Foerster (1924), *The Italian Emigration of Our Time*; Jerre Mangione (1993), *La Storia: Five Centuries of the Italian American Experience.*

39. The poor performance of agricultural crops in southern Italy was compounded by the lack of effective crop insurance and complicated patterns of land tenancy. See Francesco L. Galassi and Jon S. Cohen (1994), "The Economics of Tenancy in Early Twentieth-Century Southern Italy."

40. Herbert S. Klein (1983), "The Integration of Italian Immigrants into the United States and Argentina: A Comparative Analysis."

41. Klein (1983).

42. Perlmann (2005).

43. Ross (1914), p. 139.

44. *Congressional Record*, 68th Congress, 1st session, April 1–14, 1924, 65, pt. 6, pp. 5643–45.

45. See William J. Collins (1997), "When the Tide Turned: Immigration and the Delay of the Great Black Migration."

46. In 1939, the S.S. *St. Louis* attempted to transport German Jewish refugees to Havana, Cuba. The Cuban government ultimately refused entry.

47. Robert N. Rosen (2006), *Saving the Jews: Franklin D. Roosevelt and the Holocaust.*

48. There were some exemptions to the quotas; they never applied to nations in the Western Hemisphere, for example.

49. The adoption of NAFTA, by contrast, has been associated with a reduction in migration from Mexico to the United States. See Susan M. Richter, J. Edward Taylor, and Antonio Yunez-Naude (2007), "Impacts of Policy Reforms on Labor Migration from Rural Mexico to the United States."

50. Gordon H. Hanson and Antonio Spilimbergo (1999), "Illegal Immigration, Border Enforcement, and Relative Wages: Evidence from Apprehensions at the U.S.-Mexico Border."

51. See Sherwin Rosen (1981), "The Economics of Superstars."

## Chapter 3

1. George J. Borjas (1995), "The Economic Benefits from Immigration."

2. This figure is based on the simple methodology used in Borjas (1995). Immigrants currently form roughly 17 percent of the labor force; assuming that the elasticity of factor price for labor is –0.3 (a value widely supported in economic literature; see Daniel Hamermesh (1993), *Labor Demand*), immigrants reduce wages by about 5 percent. The economic benefit from immigration is the area of a triangle with height 5 percent and base 17 percent, $1/2 \times .17 \times .05 = 0.004$, times GDP, which in 2008 was

roughly $14.3 trillion. This is a larger estimate than that reported by Borjas, because the share of immigrants in the labor market has increased over time, and because nominal GDP has increased over time. Note that, as Borjas argues, this surplus may mark a much larger net transfer of wealth from labor to capital. This calculation also presumes that immigrants do not contribute to the nation's capital stock, only to the labor supply, and that the economy is not marked by increasing returns. Both these assumptions are debatable.

3. These arguments are frequently made by employers. See, for example, Deborah Sharp, Paul Davidson, and Tom Kenworthy, "Employers Praise Bush's 'Guest Worker' Plan," *USA Today*, January 7, 2004, 3A.

4. This counterargument can be easily found in the popular press. See, for example, "Jobs Americans Won't Do," *Wall Street Journal*, April 7, 2006, A12.

5. For example, George J. Borjas (2003a), "The Labor Demand Curve *Is* Downward Sloping" presents estimates suggesting that a 10 percent increase in the labor force through immigration depresses wages by roughly 3 percent—a figure also consistent with assumptions in the Borjas (1995) method of computing the benefits from immigration.

6. The rebuttal is stated succinctly in David Card (2005), "Is the New Immigration Really So Bad?"

7. Card credits the strategy to Jean B. Grossman (1982), "The Substitutability of Natives and Immigrants in Production."

8. Card (2005) argues that evidence of a negative impact on wages is "slight."

9. See George J. Borjas and Lynette Hilton (1996), "Immigration and the Welfare State: Immigrant Participation in Means-Tested Entitlement Programs," which shows that immigrant participation in cash or noncash welfare programs was roughly 50 percent higher than among native households, in data from the 1980s and early 1990s. Borjas (1999), "Immigration and Welfare Magnets," shows evidence that, prior to 1990, immigrants gravitated towards states with higher welfare benefits.

10. See George J. Borjas (2003b), "Welfare Reform, Labor Supply, and Health Insurance in the Immigrant Population."

11. See Thomas C. Buchmueller, Anthony T. Lo Sasso, Ithai Lurie, and Sarah Dolfin (2007), "Immigrants and Employer-Sponsored Health Insurance," and Olveen Carrasquillo, Angeles I. Carrasquillo, and Steven Shea (2000), "Health Insurance Coverage of Immigrants Living in the United States: Differences by Citizenship Status and Country of Origin." These studies document that noncitizen immigrants who work full-time are much less likely to receive health insurance from their employer, primarily because they are less likely to work for a firm that offers insurance benefits. Naturalized immigrants have insurance coverage rates very similar to those of the native-born.

12. Charles Clotfelter, Helen Ladd, and Jacob Vigdor (2006), "The Academic Achievement Gap in Grades 3–8," report that Hispanic students in North Carolina public schools, who are almost entirely immigrants or the children of immigrants, score significantly below white students upon their arrival in school. Schools do manage to close a large portion of this gap, at least among children who remain in North Carolina public schools for several years.

13. Foreign students and several other officially recognized categories of "nonresident aliens" are exempt from paying Social Security and Medicare taxes.

14. Dowell Myers (2007), *Immigrants and Boomers: Forging a New Social Contract for the Future of America.* See also Kjetil Storesletten (2000), "Sustaining Fiscal Policy through Immigration."

15. There is strong evidence that immigration raises rents, at least in the short term. See Albert Saiz (2003), "Room in the Kitchen for the Melting Pot: Immigration and Rental Prices."

16. As summarized in Borjas (1995), the question of net fiscal impact of immigrants depends on assumptions regarding the marginal cost of providing services such as national defense and highways to immigrants. Jeffrey S. Passel and Rebecca L. Clark (1994), "How Much Do Immigrants Really Cost? A Reappraisal of Huddle's 'The Cost of Immigrants,'" estimate a net gain; Donald Huddle (1993), *The Net National Costs of Immigration* estimates a net loss. Ronald Lee and Timothy Miller (2000), "Immigration, Social Security, and Broader Fiscal Impacts," estimate that the overall net impact of marginal increases in immigration are small, and reflects a combination of net fiscal contributions to social security, little impact on the federal budget, and a net drain on state and local government.

17. Borjas (2003a, p. 1370) concludes that the negative impact of immigration on high school dropouts is more than twice the magnitude of the impact on high school graduates.

18. For studies of successive cohorts, see Edward Funkhouser and Stephen J. Trejo (1995), "The Labor Market Skills of Recent Male Immigrants: Evidence from the Current Population Survey"; Guillermina Jasso, Mark Rosenzweig, and James P. Smith (1998), "The Changing Skills of New Immigrants to the United States: Recent Trends and Their Determinants"; George J. Borjas and Rachel Friedberg (2007), "The Immigrant Earning Turnaround of the 1990s." Studies of immigrant progress in the labor market will be reviewed in greater detail later in the chapter.

19. This evidence is generally consistent with George J. Borjas (1994), "Long-Run Convergence of Ethnic Skills Differentials: The Children and Grandchildren of the Great Migration." Borjas used a different scheme to impute wages to occupations.

20. George J. Borjas and Lawrence F. Katz (2007), "The Evolution of the Mexican-Born Workforce in the United States," find evidence of economic improvements in post-1960 immigrant cohorts using actual income data, which is uniformly available during this time period.

21. It is commonly asserted, for example, that Irish immigrants were subjected to discrimination, that the phrase "No Irish Need Apply" was inserted into job advertisements. Historian Richard Jensen (2002) argues that there is little physical evidence to support the claim in "'No Irish Need Apply': A Myth of Victimization." Discrimination against Chinese immigrants in the nineteenth century, however, can be more directly corroborated since it was often supported by government policy—California passed laws that placed a tax on Chinese labor in the 1850s. For a discussion, see Charles J. McClain (1994), *In Search of Equality: The Chinese Struggle Against Discrimination in Nineteenth-Century America.*

22. For a review of recent literature on discrimination, see Devah Pager and Hana Shepherd (2008), "The Sociology of Discrimination: Racial Discrimination in Employment, Housing, Credit, and Consumer Markets." Marianne Bertrand and Sendhil Mullainathan (2004), "Are Emily and Greg More Employable than Lakisha and Jamal? A Field Experiment on Labor Market Discrimination," found differential likelihood of interview requests in response to resumes sent to employers in Boston and Chicago. Magnus Carlsson and Dan-Olof Rooth (2007), "Evidence of Ethnic Discrimination in the Swedish Labor Market Using Experimental Data," found that resumes assigned Middle Eastern names were called for an interview less frequently than resumes with Swedish names.

23. Darren Lubotsky (2007), "Chutes or Ladders? A Longitudinal Analysis of Immigrant Earnings," and Harriet Duleep and Daniel Dowhan (2002), "Insights from Longitudinal Data on the Earnings Growth of U.S. Foreign-Born Men," both use SSA records.

24. The occupation score is not the only method ever derived to translate occupations into a measure of economic well-being. Alternative measures take more than just the income of workers claiming an occupation into account. Some factor in a measure of occupational prestige, and others take account of the educational attainment of workers in a given occupation. The correlation between these various factors is substantial, though. It would be rare for an individual to experience a large increase in earnings and a decrease in occupational prestige simultaneously.

25. Claudia Goldin and Robert A. Margo (1992), "The Great Compression: The Wage Structure in the United States at Mid-Century."

26. Thomas Piketty and Emmanuel Saez (2003), "Income Inequality in the United States, 1913–1998."

27. This table restricts attention to males who reported participating in the labor force, between the ages of eighteen and sixty-five.

28. See, for example, Borjas and Katz (2007).

29. Borjas and Katz (2007); see also Robert J. LaLonde and Robert H. Topel (1992), "The Assimilation of Immigrants in the U.S. Labor Market."

30. George J. Borjas and Bernt Bratsberg (1996), "Who Leaves? The Outmigration of the Foreign-Born."

31. Guillermina Jasso and Mark R. Rosenzweig (1990), *The New Chosen People: Immigrants in the United States.*

32. Borjas and Bratsberg (1996), p. 172.

33. Barry Chiswick (1980), *An Analysis of the Economic Progress and Impact of Immigrants.*

34. George J. Borjas (1989), "Immigrant and Emigrant Earnings: A Longitudinal Study."

35. Wei-Yin Hu (2000), "Immigrant Earnings Assimilation: Estimates from Longitudinal Data."

36. Lubotsky (2007); Duleep and Dowhan (2002). Lubotsky's study raises an additional concern: that the U.S. census and other surveys that ask immigrants for the date that they most recently came to stay in the country overlook the fact that a substantial fraction are in the midst of their second stay. Thus, many of the successful-looking

recent migrants to the United States actually have significantly more experience in the American labor market. This pattern will generally lead to an understatement of the progress that immigrants make over time. For further assessment of this issue, see Ilana Redstone and Douglas Massey (2004), "Coming To Stay: An Analysis of the U.S. Census Question on Immigrants' Year of Arrival."

37. Lubotsky (2007) notes that up to 38 percent of the immigrant cohorts he studies cannot be located in Social Security Administration records.

38. Natives of any of the small states that would later form the German nation are counted as Germans here.

39. Recall that by the definition of the occupation score, one point translates into $100 in annual average income for an occupation.

40. Funkhouser and Trejo (1995); Jasso, Rosenzweig, and Smith (1998); Borjas and Friedberg (2007).

41. The decline in labor force participation among older men has been noted previously; see Chinhui Juhn and Simon Potter (2006), "Changes in Labor Force Participation in the United States." The decline can be observed as early as the 1970s. Several factors have been implicated as sources of this trend. Improvements in retirement savings for some workers may be enabling them to take early retirement. For lower-skilled workers, however, the decline of the manufacturing sector has reduced job opportunities; workers who abandon the search for new employment are counted as nonparticipants. A 1984 policy change easing the process for claiming disability insurance payments has also been implicated in the decline in labor force participation; see David Autor and Mark Duggan (2003), "The Rise In The Disability Rolls and the Decline in Unemployment." Immigrants are eligible to receive disability benefits if they are either legal permanent residents or naturalized citizens and meet the service requirements set by the Social Security Administration.

42. This evidence contrasts to some extent with that of Borjas and Katz (2007), who generally show anemic wage growth for Mexican immigrants in repeat cross-section analysis. The relative wage growth for Mexican immigrants has probably been hampered by general increases in inequality in the United States; the occupation score is impervious to that trend.

43. See, for example, Borjas (1994); Perlmann (2005).

## Chapter 4

1. Language is certainly not the only cultural difference between certain immigrants and the native-born majority. Immigration introduces racial and religious differences as well. While most objective indicators suggest that the nation's tolerance for racial and religious diversity is stronger now than it was a generation ago, there are also clear signals that immigration leads to unease. David Cutler, Edward Glaeser, and Jacob Vigdor (1999), "The Rise and Decline of the American Ghetto," cite evidence on moderating racial attitudes derived from the General Social Survey. In the wake of the terrorist acts of September 11, 2001, various commentators raised concerns about the presence of Muslim immigrants in the United States. See, for

example, Daniel Pipes and Khalid Duran (2002), "Muslim Immigrants in the United States." Mark Krikorian, writing in the *National Review Online* in 2002, expressed concern that continued immigration by Muslims might undermine American support for Israel ("Muslim Invasion?" April 17; www.nationalreview.com/comment/comment-krikorian041702.asp).

2. Two nonprofit groups advocating official English policies, ProEnglish and U.S. English, both invoke the cause of assimilation in their mission statements (see www.proenglish.org and www.us-english.org, respectively). For an example of the anti-pro-English viewpoint, see Ruben Navarette (2007), "Fear of Losing Culture Fuels Immigration Debate," CNN commentary published December 4.

3. Franklin (1751).

4. Theodore Roosevelt (1918), "A Square Deal for All Americans," *Kansas City Star*, April 27, 1918.

5. Exceptions to this law were later enacted; these exceptions will be analyzed in chapter 5.

6. John Foster Carr (1911), *Guide for the Immigrant Italian in the United States of America*.

7. "Time to Catch Up," *The New York Times*, July 15, 1924, p. 8.

8. The basic idea that language ability is a form of human capital is a recurring theme in the work of Barry Chiswick, which is summarized below. For an overview, see Chiswick (2008), "The Economics of Language: An Introduction and Overview." IZA Discussion Paper #3568.

9. See Barry Chiswick (1991), "Speaking, Reading, and Earnings among Low-Skilled Immigrants"; Chiswick (1998), "Hebrew Language Usage: Determinants and Effects on Earnings among Immigrants in Israel"; Chiswick and Paul Miller (1992), "Language in the Immigrant Labor Market"; Chiswick and Miller (1994), "Language Choice among Immigrants in a Multi-lingual Destination"; Chiswick and Miller (1995), "The Endogeneity Between Language and Earnings: International Analyses"; and Chiswick and Miller (2001), "A Model of Destination-Language Acquisition: Application to Male Immigrants in Canada." See also Espenshade and Fu (1997).

10. See Alejandro Portes and Ruben Rumbout (2006), *Immigrant America*, third edition. Chapter 7 reviews the sociological literature on language adoption and presents new findings.

11. See Stanley Lieberson, Guy Dalto, and Mary Ellen Johnston (1975), "The Course of Mother-Tongue Diversity in Nations."

12. See William Easterly and Ross Levine (1997), "Africa's Growth Tragedy: Policies and Ethnic Divisions" for a discussion of ethno-linguistic fractionalization.

13. Alberto Alesina, Reza Baqir, and William Easterly (1999), "Public Goods and Ethnic Divisions."

14. Alberto Alesina and Eliana La Ferrara (2002), "Who Trusts Others?"

15. Jacob Vigdor (2004), "Community Composition and Collective Action: Analyzing Initial Mail Response to the 2000 Census."

16. Lazear (1999).

17. For an overview of the literature and a discussion of these concerns, see Alberto Alesina and Eliana La Ferrara (2005), "Ethnic Diversity and Economic Performance."

18. The Australian policy is discussed in more detail in the concluding chapter. The price differential for non-English speakers is equivalent to $4,000 at current exchange rates.

19. U.S. Citizenship and Immigration Services, Office of Citizenship (2007), *Welcome to the United States: A Guide for New Immigrants.*

20. For a series of suggestions regarding "best practices" in policies promoting the education of English as a Second Language, see Elzbieta Gozdziak and Micah Bump (2008), *New Immigrants, Changing Communities*, chapter 3.

21. Specifically, if more than half of the immigrants from a particular nation interviewed in the 2007 ACS reported speaking English at home, all immigrants from that nation were excluded. The list of excluded nations consists primarily of Commonwealth nations, most notably the United Kingdom, Ireland, Canada, former British possessions in the Caribbean, South Africa, Australia, and New Zealand.

22. See, for example, Chiswick (1991), Espenshade and Fu (1997), and the evidence presented later in this chapter.

23. There have been few studies of the extent to which apparent linguistic progress reflects return migration. Kristin E. Espinosa and Douglas S. Massey (1997), "Determinants of English Proficiency among Mexican Migrants to the United States," utilize a unique data source that combines a sample of immigrants with a sample of return migrants in Mexico, and conclude that real linguistic progress does take place within the immigrant population. The data, collected between 1987 and 1994, do not permit an analysis of whether this pattern has changed over time.

24. One additional potential skewing factor bears mentioning here: English language skills may increase for some cohorts because young children, who are more likely to acquire English skills than those arriving at older ages (see figure 4.7) are not counted in the initial sample. In the 1900–1920 period, for example, English ability is not recorded for individuals under the age of ten. In 1900, about 7 percent of the 1896–1900 arrival cohort was under the age of ten. Presuming that 100 percent of these young immigrants knew English in 1900, but were simply not asked, the proportion of English-speaking immigrants would have been 48 percent instead of the 45 percent actually recorded. The proportion of non-English speakers in this cohort who learned the language over twenty years would be recorded as 71 percent instead of 74 percent. This issue is less of a concern in the period between 1980 and 2007; English ability was recorded for children as young as three in 1980 and as young as five in later years. The general point that the likelihood of learning English after arrival was greater in later-arriving cohorts still holds after taking this concern into consideration.

25. This argument is made and supported with evidence by Barry Chiswick and Paul Miller (1996), "Ethnic Networks and Language Proficiency Among Immigrants."

26. This finding corroborates the analysis in Edward Lazear (2007), "Mexican Assimilation in the United States."

27. For a discussion of theories of language acquisition, see P. M. Lightbown and N. Spada (2006), *How Languages Are Learned.*

28. For an analysis of immigration to "new destinations," see Douglas Massey, ed. (2008), *New Faces in New Places: The Changing Geography of American Immigration.*

## Chapter 5

1. For reviews of the academic literature, see Louis DeSipio (1987), "Social Science Literature and the Naturalization Process," and Barry R. Chiswick and Paul W. Miller (2008), "Citizenship in the United States: The Roles of Immigrant Characteristics and Country of Origin."

2. One of the most commonly cited studies of naturalization, for example, analyzes the cohort of immigrants who arrived in the United States in 1971, over a ten-year period. See Jasso and Rosenzweig (1986).

3. For examples of this strategy, see Irene Bloemraad (2002), "The North American Naturalization Gap: An Institutional Approach to Citizenship Acquisition in the United States and Canada," or Rogers Brubaker (1992), *Citizenship and Nationhood in France and Germany.* James Clarke, Elsbeth van Dam, and Liz Gooster (1998), "New Europeans: Naturalisation and Citizenship in Europe," pursue a more truly cross-national strategy and note some differences in naturalization rates across nations, but do not come to any specific conclusions regarding the role of policy.

4. For example, Amelie Constant, Liliya Gataullina, and Klaus Zimmermann (2007), "Naturalization Proclivities, Ethnicity, and Integration," note that a 2000 liberalization of naturalization laws in Germany, which among other things cut the residency requirement from fifteen years down to eight, led to a one-time spike in naturalization. It is unclear, however, whether the policy actually induced naturalization or more simply accelerated the process for individuals who would have eventually become citizens.

5. Chiswick and Miller (2008).

6. Jasso and Rosenzweig (1986).

7. Clarke, van Dam, and Gooster (1998); Pieter Bevelander and Justus Vennman (2006), "Naturalisation and Socioeconomic Integration: The Case of the Netherlands"; and Jasso and Rosenzweig (1986) find higher naturalization rates among male refugees in their sample of 1971 entrants to the United States, but not females.

8. The rational choice perspective is not the only school of thought regarding the determinants of naturalization. Some authors have argued that social institutions and attitudes, whether official or popular, make a significant difference. Even these studies, however, admit an explanatory role for more traditional cost and benefit measures. Sociologists often refer to measures of "commitment," which can be interpreted in the rational choice framework as a measure of the potential costs of deportation, and hence the potential benefits of naturalization, and to "structural" factors, such as income or education, which factor into the cost-benefit framework when nations use these factors in setting priorities in their naturalization policies. See Alejandro Portes and John W. Curtis (1987), "Changing Flags: Naturalization and its Determinants Among Mexican Immigrants"; M. D. R. Evans (1988), "Choosing to Be a Citizen: The Time-Path of Citizenship in Australia"; Bloemraad (2002).

9. Technically speaking, the unskilled European could join the path to citizenship if he or she were related by blood or marriage to a citizen, or in some cases a legal permanent resident.

10. We will temper this conclusion somewhat later in the chapter, noting that there are many individuals favored under current naturalization policy that nonetheless rarely opt to become citizens.

11. Current requirements for naturalization are covered in "A Guide to Naturalization," published by the U.S. Citizenship and Immigration Services, publication M-476, most recently revised in January 2009.

12. Much of the information in this table was culled from Michael LeMay and Elliott Barkan, eds. (1999), *U.S. Immigration and Naturalization Laws and Issues: A Documentary History.*

13. The U.S. Citizenship and Immigration Services maintains information regarding the various paths to legal permanent residence online: www.uscis.gov/greencard.

14. The U.S. State Department's *Visa Bulletin* for March 2009, for example, indicated that the waiting period for an adult Mexican-born child of a naturalized U.S. citizen was approximately sixteen years. See travel.state.gov/visa/frvi/bulletin/bulletin_4428.html.

15. See travel.state.gov/visa/immigrants/types/types_1317.html.

16. The number of permanent resident visas actually awarded through the diversity lottery exceeds fifty thousand, because the spouse and unmarried minor children of a lottery winner are also eligible for visas. In the 2008 lottery, a total of ninety-six thousand individuals became eligible for visas as a result of the lottery.

17. For example, the odds in scratch-off games sold by the District of Columbia lottery as of February 2009 offered odds between 1:3.31 and 1:4.86. At the midpoint of this range, a player would expect to win about once in every five tickets purchased, or 20 percent of the time.

18. The U.S. State Department "recognizes that dual nationality exists, but does not encourage it as a matter of policy because of the problems it may cause." See travel.state.gov/travel/cis_pa_tw/cis/cis_1753.html.

19. For example, Australia, Canada, New Zealand, and the United Kingdom all maintain preferential immigration programs for highly skilled workers.

20. Not all countries of origin are represented in this figure. Only those nations with one hundred or more natives represented in the relevant ACS sample are included in the figure. Statistically, naturalization rates cannot be computed with reasonable confidence for those nations represented by only a handful of immigrants.

21. Jasso and Rosenzweig (1986); Chiswick and Miller (2008). Interestingly, this pattern is not present in earlier eras. Among immigrants arriving between 1906 and 1910, the naturalization rate as of 1920 was 50 percent for natives of the United Kingdom, compared with 21 percent for Italians, 15 percent for Poles, and 31 percent for Russians. In this earlier era of expensive transportation, natives of wealthy countries may have chosen to emigrate only if they anticipated taking up residence in a new country on a permanent basis. In the modern era, natives of wealthy countries may be more likely to view their residence in a foreign country as temporary.

22. Michale Hoefer, Nancy Rytina, and Bryan C. Baker (2009), "Estimates of the Unauthorized Immigrant Population Residing in the United States: January 2008."

23. As noted above, the spouse and minor children of a lottery winner are immediately eligible for permanent resident visas. These individuals may then sponsor

additional relatives once they transition to citizenship. The "multiplier effect" associated with granting permanent residency or citizenship to individuals who may then nominate relatives is the central focus of Jasso and Rosenzweig (1986), who estimate that each immigrant receiving an employment-related green card introduces an average of 1.2 additional citizens in the long run. Jasso and Rosenzweig do not study lottery winners because the diversity lottery was not instituted until 1995.

24. Jasso and Rosenzweig (1986); Evans (1988); Chiswick and Miller (2008).

25. Recall that the figure is restricted to nations represented by at least one hundred natives arriving in the United States between 1995 and 1999 in the 2007 ACS. Liberia barely misses this criterion, with ninety-six sample members.

26. In fiscal year 2007, for example, the cap was 70,000, and 48,217 refugees were admitted. See Kelly J. Jefferys and Daniel C. Martin (2008), "Annual Flow Report: Refguees and Asylees, 2007."

27. Complete information on the relative economic position of the United States and other nations is difficult to acquire for the early twentieth century or any earlier period. According to the estimates of Angus Maddison, economic historian at the University of Groningen in the Netherlands, the ratio of U.S. GDP per capita to Mexican GDP per capita rose from three to four between 1900 and 2006. Over a comparable time period, the ratio between the United States and the Philippines rose from seven to eleven. This is consistent with the notion that the value of access to the U.S. labor market has increased over time.

## Chapter 6

1. Based on 2000 census tract data for tract 240, Philadelphia County, Pennsylvania.

2. Based on 2000 census tract data for tract 43, New York County, New York.

3. See, in particular, Robert E. Park (1926b), "The Urban Community as a Spatial Pattern and a Moral Order."

4. For an explicit rational choice model of an immigrant's decision to enter an ethnic enclave, see George J. Borjas (1998), "To Ghetto or Not To Ghetto: Ethnicity and Residential Segregation."

5. For further discussion of these trade-offs, see David M. Cutler, Edward L. Glaeser, and Jacob L. Vigdor (2005), "Ghettos and the Transmission of Ethnic Capital."

6. Herbert J. Gans (1962), *The Urban Villagers: Group and Class in the Life of Italian-Americans*; Glazer and Moynihan (1963); Olivier Zunz (1982), *The Changing Face of Inequality: Urbanization, Industrial Development, and Immigrants in Detroit, 1880–1920*.

7. Lieberson (1980).

8. See Douglas Massey (1985), "Ethnic Residential Segregation: A Theoretical Synthesis and Empirical Review"; Mary J. Fischer and Douglas Massey (2000), "Residential Segregation and Ethnic Enterprise in U.S. Metropolitan Areas."

9. Recall that parents' birthplace has not been recorded in recent census and ACS enumerations. Parents' birthplace can be recorded, however, for children still residing with their parents. David Cutler, Edward Glaeser, and Jacob Vigdor (2008), "Is the

Melting Pot Still Hot? Explaining the Resurgence of Immigrant Segregation," present an analysis of the impact of immigrant childbearing on measures of foreign-born segregation. The results are described later in the chapter.

10. See, for example, Jacob Riis (1891), *How The Other Half Lives: Studies Among the Tenements of New York.* See also Gans (1962), Glazer and Moynihan (1963), Zunz (1982).

11. For an overview of segregation measures, see Douglas Massey and Nancy Denton (1988), "The Dimensions of Residential Segregation."

12. Aside from examples of ethnic segregation through government policy, black-white segregation in several American cities neared the "perfect" point at the midpoint of the twentieth century. See Cutler, Glaeser, and Vigdor (1999).

13. Julius Jahn, Calvin F. Schmid, and Clarence Schrag (1947), "The Measurement of Ecological Segregation." The formula for the dissimilarity index measuring segregation of ethnic group *j* from the native population in a city or metropolitan area can be expressed as follows:

$$D = \frac{1}{2} \sum_{i=1}^{I} \left| \frac{e_{ij}}{e_j} - \frac{n_i}{n} \right|$$

where $e_j$ and $n$ are the number of ethnic group *j* members and natives in the city, respectively, and $e_{ij}$ and $n_i$ track the number of group members and natives in each of the *I* neighborhoods within the city.

14. The isolation index is one of several measures of the relative concentration of immigrants in the neighborhoods they occupy (Massey and Denton 1988). The specific formula used here is derived from Cutler, Glaeser, and Vigdor (1999):

$$I = \frac{\displaystyle\sum_{i=1}^{I} \frac{e_{ij}}{p_i} e_{ij} - \frac{e_j}{p}}{\min\left(1, \dfrac{e_j}{p_{\min}}\right) - \dfrac{e_j}{p}}$$

where $e_{ij}$ is a count of the population of group *j* in neighborhood *i*, $e_j$ is the citywide population of group *j*, $p_i$ is the population of neighborhood *i*, *p* the citywide population, and $p_{\min}$ the population of the least populated neighborhood. The numerator is the difference between the average neighborhood-level group share experienced by the group and the theoretical minimum that would exist under perfect integration. The denominator is used to scale the index so that it has a theoretical maximum value of 1; without this scaling factor the maximum would be 1 minus group *j*'s share of the citywide population.

15. The most commonly cited multigroup segregation measure is the entropy index, derived from Henri Thiel and Anthony J. Finezza (1971), "A Note on the Measurement of Racial Integration of Schools by Means of Informational Concepts."

16. Several such measures are catalogued by Massey and Denton (1988). See also Federico Echenique and Roland G. Fryer Jr. (2007), "A Measure of Segregation Based on Social Interactions."

17. Analysis here will take advantage of recently released information from the 1930 census, which permits identification of an immigrant's ward of residence in IPUMS microdata.

18. For example, many states delineate enterprise zones, disadvantaged areas in which special tax exemptions are available for expanding or relocating businesses, using census tract boundaries.

19. Cutler, Glaeser, and Vigdor (1999) use data from 1940, when both ward- and tract-level tabulations of race were available in a subset of cities, to show that tract-level indices of dissimilarity and isolation were on average fifteen percentage points higher than equivalent ward-level indices.

20. Echenique and Fryer (2007).

21. Cutler, Glaeser, and Vigdor (1999) find that the exclusion of suburbs from post-1960 data in the computation of black-white segregation indices leads to a modest decrease in index values, consistent with expectations for a group concentrated in the city rather than the suburbs.

22. The complete analysis is described in the appendix to Cutler, Glaeser, and Vigdor (2008). To complete the analysis, I became a research affiliate of the Center for Economic Studies at the U.S. Census Bureau. The analysis underwent a Census Bureau review prior to public release. The purpose of the screening was to ensure that no confidential information was revealed. This review is more limited in scope than that given to official Census Bureau publications. Research results and conclusions summarized here are my own and do not necessarily indicate concurrence by the Census Bureau.

23. Immigrant communities are defined as a set of immigrants from a common origin country living in the same city. Mexican immigrants in the Los Angeles metropolitan area and Cubans in Miami-Dade would be two examples of immigrant communities. This figure is taken from Cutler, Glaeser, and Vigdor (2008).

24. This figure is derived from Cutler, Glaeser, and Vigdor (2008).

25. Indeed, the urban economics literature has devoted considerable effort to rework the economic analog to the concentric ring model, the monocentric city model. See, for example, Masahisa Fujita and Hideaki Ogawa (1982), "Multiple Equilibria and Structural Transition of Non-Monocentric Urban Configurations"; Kenneth F. Weiand (1987), "An Extension of the Monocentric Urban Spatial Equilibrium Model to a Multicenter Setting: The Case of the Two-Center City."

26. A recent Brookings Institution report examining census data for thirty-five large metropolitan areas indicates that the average suburban population is more than twice the average central city population; suburbs grew at twice the rate of central cities in the 1990s. See William H. Lucy and David L. Phillips (2001), "Suburbs and the Census: Patterns of Growth and Decline."

27. For a case study on the impact of land use regulation on housing prices, see Edward L. Glaeser and Bryce A. Ward (2006), "The Causes and Consequences of Land Use Regulation: Evidence from Greater Boston."

28. To be fair, there are some analyses suggesting that housing market discrimination is still a problem for immigrants. See, for example, Lauren J. Krivo (1995), "Immigrant Characteristics and Hispanic-Anglo Housing Inequality." The claim that housing market discrimination has declined in importance is supported by evidence of declining black-white segregation since the passage of the Fair Housing Act in 1968. See Cutler, Glaeser, and Vigdor (1999).

29. In a database of 414 restrictive covenants in the Seattle area, University of Washington researchers found 24 prohibitions against "Hebrews" or "Semites," along with numerous references to persons of "Malay," "Mongolian," "Asiatic," or "Ethiopian" races. Seattle Civil Rights and Labor History Project (2006), *Database of 414 Racial Restrictive Covenants from King County Recorder's Office.*

30. For a study of housing market discrimination and the laws that curtailed it, see William J. Collins (2006), "The Political Economy of State Fair Housing Laws Before 1968." Collins notes that states with sizable Jewish populations were more likely to pass fair housing laws ahead of the federal government in 1968.

31. To be precise, the Census Bureau estimated that 30.1 out of the nation's 31.1 million foreign-born residents in 2000 lived in census tracts where the proportion of foreign-born was 33 percent or less.

32. The ethnic concentration of each ward is determined using the IPUMS sample data. This introduces sampling error into the determination of percent immigrant in each ward. Actual census counts of individuals by birthplace in each ward would be preferable; such counts are unfortunately unavailable for 1900 and 1930. Moreover, it is not always possible to link ward numbers from original Census Bureau publications to the IPUMS, as some cities used nonnumeric names for their wards.

33. Only cities with twenty-five thousand or more inhabitants at the time of enumeration are counted for purposes of this chart.

34. While New York City itself was fairly homogenized by 1930, it should also be noted that significant suburbanization was already well underway by this point in time. The population of Westchester County octupled between 1850 and 1910; the opening of Penn Station in 1910 fostered additional growth of commuter-oriented suburbs in New Jersey and on Long Island. In 1910, whereas the five boroughs of New York were 40 percent foreign-born, only 28 percent of the population of Westchester County was foreign-born; Nassau County was 23 percent foreign-born. Note that all these areas were substantially above the national average of 14 percent. For a detailed history of suburbanization in general and in New York specifically, see Kenneth T. Jackson (1985), *Crabgrass Frontier: The Suburbanization of the United States.*

35. For purposes of this analysis, metropolitan areas were defined according to the guidelines released by the Office of Management and Budget in November 2007.

36. Cutler, Glaeser, and Vigdor (2008) argue that much of the lower suburbanization of immigrants can be attributed to their increased reliance on shared transportation—whether public transport or carpools. An alternative view is that native suburbanization is a form of flight; that natives have abandoned neighborhoods where immigrants now reside in order to avoid living near them. For evidence on this view, see Albert Saiz and Susan Wachter (2006), "Immigration and the Neighborhood."

37. In previous chapters, we've analyzed assimilation for individual country-of-origin groups. This is not possible using neighborhood-level data for 1990 or 2000, as the Census Bureau does not publish tabulations of residents by country of birth and year of arrival.

38. For an assessment and analysis of migration to "new destinations," see Massey, ed. (2008).

## Chapter 7

1. Much of the literature on intermarriage concerns individuals of different races, religions, or socioeconomic status rather than nativity. A review of scholarship on interethnic marriage appears below. For a review of various types of intermarriage, see Matthijs Kalmijn (1998), "Intermarriage and Homogamy: Causes, Patterns, Trends." For a more recent economic analysis of religious intermarriage, see Alberto Bisin, Giorgio Topa, and Thierry Verdier (2004), "Religious Intermarriage and Socialization in the United States."

2. As of April 2009, the queue for spouses of legal permanent residents was roughly five years, except for those born in Mexico, who faced a wait of seven to eight years. The U.S. State Department publishes a monthly *Visa Bulletin* updating the state of the queue for legal permanent residency.

3. The intergenerational implications of intermarriage are emphasized in the conceptual discussion beginning in Kalmijn (1998).

4. For purposes of this figure, adults are considered to be those individuals at least eighteen years of age.

5. Julius Drachsler (1920), *Democracy and Assimilation: The Blending of Immigrant Heritages in America.*

6. Drachsler's analysis is complicated by efforts to determine the nationality of "third generation" brides and grooms, using marriage certificates that included only information on birthplace, parents' birthplace, race, and religion.

7. Drachsler (1920), p. 103.

8. Deanna Pagnini and S. Philip Morgan (1990), "Intermarriage and Social Distance Among U.S. Immigrants at the Turn of the Century."

9. Zhenchao Qian and Daniel Lichter (2001), "Measuring Marital Assimilation: Intermarriage among Natives and Immigrants."

10. Gary S. Becker (1973), "A Theory of Marriage: Part I."

11. Donn Erwin Byrne (1971), *The Attraction Paradigm*; for additional conceptual discussion of the causes of homogamy see also Kalmijn (1998).

12. Kalmijn (1998), p. 400.

13. For an assessment of the potential role of geographic segregation in restricting intermarriage, see Stanley Lieberson and Mary C. Waters (1988), *From Many Strands: Ethnic and Racial Groups in Contemporary America*, chapter 7.

14. Much of the literature on intermarriage fails to analyze the decision to remain unmarried, because the unit of analysis is the marriage rather than the individual. In

the analysis that follows, marital status is analyzed for all immigrants rather than just married ones.

15. The set of European nations included in these statistics includes the United Kingdom, Ireland, Belgium, France, the Netherlands, Switzerland, Greece, Italy, Spain, Austria, and Germany.

16. The set of nations included here consists of those listed in table 7.1, as well as Costa Rica, Panama, and the remainder of the Caribbean.

17. Israeli nationals have intermarriage rates that approach European levels, but presumably many of these marriages are "within-ethnicity," if Jewish religious affiliation is considered an ethnicity. The U.S. Census Bureau does not collect information on religious affiliation.

18. Vietnamese immigrants of both genders show a strong tendency to marry naturalized citizens—an artifact of the high naturalization rates we observed for this group in chapter 5.

19. Drachsler (1920) and Pagnini and Morgan (1990) report higher rates largely because they restrict attention to marriages that took place after emigration.

## Chapter 8

1. For example, Mark Krikorian (2008), *The New Case Against Immigration: Both Legal and Illegal.*

2. For example, a 2006 novel by Matthew Bracken titled *Domestic Enemies: The Reconquista* detailed a hypothetical "low intensity civil war" in the southwestern United States.

3. See, for example, Krikorian (2008).

4. Jason L. Riley (2008), *Let Them In: The Case for Open Borders.*

5. Joshua S. Reichert and Douglas S. Massey (1982), "Guestworker Programs: Evidence form Europe and the United States and Some Implications for U.S. Policy."

6. Reichert and Massey (1982) go so far as to call illegal immigration "an unintended result of the Bracero program" (p. 6). For a more recent critique of the role of the Bracero program in promoting illegal immigration, see Philip L. Martin and Michael S. Teitelbaum (2001), "The Mirage of Mexican Guest Workers."

7. Both Reichert and Massey (1982) and Martin and Teitelbaum (2001) discuss European guest worker programs.

8. Reichert and Massey (1982) note that the termination of the Bracero program was associated with increases in the population of both legal and illegal immigrants from Mexico.

9. Martin and Teitelbaum (2001), p. 119.

10. For details on the IRCA and its provisions, see Pia Orrenius and Madeline Zavodny (2003), "Do Amnesty Programs Reduce Undocumented Immigration? Evidence from IRCA."

11. See, for example, Orrenius and Zavodny (2003); Katherine Donato, Jorge Durand, and Douglas Massey (1992), "Stemming the Tide? Assessing the Deterrent

Effects of the Immigration Reform and Control Act"; Karen A. Woodrow and Jeffrey S. Passel (1990), "Post-IRCA Undocumented Immigration to the United States: An Assessment Based on the June 1988 CPS"; Frank D. Bean, Thomas J. Espenshade, Michael J. White, and Robert F. Dymowski (1990), "Post-IRCA Changes in the Volume and Composition of Undocumented Migration to the United States"; Michael J. White, Frank D. Bean, and Thomas J. Espenshade (1997), "The U.S. 1986 Immigration Reform and Control Act and Undocumented Immigration to the United States."

12. See Donato, Durand, and Massey (1992); Woodrow and Passel (1990).

13. See Orrenius and Zavodny (2003); Bean et al. (1990); White, Bean, and Espenshade (1997).

14. This is not a perfect empirical test, because agricultural migrant workers were in some cases eligible for amnesty even if they had not initially arrived before 1982. Nonetheless, the majority of amnesty applications were in the category for which January 1, 1982, was a strict eligibility cutoff.

15. For evidence on the prevalence of fraudulent amnesty applications in the wake of IRCA, see Jeffrey S. Passel (1999), "Undocumented Immigration to the United States: Numbers, Trends, and Characteristics"; Katherine M. Donato and Rebecca S. Carter (1999), "Mexico and U.S. Policy on Illegal Immigration: A Fifty-Year Retrospective"; and Wayne A. Cornelius (1989), "Impacts of the 1986 U.S. Immigration Law on Emigration from Rural Mexican Sending Communities."

16. For reasons explained below, this credit would ideally not be a refundable credit such as the Earned Income Tax Credit, which is payable regardless of whether a worker had any federal income tax liability. A "nonrefundable" credit creates an incentive to obtain legal employment, and to report earnings sufficient to generate an income tax liability. In the context of an assimilation bond, these are desirable things.

# Works Cited

Alba, Richard D., and Victor Nee. (2003). *Remaking the American Mainstream: Assimilation and Contemporary Immigration.* Cambridge, Mass.: Harvard University Press.

Alesina, Alberto, Reza Baqir, and William Easterly. (1999). "Public Goods and Ethnic Divisions." *Quarterly Journal of Economics* 114, no. 4, pp. 1243–84.

Alesina, Alberto, and Eliana La Ferrara. (2002). "Who Trusts Others?" *Journal of Public Economics* 85, pp. 207–34.

———. (2005). "Ethnic Diversity and Economic Performance." *Journal of Economic Literature* 43, pp. 762–800.

Ander, O. Fritiof. (1979). "Reflections on the Causes of Emigration from Sweden," in Hildor Arnold Barton, ed., *Clipper Ship and Covered Wagon: Essays from the Swedish Pioneer Historical Quarterly.* New York: Arno Press.

Ariely, Dan. (2008). *Predictably Irrational: The Hidden Forces that Shape our Decisions.* New York: HarperCollins.

Aronson, I. Michael. (1992). "The Anti-Jewish Pogroms in Russia in 1881," in John Doyle Klier and Shlomo Lambroza, eds., *Pogroms: Anti-Jewish Violence in Modern Russian History.* Cambridge: Cambridge University Press.

Austen-Smith, David, and Roland G. Fryer Jr. (2005). "An Economic Analysis of 'Acting White.'" *Quarterly Journal of Economics* 120, no. 2, pp. 551–83.

Autor, David, and Mark Duggan. (2003). "The Rise In The Disability Rolls and the Decline in Unemployment." *Quarterly Journal of Economics* 118, no. 1, pp. 157–205.

Babcock, Kendric Charles. (1914). *The Scandinavian Element in the United States.* Urbana: University of Illinois Press.

Bassler, Roy P., ed. (1953). *The Collected Works of Abraham Lincoln.* New Brunswick, N.J.: Rutgers University Press.

Bean, Frank D., Thomas J. Espenshade, Michael J. White, and Robert F. Dymowski (1990). "Post-IRCA Changes in the Volume and Composition of Undocumented Migration to the United States," in Frank D. Bean, Barry Edmonston, and Jeffrey S. Passell, eds., *Undocumented Migration to the United States: IRCA and the Experience of the 1980s.* Washington, D.C.: Urban Institute Press.

Becker, Gary S. (1973). "A Theory of Marriage: Part I." *Journal of Political Economy* 81, no. 4, pp. 813–46.

Belanger, Damien-Claude. (2000). "French Canadian Emigration to the United States, 1840–1930." *Readings in Quebec History.* Montreal: Marianopolis College.

Bertrand, Marianne, and Sendhil Mullainathan. (2004). "Are Emily and Greg More Employable than Lakisha and Jamal? A Field Experiment on Labor Market Discrimination." *American Economic Review* 94, no. 4, pp. 991–1013.

Bevelander, Pieter, and Justus Vennman. (2006). "Naturalisation and Socioeconomic Integration: The Case of the Netherlands." Institute for the Study of Labor (IZA) Discussion Paper #2153.

Bisin, Alberto, Giorgio Topa, and Thierry Verdier. (2004). "Religious Intermarriage and Socialization in the United States." *Journal of Political Economy* 112, no. 3, pp. 615–64.

Black, Dan, Seth Sanders, and Lowell Taylor. (2003). "Measurement of Higher Education in the Census and Current Population Survey." *Journal of the American Statistical Association* 98, no. 463, pp. 545–54.

Blobaum, Robert. (1988). "The Revolution of 1905–1907 and the Crisis of Polish Catholicism." *Slavic Review* 47, no. 4, pp. 667–86.

Bloemraad, Irene. (2002). "The North American Naturalization Gap: An Institutional Approach to Citizenship Acquisition in the United States and Canada." *International Migration Review* 36, no. 1, pp. 193–229.

Borjas, George J. (1989). "Immigrant and Emigrant Earnings: A Longitudinal Study." *Economic Inquiry* 27, no. 1, pp. 21–37.

———. (1994). "Long-Run Convergence of Ethnic Skills Differentials: The Children and Grandchildren of the Great Migration." *Industrial and Labor Relations Review* 47, no. 4, pp. 553–73.

———. (1995). "The Economic Benefits from Immigration." *Journal of Economic Perspectives* 9, no. 2, pp. 3–22.

———. (1998). "To Ghetto or Not To Ghetto: Ethnicity and Residential Segregation." *Journal of Urban Economics* 44, pp. 228–53.

———. (1999). "Immigration and Welfare Magnets." *Journal of Labor Economics* 17, no. 4, pp. 607–37.

———. (2003a). "The Labor Demand Curve *Is* Downward Sloping: Reexamining the Impact of Immigration on the Labor Market." *Quarterly Journal of Economics* 118, no. 4, pp. 1335–74.

———. (2003b). "Welfare Reform, Labor Supply, and Health Insurance in the Immigrant Population." National Bureau of Economic Research Working Paper #9781.

Borjas, George J., and Bernt Bratsberg. (1996). "Who Leaves? The Outmigration of the Foreign-Born." *Review of Economics and Statistics* 78, no. 1, pp. 165–76.

Borjas, George J., and Rachel Friedberg. (2007). "The Immigrant Earning Turnaround of the 1990s." Brown University manuscript.

Borjas, George J., and Lynette Hilton. (1996). "Immigration and the Welfare State: Immigrant Participation in Means-Tested Entitlement Programs." *Quarterly Journal of Economics* 111, no. 2, pp. 575–604.

Borjas, George J., and Lawrence F. Katz. (2007). "The Evolution of the Mexican-Born Workforce in the United States," in George J. Borjas, ed., *Mexican Immigration to the United States*. Chicago: University of Chicago Press.

Bracken, Matthew. (2006). *Domestic Enemies: The Reconquista*. San Diego: Steelcutter Publishing.

Brubaker, Rogers. (1992). *Citizenship and Nationhood in France and Germany*. Cambridge, Mass.: Harvard University Press.

Buchmueller, Thomas C., Anthony T. Lo Sasso, Ithai Lurie, and Sarah Dolfin. (2007). "Immigrants and Employer-Sponsored Health Insurance." *Health Services Research* 42, no. 1, pp. 286–310.

Byrne, Donn Erwin. (1971). *The Attraction Paradigm*. New York: Academic Press.

Card, David. (2005). "Is the New Immigration Really So Bad?" *The Economic Journal* 115, pp. 300–23.

Carlsson, Magnus, and Dan-Olof Rooth. (2007). "Evidence of Ethnic Discrimination in the Swedish Labor Market Using Experimental Data." *Labour Economics* 14, no. 4, pp. 716–29.

Carr, John Foster. (1911). *Guide for the Immigrant Italian in the United States of America*. Garden City, N.Y.: Doubleday, Page and Co.

Carrasquillo, Olveen, Angeles I. Carrasquillo, and Steven Shea. (2000). "Health Insurance Coverage of Immigrants Living in the United States: Differences by Citizenship Status and Country of Origin." *American Journal of Public Health* 90, no. 6, pp. 917–23.

Carrington, William J., Enrica Detragiache, and Tara Vishwanath. (1996). "Migration with Endogenous Moving Costs." *American Economic Review* 86, no. 4, pp. 909–30.

Central Intelligence Agency. (2008). *The 2008 World Factbook*. Washington, D.C.: U.S. Government Printing Office.

Chiswick, Barry. (1980). *An Analysis of the Economic Progress and Impact of Immigrants*. National Technical Information Service #PB80-200454. Washington, D.C.: U.S. Department of Labor.

———. (1991). "Speaking, Reading, and Earnings among Low-Skilled Immigrants." *Journal of Labor Economics* 9, pp. 149–70.

———. (1998). "Hebrew Language Usage: Determinants and Effects on Earnings among Immigrants in Israel." *Journal of Population Economics* 11, pp. 253–71.

———. (2008). "The Economics of Language: An Introduction and Overview." IZA Discussion Paper #3568.

Chiswick, Barry, and Paul Miller. (1992). "Language in the Immigrant Labor Market," in Barry Chiswick, ed., *Immigration, Language and Ethnicity*. Washington, D.C.: AEI Press.

———. (1994). "Language Choice among Immigrants in a Multi-lingual Destination." *Journal of Population Economics* 7, pp. 119–31.

———. (1995). "The Endogeneity Between Language and Earnings: International Analyses." *Journal of Labor Economics* 13, pp. 246–88.

———. (1996). "Ethnic Networks and Language Proficiency Among Immigrants." *Journal of Population Economics* 9, pp. 19–35.

———. (2001). "A Model of Destination-Language Acquisition: Application to Male Immigrants in Canada." *Demography* 38, pp. 391–409.

———. (2008). "Citizenship in the United States: The Roles of Immigrant Characteristics and Country of Origin." IZA Discussion Paper #3596.

Clarke, James, Elsbeth van Dam, and Liz Gooster. (1998). "New Europeans: Naturalisation and Citizenship in Europe." *Citizenship Studies* 2, no. 1, pp. 43–67.

Clements, Kenneth W. (2005). "Larry Sjaastad, the Last Chicagoan." *Journal of International Money and Finance* 24, no. 6, pp. 859–72.

Clotfelter, Charles, Helen Ladd, and Jacob Vigdor. (2006). "The Academic Achievement Gap in Grades 3–8." National Bureau of Economic Research Working Paper #12207.

Collins, William J. (1997). "When the Tide Turned: Immigration and the Delay of the Great Black Migration." *Journal of Economic History* 57, no. 3, pp. 607–32.

———. (2006). "The Political Economy of State Fair Housing Laws Before 1968." *Social Science History* 30, no. 1, pp. 15–49.

Constant, Amelie, Liliya Gataullina, and Klaus Zimmermann. (2007). "Naturalization Proclivities, Ethnicity, and Integration." DIW Berlin Discussion Paper #75.

Constantine, Stephen. (2003). "British Emigration to the Empire-Commonweath since 1880: From Overseas Settlement to Diaspora?" *Journal of Imperial and Commonwealth History* 31, no. 2, pp. 16–35.

Conzen, Kathleen Neils. (1980). "Germans," in Stephan Thernstrom, ed., *Harvard Encyclopedia of American Ethnic Groups*. Cambridge, Mass.: Belknap Press.

Cornelius, Wayne A. (1989). "Impacts of the 1986 U.S. Immigration Law on Emigration from Rural Mexican Sending Communities." *Population and Development Review* 15, pp. 689–705.

Costa, Dora L., and Matthew E. Kahn. (2008). *Heroes and Cowards: The Social Face of War*. Princeton, N.J.: Princeton University Press.

Cutler, David, Edward Glaeser, and Jacob Vigdor. (1999). "The Rise and Decline of the American Ghetto." *Journal of Political Economy* 107, no. 3, pp. 455–506.

———. (2005). "Ghettos and the Transmission of Ethnic Capital," in Glenn C. Loury, Tariq Modood, and Steven M. Teles, eds., *Ethnicity, Social Mobility and Public Policy: Comparing the US and UK*. Cambridge: Cambridge University Press.

———. (2008). "Is the Melting Pot Still Hot? Explaining the Resurgence of Immigrant Segregation." *Review of Economics and Statistics* 90, no. 3, pp. 478–97.

DeSipio, Louis. (1987). "Social Science Literature and the Naturalization Process." *International Migration Review* 21, no. 2, pp. 390–405.

Donato, Katherine M., and Rebecca S. Carter. (1999). "Mexico and U.S. Policy on Illegal Immigration: A Fifty-Year Retrospective," in David W. Haines and Karen E.

Rosenblum, eds., *Illegal Immigration in America: A Reference Handbook*. Westport, Conn.: Greenwood Press.

Donato, Katherine, Jorge Durand, and Douglas Massey. (1992). "Stemming the Tide? Assessing the Deterrent Effects of the Immigration Reform and Control Act." *Demography* 29, pp. 139–57.

Drachsler, Julius. (1920). *Democracy and Assimilation: The Blending of Immigrant Heritages in America*. New York: The Macmillan Company.

Duleep, Harriet, and Daniel Dowhan. (2002). "Insights from Longitudinal Data on the Earnings Growth of U.S. Foreign-Born Men." *Demography* 39, no. 3, pp. 485–506.

Easterly, William, and Ross Levine. (1997). "Africa's Growth Tragedy: Policies and Ethnic Divisions." *Quarterly Journal of Economics* 112, pp. 1203–50.

Echenique, Federico, and Roland G. Fryer Jr. (2007). "A Measure of Segregation Based on Social Interactions." *Quarterly Journal of Economics* 122, no. 2, pp. 441–85.

Erickson, C. (1972). *Invisible Immigrants: The Adaptation of English and Scottish Immigrants in 19th Century America*. Leicester: Littlehampton Book Services Ltd.

Espenshade, Thomas J., and Haishan Fu. (1997). "An Analysis of English-Language Proficiency Among U.S. Immigrants." *American Sociological Review* 62, pp. 288–305.

Espinosa, Kristin E., and Douglas S. Massey. (1997). "Determinants of English Proficiency among Mexican Migrants to the United States." *International Migration Review* 31, pp. 28–50.

Evans, M. D. R. (1988). "Choosing to Be a Citizen: The Time-Path of Citizenship in Australia." *International Migration Review* 22, no. 2, pp. 243–64.

Fischer, Mary J., and Douglas Massey. (2000). "Residential Segregation and Ethnic Enterprise in U.S. Metropolitan Areas." *Social Problems* 47, no. 3, pp. 408–24.

Foerster, Robert Franz. (1924). *The Italian Emigration of Our Times*. Manchester, N.H.: Ayer Co.

Foot, David K., and William J. Milne. (1984). "Net Migration Estimation in an Extended, Multiregional Gravity Model." *Journal of Regional Science* 24, no. 1, pp. 119–33.

Fox, Paul. (1922). *The Poles in America*. New York: George H. Doran Co.

Franklin, Benjamin. (1751). "Observations Concerning the Increase of Mankind." Papers of Benjamin Franklin, Yale University.

Fujita, Masahisa, and Hideaki Ogawa. (1982). "Multiple Equilibria and Structural Transition of Non-Monocentric Urban Configurations." *Regional Science and Urban Economics* 12, no. 2, pp. 161–96.

Funkhouser, Edward, and Stephen J. Trejo. (1995). "The Labor Market Skills of Recent Male Immigrants: Evidence from the Current Population Survey." *Industrial and Labor Relations Review* 48, pp. 792–811.

Galassi, Francesco L., and Jon S. Cohen. (1994). "The Economics of Tenancy in Early Twentieth-Century Southern Italy." *Economic History Review* 47, no. 3, pp. 585–600.

Gans, Herbert J. (1962). *The Urban Villagers: Group and Class in the Life of Italian-Americans*. New York: Free Press of Glencoe.

Glaeser, Edward L., and Bryce A. Ward. (2006). "The Causes and Consequences of Land Use Regulation: Evidence from Greater Boston." Harvard Institute of Economic Research Discussion Paper #2124.

Glazer, Nathan, and Daniel P. Moynihan. (1963). *Beyond the Melting Pot: The Negroes, Puerto Ricans, Jews, Italians and Irish of New York City.* Cambridge, Mass.: MIT Press.

Goldin, Claudia, and Robert A. Margo. (1992). "The Great Compression: The Wage Structure in the United States at Mid-Century." *Quarterly Journal of Economics* 107, no. 1, pp. 1–34.

Gordon, Milton M. (1964). *Assimilation in American Life: The Role of Race, Religion, and National Origins.* Oxford: Oxford University Press.

Gozdziak, Elzbieta, and Micah Bump. (2008). *New Immigrants, Changing Communities.* Lanham, Md.: Lexington Books.

Green, Donald, and Ian Shapiro. (1996). *Pathologies of Rational Choice Theory: A Critique of Applications in Political Science.* New Haven, Conn.: Yale University Press.

Grig, D. B. (1977). "E.G. Ravenstein and the 'Laws of Migration.'" *Journal of Historical Geography* 3, no. 1, pp. 41–54.

Grossman, Jean B. (1982). "The Substitutability of Natives and Immigrants in Production." *Review of Economics and Statistics* 64, pp. 596–603.

Gurak, Douglas T., and Fe Caces. (1992). "Migration Networks and the Shaping of Migration Systems," in Mary Kritz, Lin Lean Lim, and Hania Zlotnik, eds., *International Migration Systems: A Global Approach.* Oxford: Clarendon Press.

Hamermesh, Daniel. (1993). *Labor Demand.* Princeton, N.J.: Princeton University Press.

Hanson, Gordon H., and Antonio Spilimbergo. (1999). "Illegal Immigration, Border Enforcement, and Relative Wages: Evidence from Apprehensions at the U.S.-Mexico Border." *American Economic Review* 89, no. 5, pp. 1337–57.

Hoefer, Michale, Nancy Rytina, and Bryan C. Baker. (2009). "Estimates of the Unauthorized Immigrant Population Residing in the United States: January 2008." Washington, D.C.: U.S. Department of Homeland Security, Office of Immigration Statistics.

Hu, Wei-Yin. (2000). "Immigrant Earnings Assimilation: Estimates from Longitudinal Data." *American Economic Review* 90, no. 2, pp. 368–72.

Huddle, Donald. (1993). *The Net National Costs of Immigration.* Washington, D.C.: Carrying Capacity Network.

Ibarraran, Pablo, and Darren Lubotsky. (2007). "Mexican Immigration and Self-Selection: New Evidence from the 2000 Mexican Census," in George J. Borjas, ed., *Mexican Immigration to the United States.* Chicago: University of Chicago Press.

Jackson, Kenneth T. (1985). *Crabgrass Frontier: The Suburbanization of the United States.* Oxford: Oxford University Press.

Jahn, Julius, Calvin F. Schmid, and Clarence Schrag. (1947). "The Measurement of Ecological Segregation." *American Sociological Review* 12, pp. 293–303.

Jasso, Guillermina, and Mark Rosenzweig. (1986). "Family Reunification and the Immigration Multiplier: U.S. Immigration Law, Origin-Country Conditions, and the Reproduction of Immigrants." *Demography* 23, no. 3, pp. 291–311.

————. (1990). *The New Chosen People: Immigrants in the United States.* New York: Russell Sage Foundation.

Jasso, Guillermina, Mark Rosenzweig, and James P. Smith. (1998). "The Changing Skills of New Immigrants to the United States: Recent Trends and Their Determinants." National Bureau of Economic Research Working Paper #6764.

Jefferys, Kelly J., and Daniel C. Martin. (2008). "Annual Flow Report: Refugees and Asylees, 2007." Washington, D.C.: U.S. Department of Homeland Security, Office of Immigration Statistics.

Jensen, Richard. (2002). "'No Irish Need Apply': A Myth of Victimization." *Journal of Social History* 36, no. 2, pp. 405–29.

Juhn, Chinhui, and Simon Potter. (2006). "Changes in Labor Force Participation in the United States." *Journal of Economic Perspectives* 20, no. 3, pp. 27–46.

Kahneman, Daniel, Paul Slovic, and Amos Tversky, eds. (1982). *Judgment Under Uncertainty: Heuristics and Biases.* Cambridge: Cambridge University Press.

Kalmijn, Matthijs. (1998). "Intermarriage and Homogamy: Causes, Patterns, Trends." *Annual Review of Sociology* 24, pp. 395–421.

Karemera, David, Victor I. Oguledo, and Bobby Davis. (2000). "A Gravity Model Analysis of International Migration to North America." *Applied Economics* 32, no. 13, pp. 1745–55.

Khwaja, Ahmed, Dan Silverman, and Frank Sloan (2006). "Time Preference, Time Discounting, and Smoking Decisions." National Bureau of Economic Research Working Paper #12615.

Klein, Herbert S. (1983). "The Integration of Italian Immigrants into the United States and Argentina: A Comparative Analysis." *The American Historical Review* 88, no. 2, pp. 306–29.

Krikorian, Mark. (2008). *The New Case Against Immigration: Both Legal and Illegal.* New York: Sentinel.

Krivo, Lauren J. (1995). "Immigrant Characteristics and Hispanic-Anglo Housing Inequality." *Demography* 32, no. 4, pp. 599–615.

LaLonde, Robert J., and Robert H. Topel. (1992). "The Assimilation of Immigrants in the U.S. Labor Market," in George J. Borjas and Richard B. Freeman, eds., *Immigration and the Work Force.* Chicago: University of Chicago Press.

Lazear, Edward. (1999). "Culture and Language." *Journal of Political Economy* 107, pp. S95–S129.

————. (2007). "Mexican Assimilation in the United States," in George J. Borjas, ed., *Mexican Immigration to the United States.* Chicago: University of Chicago Press.

Lee, Ronald, and Timothy Miller. (2000). "Immigration, Social Security, and Broader Fiscal Impacts." *American Economic Review* 90, no. 2, pp. 350–54.

LeMay, Michael, and Elliott Barkan, eds. (1999). *U.S. Immigration and Naturalization Laws and Issues: A Documentary History.* Westport, Conn.: Greenwood Press.

Lewis, G. J. (1982). *Human Migration: A Geographical Perspective.* London: Croom Helm.

Lieberson, Stanley. (1980). *A Piece of the Pie: Blacks and White Immigrants Since 1880.* Berkeley: University of California Press.

Lieberson, Stanley, Guy Dalto, and Mary Ellen Johnston. (1975). "The Course of Mother-Tongue Diversity in Nations." *American Journal of Sociology* 81, pp. 34–61.

Lieberson, Stanley, and Mary C. Waters. (1988). *From Many Strands: Ethnic and Racial Groups in Contemporary America.* New York: Russell Sage Foundation.

Lightbown, P. M., and N. Spada. (2006). *How Languages Are Learned,* third edition. Oxford: Oxford University Press.

Loewen, James. (1971). *The Mississippi Chinese: Between Black and White.* Cambridge, Mass.: Harvard University Press.

Lubotsky, Darren. (2007). "Chutes or Ladders? A Longitudinal Analysis of Immigrant Earnings." *Journal of Political Economy* 115, no. 5, pp. 820–67.

Lucy, William H., and David L. Phillips. (2001). "Suburbs and the Census: Patterns of Growth and Decline." Washington, D.C.: Brookings Institution Center on Urban and Metropolitan Policy.

Madrian, Brigitte C., and Dennis F. Shea. (2001). "The Power of Suggestion: Inertia in 401(k) Participation and Savings Behavior." *Quarterly Journal of Economics* 116, no. 4, pp. 1149–87.

Mangione, Jerre. (1993). *La Storia: Five Centuries of the Italian American Experience.* New York: Harper Perennial.

Marshall, Alfred. (1890). *Principles of Economics.* London: Macmillan and Co.

Martin, Philip L., and Michael S. Teitelbaum. (2001). "The Mirage of Mexican Guest Workers." *Foreign Affairs* 80, no. 6, pp. 117–31.

Massey, Douglas S. (1985). "Ethnic Residential Segregation: A Theoretical Synthesis and Empirical Review." *Sociology and Social Research* 69, pp. 315–50.

———, ed. (2008). *New Faces in New Places: The Changing Geography of American Immigration.* New York: Russell Sage Foundation.

Massey, Douglas S., Joaquin Arango, Graeme Hugo, Ali Kouaouci, Adela Pellegrino, and J. Edward Taylor. (1993). "Theories of International Migration: A Review and Appraisal." *Population and Development Review* 19, no. 3, pp. 431–66.

Massey, Douglas S., and Nancy Denton. (1988). "The Dimensions of Residential Segregation." *Social Forces* 67, pp. 281–315.

McClain, Charles J. (1994). *In Search of Equality: The Chinese Struggle Against Discrimination in Nineteenth-Century America.* Berkeley: University of California Press.

Mulkern, John R. (1990). *The Know-Nothing Party in Massachusetts: The Rise and Fall of a People's Movement.* Boston: Northeastern University Press.

Myers, Dowell. (2007). *Immigrants and Boomers: Forging a New Social Contract for the Future of America.* New York: Russell Sage Foundation.

Ong, Paul M., and Doug Houston. (2002). "The 2000 Census Undercount in Los Angeles County." Ralph and Goldy Lewis Center for Regional Policy Studies, Working Paper #42, University of California, Los Angeles.

Oreopoulos, Philip. (2007). "Do Dropouts Drop Out Too Soon? Wealth, Health, and Happiness from Compulsory Schooling." *Journal of Public Economics* 91, no. 11–12, pp. 2213–29.

Orrenius, Pia, and Madeline Zavodny. (2003). "Do Amnesty Programs Reduce Undocumented Immigration? Evidence from IRCA." *Demography* 40, no. 3, pp. 437–50.

Pager, Devah, and Hana Shepherd. (2008). "The Sociology of Discrimination: Racial Discrimination in Employment, Housing, Credit, and Consumer Markets." *Annual Review of Sociology* 34, pp. 181–209.

Pagnini, Deanna, and S. Philip Morgan. (1990). "Intermarriage and Social Distance Among U.S. Immigrants at the Turn of the Century." *American Journal of Sociology* 96, no. 2, pp. 405–32.

Park, Robert. (1926a). "Behind our Masks." *Survey Graphic* 56, pp. 135–39.

———. (1926b). "The Urban Community as a Spatial Pattern and a Moral Order," in Edward Burgess, ed., *The Urban Community*. Chicago: University of Chicago Press.

Passel, Jeffrey S. (1999). "Undocumented Immigration to the United States: Numbers, Trends, and Characteristics," in David W. Haines and Karen E. Rosenblum, eds., *Illegal Immigration in America: A Reference Handbook*. Westport, Conn.: Greenwood Press.

Passel, Jeffrey S., and Rebecca L. Clark. (1994). "How Much Do Immigrants Really Cost? A Reappraisal of Huddle's 'The Cost of Immigrants.'" Washington, D.C.: Urban Institute.

Perlmann, Joel. (2005). *Italians Then, Mexicans Now: Immigrant Origins and Second-Generation Progress, 1890–2000*. New York: Russell Sage Foundation.

Piketty, Thomas, and Emmanuel Saez. (2003). "Income Inequality in the United States, 1913–1998." *Quarterly Journal of Economics* 118, no. 1, pp. 1–39.

Pipes, Daniel, and Khalid Duran. (2002). "Muslim Immigrants in the United States." Center for Immigration Studies *Backgrounder*, August.

Portes, Alejandro, and John W. Curtis. (1987). "Changing Flags: Naturalization and its Determinants Among Mexican Immigrants." *International Migration Review* 21, no. 2, pp. 352–71.

Portes, Alejandro, and Ruben Rumbout. (2006). *Immigrant America*, third edition. Berkeley: University of California Press.

Pula, James S. (1995). *Polish Americans: An Ethnic Community*. New York: Twayne Publishers.

Qian, Zhenchao, and Daniel Lichter. (2001). "Measuring Marital Assimilation: Intermarriage among Natives and Immigrants." *Social Science Research* 30, pp. 289–312.

Ramirez, Bruno. (2001). *Crossing the 49th Parallel: Migration from Canada to the United States, 1900–1930*. Ithaca, N.Y.: Cornell University Press.

Ravenstein, E. G. (1876). "Census of the British Isles, 1871; Birthplaces and Migration." *Geographical Magazine* 3, pp. 173–77.

———. (1885). "The Laws of Migration." *Journal of the Statistical Society* 48, no. 2, pp. 167–227.

———. (1889). "The Laws of Migration." *Journal of the Statistical Society* 52, pp. 214–301.

Redstone, Ilana, and Douglas Massey. (2004). "Coming To Stay: An Analysis of the U.S. Census Question on Immigrants' Year of Arrival." *Demography* 41, pp. 721–38.

Reichert, Joshua S., and Douglas S. Massey. (1982). "Guestworker Programs: Evidence form Europe and the United States and Some Implications for U.S. Policy." *Population Research and Policy Review* 1, no. 1, pp. 1–17.

Richter, Susan M., J. Edward Taylor, and Antonio Yunez–Naude. (2007). "Impacts of Policy Reforms on Labor Migration from Rural Mexico to the United States," in George J. Borjas, ed., *Mexican Immigration to the United States*. Chicago: University of Chicago Press.

Riis, Jacob. (1891). *How The Other Half Lives: Studies Among the Tenements of New York*. New York: Charles Scribner's Sons.

Riley, Jason L. (2008). *Let Them In: The Case for Open Borders*. New York: Gotham Press.

Roback, Jennifer. (1982). "Wages, Rents, and the Quality of Life." *Journal of Political Economy* 90, no. 6, pp. 1257–78.

Rosen, Robert N. (2006). *Saving the Jews: Franklin D. Roosevelt and the Holocaust*. New York: Basic Books.

Rosen, Sherwin. (1981). "The Economics of Superstars." *American Economic Review* 71, no. 5, pp. 845–58.

Ross, Edward Alsworth. (1914). *The Old World in the New: The Significance of Past and Present Immigration to the American People*. New York: The Century Co.

Roy, A. D. (1951). "Some Thoughts on the Distribution of Earnings." *Oxford Economic Papers* 3, no. 2, pp. 135–46.

Ruggles, Steven, Matthew Sobek, Trent Alexander, Catherine A. Fitch, Ronald Goeken, Patricia Kelly Hall, Miriam King, and Chad Ronnander. (2008). *Integrated Public Use Microdata Series: Version 4.0*. [Machine-readable database] Minneapolis: Minnesota Population Center.

Saiz, Albert. (2003). "Room in the Kitchen for the Melting Pot: Immigration and Rental Prices." *Review of Economics and Statistics* 85, no. 3, pp. 502–21.

Saiz, Albert, and Susan Wachter. (2006). "Immigration and the Neighborhood." IZA Discussion Paper #2503.

Seattle Civil Rights and Labor History Project. (2006). Database of 414 Racial Restrictive Covenants from King County Recorder's Office.

Silvia, Philip T., Jr. (1979). "The 'Flint Affair': French-Canadian Struggle for 'Survivance.'" *The Catholic Historical Review* 65, no. 3, pp. 414–35.

Simon, Herbert A. (1957). *Models of Man: Social and Rational*. New York: John Wiley and Sons.

Sjaastad, Larry. (1962). "The Costs and Returns of Human Migration." *Journal of Political Economy* 70, no. 5 part 2, pp. 80–93.

Storesletten, Kjetil. (2000). "Sustaining Fiscal Policy through Immigration." *Journal of Political Economy* 108, no. 2, pp. 300–323.

Taylor, J. Edward. (1986). "Differential Migration, Networks, Information, and Risk," in Oded Stark, ed., *Research in Human Capital and Development, volume 4: Migration, Human Capital, and Development*. Greenwich, Conn.: JAI Press.

Thernstrom, Stephan, ed. (1980). *Harvard Encyclopedia of American Ethnic Groups.* Cambridge, Mass.: Belknap Press.

Thiel, Henri, and Anthony J. Finezza. (1971). "A Note on the Measurement of Racial Integration of Schools by Means of Informational Concepts." *Journal of Mathematical Sociology* 1, pp. 187–94.

Tobler, Waldo. (1995). "Migration: Ravenstein, Thornthwaite, and Beyond." *Urban Geography* 16, no. 4, pp. 327–43.

U.S. Bureau of Transportation Statistics. (2007). Transportation Statistics Annual Report.

U.S. Citizenship and Immigration Services, Office of Citizenship. (2007). *Welcome to the United States: A Guide for New Immigrants* (revised edition). Washington, D.C.: U.S. Department of Homeland Security.

Van Vugt, William E. (1988). "Running from Ruin? The Emigration of British Farmers to the U.S.A. in the Wake of the Repeal of the Corn Laws." *Economic History Review* 41, no. 3, pp. 411–28.

———. (1999). *Britain to America: Mid-Nineteenth-Century Immigrants to the United States.* Urbana: University of Illinois Press.

Vigdor, Jacob. (2004). "Community Composition and Collective Action: Analyzing Initial Mail Response to the 2000 Census." *Review of Economics and Statistics* 86, pp. 303–12.

Viscusi, W. Kip, and Joseph E. Aldy. (2003). "The Value of a Statistical Life: A Critical Review of Market Estimates Throughout the World." *Journal of Risk and Uncertainty* 27, no. 1, pp. 5–76.

Weiand, Kenneth F. (1987). "An Extension of the Monocentric Urban Spatial Equilibrium Model to a Multicenter Setting: The Case of the Two-Center City." *Journal of Urban Economics* 21, no. 3, pp. 259–71.

White, Michael J., Frank D. Bean, and Thomas J. Espenshade. (1997). "The U.S. 1986 Immigration Reform and Control Act and Undocumented Immigration to the United States." *Population Research and Policy Review* 9, pp. 93–116.

Woodrow, Karen A., and Jeffrey S. Passel. (1990). "Post-IRCA Undocumented Immigration to the United States: An Assessment Based on the June 1988 CPS," in Frank D. Bean, Barry Edmonston, and Jeffrey S. Passell, eds., *Undocumented Migration to the United States: IRCA and the Experience of the 1980s.* Washington, D.C.: Urban Institute Press.

Zunz, Olivier. (1982). *The Changing Face of Inequality: Urbanization, Industrial Development, and Immigrants in Detroit, 1880–1920.* Chicago: University of Chicago Press.

# Index

across-generation economic assimilation, 73–74
ACS. *See* American Community Survey
Africa, 81
African Americans, 132
age: assimilation and, 58–60; English language ability and, 92, *98*; naturalization rate and, 115–16, *116–17. See also* children of immigrants
Alba, Richard, 16–17, 22
Alexander II, assassination of, 36
Alien and Sedition acts, 106
amenities, 11, 12, 14
American colonies, 13, 30, 175n22; Great Britain and, 7–8, 28
American Community Survey (ACS), 23–25, 173n2, 174n14; English language and, 79, 84–85, 185n21; margin of error, 58; on marriage, 142, 151; naturalization and, 110, 187n20; occupations in, 53; tracking by, 63
amnesty, 113, 162–66
anti-immigrant movements: Chinese and Japanese immigrants, 33; job-

seeking migrants and, 4, 41; Know-Nothing party, 32, 35
Aristide, Jean-Bertrand, 42
armed forces, naturalization and, 107, 108, 168
Asian immigrants: marriage and, 149; occupation scores of, 64; segregation of, 130. *See also specific countries*
assimilation: age and, 58–60; amnesty and, 162–66; between-generation, 73; books on, 2; Chinese immigrants and, 176n41; civic, 165; costs and benefits of, 16–22, *21*, 140, 161, 167; culture and, 15, 19–20, 22, 163; defined, 57; economic, 45, 51, 58–59, 62–74; guest worker programs and, 161–62; home-seeking migrants and, 4, 10, 20–21; immigration law enforcement and, 167–68; impacts on, 4–5; as investment, 79, 92, 141; job-seeking migrants and, 10, 21; linguistic, 16, 77, 82, 83, 87–99, 122, 184n2; longitudinal data and, 57, 59–61; marital, 143, 156; naturalization and, 101; obstacle to studying, 57–62;

to, 28, 35. *See also* migration; policy, immigration
Immigration Act of 1917, 37
Immigration and Nationality Act, 175n32
Immigration Reform and Control Act (IRCA), 163–64, 166
income, 54–55, 183n39. *See also* wages
income tax, 45, 168–69, 194n16
India: linguistic fractionalization, 81; partition of, 12
Indian immigrants, 41, 57; economic standing of, 66–67; labor force participation rates, 68, 69; marriage and, 149; occupation scores of, 68, 69
industrialization, 28, 34, 75
insurance: disability, 71, 183n41; health, 180n11
intangible benefits and costs, of migration, 11, 13–14, 14, 175n23
Integrated Public Use Microdata Series (IPUMS) project, 24–25, 73; data, 24, 131; margin of error, 58; occupations and, 53–54
integration: perfect, 123–24; residential, 5
intermarriage, 5, 141–56; children of, 142; constraints on, 144–46; costs and benefits of, 20, 146; culture and, 19, 146, 147, 157; current statistics on, 146–50, 147–50; defined, 147; by European immigrants, 147, 151, 193n15; history of, 150–56, 151–55; naturalization and, 4, 143
IPUMS. *See* Integrated Public Use Microdata Series project
Iran, 149
IRCA (Immigration Reform and Control Act), 163–64, 166
Irish immigrants, 27, 31, 33, 177n8; acceptance of, 38; discrimination against, 181n21; marriage and, 152, 154; motivations for, 31–32; occupations of, 61, 61, 75
isolation, 122, 127–28, 130, 136, 137; defined, 124

isolation index, 124, 127, 129, 189n14; dissimilarity index compared to, 128
Israel, 149, 193n17
Italian immigrants, 36, 36, 37–39, 73, 179n39; in Boston, 122; English language and, 78, 84; isolation of, 130; labor force participation rates, 71, 72; marriage and, 152, 155, 156; naturalization rate of, 117, 118, 187n21; occupation scores of, 71, 72

Jahn, Julius, 123
Jamaica, 41, 43
Japanese immigrants: marriage by, 147; motivations for, 42; naturalization rate, 111; opposition to, 33
Jasso, Guillermina, 59, 102
Jewish immigrants: Cuba and, 179n46; discrimination against, 36, 191n30; immigration quotas, 40; motivations for, 32, 36–37, 175n22, 178n27
job-seeking migrants, 4, 162; assimilation and, 10, 21; classification of, 13; globalization and, 30; Italians, 36; motivations for, 14, 39; opposition to, 28, 40–41
Johnson, Lyndon B., 41
Johnson-Reed Act, 39

Kahn, Matthew, 32–33
Kalmijn, Matthijs, 145
"knowledge sector" jobs, 75
Know-Nothing party, 32, 35, 171
Korean immigrants, 41, 42, 57; "Generation 1.5," 74; marriage and, 149; naturalization rate, 113; segregation of, 130
Krikorian, Mark, 159

labor force participation rates, 65–67, 65–66, 183n41; Indian immigrants, 68, 69; Italian immigrants, 71, 72; Mexican immigrants, 67, 68; Vietnamese immigrants, 70, 71

residency requirement, for
naturalization, 104, 107, 117, 186n4
residential assimilation, 123, 138–40
residential integration, 5
restrictions, immigration: policy debate
on, 159; U.S. policy, 3, 28–29, 35, 87,
160
restrictions, on emigration, 33
restrictions, racial: on citizenship, 104,
106, 110; on immigration, 52
restrictive covenants, 131, 191n29
retirees: benefits for, 49, 183n41;
migration of, 14
return migration, 13, 58, 61, 91; English
language and, 91, 92, 185n23; of
Mexican immigrants, 95, 185n23;
naturalization *vs.*, 102
return to capital, 46–47
Revolution of 1905–1907, 37
Riley, Jason, 159
risks: labor market success and, 52;
rational choice and, 11, 18
Roosevelt, Theodore, 78
Rosenzweig, Mark, 59, 102
Ross, Edward Alsworth, 37–38, 39,
179n37
Rumbout, Ruben, 80
Russia, 32
Russian immigrants, *36*, 36–37, 130,
178n27, 187n21
Russian Revolution of 1917, 39

"salad bowl," 1, 2
Scandinavian immigrants, 11, *31*, 33–34,
35, 73
Schmid, Calvin, 123
schools: cities, bidirectional migration
and, 12; ethnic profile of, 1–2. *See
also* education
Schrag, Clarence, 123
second-generation immigrants, 127, 143,
144, 147, 151
segregation, 122–27, 128, 130–31, 138,
189nn12–13; black-white, 189n12,
190n21, 191n28; childbearing and,

123, 127, 189n9; multigroup, 125,
189n15
segregation indices, 123, 125–27,
190n21
selective emigration, 58–59, 62, 89
selective return migration, 65
Sephardic Jews, 175n22
September 11, 2001, terrorist attacks,
183n1
services, fiscal impact of immigration
and, 45–46, 49, 181n16
Sjaastad, Larry, 11, 12
skilled workers: immigration programs
for, 187n19; income of, 54–55;
naturalization of, 102, 109; net fiscal
contributions by, 49–50; occupations
of, 1, 50; opportunities for, 12, 28–
29, 41–42, 45, 48
slave trade, Atlantic, 12
Smith, Adam, 7
"snowballing" effect, 3, 5
Social Security Administration (SSA),
53, 60, 183n37, 183n41
Social Security taxes, 49, 60, 181n13
sociological models, 9–10, 15–16, 19
Somalia, 104
South America, migration to, 38
South American immigrants, 41, 112
Spain, Basques in, 80
Spanish language, 77; Census Bureau
questionnaire in, 84
sponsored immigrants, 169, 170
spouses. *See* marriage
S.S. *St. Louis*, 40, 179n46
SSA (Social Security Administration),
53, 60, 183n37, 183n41
Standard Metropolitan Statistical Areas,
126
State Department, U.S., 187n14, 187n18,
192n2
Statue of Liberty, 177n1
students. *See* education
suburbanization, 126, 130–31, 138,
191n34, 191n36
suburbs, 128, 138, 190n26